# SHAKESPEARE'S

# WILDERNESS

———

DAVID RAINS WALLACE

Other books by David Rains Wallace

Natural History

*The Dark Range: A Naturalist's Night Notebook*
*Idle Weeds: Life on a Sandstone Ridge*
*The Klamath Knot: Explorations in Myth and Evolution*
*The Untamed Garden and Other Personal Essays*
*Bulow Hammock: Mind in a Forest*
*The Monkey's Bridge: Mysteries of Evolution in Central America*
*Neptune's Ark: From Ichthyosaurs to Orcas*
*Chuckwalla Land: The Riddle of California's Desert*
*Mountains and Marshes: Exploring the Bay Area's Natural History*

History of Science

*The Bonehunters' Revenge*
*Beasts of Eden*

Fiction

*The Turquoise Dragon: A Novel*
*The Vermilion Parrot: A Novel*

Conservation

*Life in the Balance: Companion to the Audubon Television Specials*
*The Quetzal and the Macaw: The Story of Costa Rica's National Parks*

Literary Criticism

*The Wilder Shore: California Landscape and Literature*
*Articulate Earth: Adventures in Ecocriticism*

Travel Guides

*Adventuring in Central America: Paseo Pantera Ecotourism Guide*
*Redwood National Park: Official Handbook 151*
*Yellowstone National Park: Official Handbook 150*
*Mammoth Cave National Park: Official Handbook 158*
*The Walker's Companion*
*New River Gorge National Park*

Then to the rolling Heav'n itself I cried,
Asking, "What lamp has Destiny to guide
Her little children stumbling in the Dark?"
And--"A blind understanding!" Heav'n replied.

Then to this earthen Bowl did I adjourn
My Lip the secret Well of Life to learn:
And Lip to Lip it murmur'd-- "While you live,
Drink! -- For once dead you never shall return."

I think the Vessel, that with fugitive
Articulation answer'd, once did live,
And merry-make; and the cold Lip I kiss'd
How many Kisses might it take, and give.

Edward Fitzgerald, *Rubaiyat*

# CONTENTS

# FOREWORD

---

Writers tend to interpret Shakespeare more idiosyncratically than critics and scholars. This can make little sense, as with Leo Tolstoy's essay, "Shakespeare and the Drama," which judges the plays according to a nineteenth century Russian novelist's ideas of Orthodox Christianity and dismisses their high reputation as a mass delusion induced by depraved critics: "The undisputed fame that Shakespeare enjoys as a great genius, which makes writers of our time imitate him and readers and spectators, distorting their esthetic and ethical sense, seek non-existent qualities in him, is a great evil… a drama that has no religious basis is not only not an important or good thing, as is now supposed, but is a most trivial and contemptible affair."

It can also make a special kind of sense, as with Ted Hughes's book, *Shakespeare and the Goddess of Complete Being,* which judges the plays according to a twentieth century English poet's ideas of Social Anthropology and does find a "religious basis" in them. Hughes perceives in the Shakespeare "canon" an impulse to reach back past modern civilization's anthropocentric traditions to one more akin to the natural world. He calls it "the myth of the Great Goddess and her consort, the sacrificed god, the myth of one of the most widespread and profoundly rooted religions of the archaic world." Like Tolstoy's, Hughes's interpretation reflects his own life and work, perhaps too much in some ways. It does take into account Shakespeare's "undisputed fame."

This book tries to interpret Shakespeare according to my own idiosyncratic ideas as a marginally twenty-first century nature writer. I think Shakespeare was the first major writer in English to see a positive religious dimension in wild nature, and since he is *the* major writer in English, this seems important, but I'm uncertain why it is or what it means. Hughes's interpretation helps to address my uncertainties, yet I think a tendency to abstraction flaws it. So I try to bring it down to earth by questioning some things that he abstractedly takes for granted.

# HISTORY

---

This precious stone set in a silver sea…

Whose rocky shore beats back the envious siege

Of wat'ry Neptune, is now bound in with shame,

With inky blots and rotten parchment bonds.

That England that was wont to conquer others

Hath made a shameful conquest of itself.

(*Richard II,* 2,1)

# Chapter One

## Monument and Monolith

———————

Poetry came alive to me suddenly in early adolescence while I idly browsed an old red leather volume of Shakespeare plays in my parents' bookcase. I read Ariel's song from *The Tempest*, and it evoked a kind of trance:

> Full fathom five they father lies.
> Of his bones are coral made;
> Those are pearls that were his eyes;
> Nothing of him that doth fade
> But doth suffer a sea-change,
> Into something rich and strange…
> (1, 2)

The song was like a magic spell, not the fairy tale, wish-fulfillment kind but one that just existed, inscrutably, apart from the everyday world of classrooms and playgrounds. All I could connect it with was a New England swamp called Mooney's Woods that I walked through on the way to school. The song seemed congruent with the trout lilies in the spring leaf litter and the suckers in the creek's blue-green pools. One morning as I watched the fish, a big snapping turtle emerged from under the bank and crept across the bottom through the waterweed. One evening I followed a wood thrush's song under the trees trying to locate the bird but saw only wing flashes through the leaves. Ariel's song had that elusive resonance.

The song also seemed apart from the red leather volume's Shakespeare, with its breezy biographical foreword and lithographs redolent of Edwin Booth productions, all Van dykes, doublets, and epees. In his quaint way, he fit right into the everyday world my homeroom teacher epitomized as he strutted among our desks after the Pledge of Allegiance and Lord's Prayer, crowing from bard and Bible: "Neither a borrower nor a lender be!" ... "Bring up a child in the way that he will go and when he is a man he will not depart from it!" ... "How sharper than a serpent's tooth to have a thankless child!" ... "The Lord is my shepherd, I shall not want!"

The classroom Shakespeare was a model success story for mid-twentieth century suburbia: his modest Stratford roots, grammar school education, teaching and/or law clerking, wild oats of teenage fatherhood and deer poaching, flight to London, meteoric theatrical career, carousing with fellow actors and writers, racy but respected, sublime but popular masterpieces, hobnobbing with noble patrons and sophisticated ladies, London-Stratford commuting, wealthy retirement, deathless fame.

The "Full Fathom Five" resonance seemed confined to my head. Nobody questioned Shakespeare's everyday greatness, not even the more intense English teachers. His plays epitomized 1950s America's "Whiggish history" of progress from dark age barbarism to modern prosperity and liberty-- the rise of the common man. (Early English liberals, "Whigs," saw history as leading inevitably toward their own utilitarian goals and wrote it that way.) The histories and tragedies, like Charlton Heston movies, dramatized the splendors and miseries of tyranny, crime, war, and sex. The comedies and romances, like Doris Day ones, celebrated the pluck and luck whereby modest goodness conquers pretentious badness. Ordinary yet supreme, William was just the one to have written them—a Whiggish Bard.

That was not just the suburban school version. In 1957, around the time I was having my "Full Fathom Five" epiphany, the editors of the *Folger Library General Reader's Shakespeare* declared that Elizabethan plays "were not considered 'literature' any more than radio and television scripts today are considered literature" and that "when Shakespeare's audience went to the Globe in 1600, they expected to see a rousing melodrama."

William, they explained, "probably never dreamed that his plays would establish his reputation as a literary genius. His learning in books was anything but profound, but he clearly had the probing curiosity that sent him in search of information, and he had a keenness in the observation of nature and of humankind that finds reflection in his poetry."

As adolescents do, I swallowed the gap between the normal perception of Shakespeare as a media hack who happened to be a supreme genius and my unexpected one. That he was somehow schizoid, unlike Longfellow and other model poets who bored me in class was, like puberty and its surprises, just another tacit fact of life. *Evangeline*'s author also may have had "a keenness in the observation of nature and of humankind" but his poems didn't entrance me.

The excitement that linked Ariel's song to Mooney's Woods and gave the song its resonance did not exist in the everyday world. My father was the authority on that. He was a success: a PhD in Psychology, the Director of Research at a life insurance company, a Lieutenant Colonel in the Air Force Reserve, frequently abroad on Pentagon affairs. He too quoted the Bard, not bombastically like my homeroom teacher but still Whiggishly: "Costly thy habit as thy purse can buy, but not expressed in fancy; rich, not gaudy, for the apparel oft proclaims the man... This above all-- to thine own self be true, and it must follow, as the night the day, that thou cans't not be false to any man."

He often asked me what I'd "learned today" and shook his head at the vacuity of my responses. When I told him, for once excitedly, about seeing deer at Mooney's Woods, the first I'd seen, he was unimpressed.

"What would the world be without forests?" I asked, as tracts and malls spread around the Woods.

"We'll have forests of tomato plants," my father said.

## Isms and Bios

The Whiggish Bard was entertaining. We watched him on network television: *Richard III* with creepy Lawrence Olivier; *Macbeth* with gaunt Edith Evans, who embarrassed me by clutching her breasts during Lady Macbeth's "I have given suck" soliloquy; *The Tempest* with magisterial Maurice Evans. TV's version of "Full Fathom Five" evoked no trance-like epiphany. *The Tempest*'s fantastic side might have been a *Star Trek* episode with Ariel as Peter Pan and Caliban as The Creature from the Black Lagoon. But that didn't surprise me.

The suburbs' fun Bard evaporated when I got to college. Freshman English spent weeks on a sonnet, and Shakespeare criticism comprised a daunting part of the library. An inviting monument became a forbidding monolith carved over with cryptic cuneiforms. And the elusive voice that I heard in Ariel's song wasn't part of academia either. Despite Shakespeare criticism's august diversity-- Formalist, Marxist, New—it converged on the canon's meaning for everyday world concerns, weightier ones than the suburbs' but Whiggish-- the socioeconomic and psycho-philosophical progress from barbaric to modern.

I felt a vague desire to evade the monolith, and the youngish assistant professors and aging non-tenured instructors in my "Letters" major seemed to share it. They dropped the Bard's obscure *Coriolanus* into the mix with plays by Christopher Marlowe, George Chapman, and Ben Jonson: writers for whom the bar of exegesis was lower. This evasion continued in graduate school. When I wrote a paper on wilderness in English literature as an M.A. tutorial, I didn't even think of including Shakespeare, whose Stratford to London orbit seemed too monumentally monolithic for such marginalities. Hack work schedules wouldn't allow backwoods adventures: supreme imaginative genius wouldn't require them. This arguably glaring omission was fine with my tutor, who gave the paper a high mark.

Any feeling for an inner-other Shakespeare slumped for decades under a growing weight of isms. As post-structuralism, neo-historicism and multiculturalism came along, Whiggishness persisted in new "narratives." Twentieth century America wasn't civilization's apogee anymore, but its common man's Bard morphed smoothly into a twenty-first century common person's one. A popular 2004 narrative, appropriately titled *Will in the World*, begins like the Folger Library's 1957 introduction: "Not only did Shakespeare write and act for a cutthroat commercial entertainment industry, he also wrote scripts that were intensely alert to the social and political realities of his times... This is a book, then, about an amazing success story..."

Then, unexpectedly, television revived my feelings for an inner-other Shakespeare. A 2003-05 Canadian mini-series, *Slings and Arrows*, brilliantly satirizes the new narrative Bard in the form of a postmodern "Burbage Festival" wherein the plays are so embalmed for tradition or dissected for novelty that they provoke a borderline psychotic actor-director-- with hallucinatory help from another's ghost— to try to resurrect them. Beyond disgust with the industry, the madman and the ghost aren't sure just what they are trying to resurrect, so their attempt is confused. They aim shakily at the conflicts that unhappy women pose for male authority in *Hamlet*, *Macbeth*, and *King Lear*, with their trouble-making heroines played by an actress who has made trouble for both men. They manage to mount surprisingly successful productions of *Hamlet* and *Macbeth*, but their revival collapses as corporate sponsors move back in. They end up presenting *King Lear*-- with Lear played by a heroin addict dying of colon cancer—to an audience of five in a neighboring church's rumpus room.

The madman has a nemesis, a post-structuralist-conceptualist director who lurks in the wings through all this. Assigned to direct *Hamlet* as the series begins, he brandishes the script at the cast and proclaims: "This play is *dead*! It's been *dead* for *400 years*!" The madman drives him away with an epee, but he returns at the series end to reclaim the Festival for its sponsors.

It struck me that *Hamlet* probably *would* be dead now if a media-hack Whiggish Bard had written it. But, as the madman and the ghost try to show, the plays *are* more than fossil fuel for the entertainment and academic industries. *Slings and Arrows* interested me in Shakespeare as a writer, and I started reading biographies like *Will in the World.* I found them surprisingly vague, although one thing was clear: the breezy story I learned in high school is largely unsupported by contemporary evidence. So what I read was so conjectural and padded with genealogy, history, sociology, and dramaturgy that the writer faded into the background. Like decaf coffee, he lacked a stimulating ingredient— a personality. I tried stronger scholarly brews like James Shapiro's *A Year in the Life of Shakespeare: 1599*, but, again, a lot went on around little in the way of a personage. Shapiro's book says much about what William might have done in response to events in the year 1599: little about what he did.

The mass of stuff about a biographical wraith was mind numbing. I tried books about Shakespeare's development as a historical figure, which told me how the Bard became Whiggish as Whigs made him exemplary of progress, but no more. One of these, Jack Lynch's *Becoming Shakespeare*, starts with several different accounts of William's funeral and suggests how each might affect our idea of him. Lynch then acknowledges that no contemporary account exists. That made an impression, not least in that another source, Peter Ackroyd's 500-page *Shakespeare: The Biography*, has a detailed account:

"He was embalmed and laid upon the bed, wrapped in flowers and herbs in the process known as 'winding' the corpse. His friends and neighbors walked solemnly through New Place to view the body; the principal rooms and staircases were draped with black cloths. The corpse was then 'watched' until interment. He was wrapped in a linen winding sheet and, two days later, carried down the well-worn 'burying path' to the old church."

## A Radical

I'm not the first nature writer to see incongruity between canon and Bard. Henry Thoreau complains of it in his journal: "Shakespeare has left us his fancies and imaginings, but the truth of his life, with its becoming circumstances, we know nothing about. The writer is reported, the liver not at all. Shakespeare's house! How hollow it is! No man can conceive of Shakespeare in that house." In his essay, "Walking," Thoreau links this to a general dissatisfaction with Anglo-American attitudes to nature: "English literature, from the days of the minstrels to the Lake Poets—Chaucer and Spencer and Milton, and even Shakespeare, included—breathes no quite fresh and, in this sense, wild strain. It is essentially tame and civilized literature… Her wilderness is a greenwood, her wild man a Robin Hood…

"Where is the literature which gives expression to Nature? He would be a poet who could impress the winds and streams into his service… You will perceive that I demand something which no Augustan nor Elizabethan age, which no culture, in short, can give. Mythology comes nearer to it than anything. How much more fertile a Nature, at least, has Grecian mythology its root in than English literature! Mythology was the crop which the Old World bore before its soil was exhausted, before the fancy and imagination were affected with blight; and which it still bears, wherever its pristine vigor is unabated. All other literatures endure only as the elms which overshadow our houses; but this is like the great dragon-tree of the Western Isles, as old as mankind, and, whether that does or not, will endure as long; for the decay of other literature makes the soil in which it thrives."

Thoreau's idea that mythology is the living root of literature seems right, although his linking it with wild nature is radical. A leading twentieth century critic, Northrop Frye, sees myth as the root of literature but thinks that it concerns only culture: "As a type of story, myth is a form of verbal art, and belongs to the world of art. Like art, and unlike science, it deals, not with the world that man contemplates, but with the world that man creates." Frye associates verbal art's origins with the elaboration of primitive magic-- fertility dances and so on--into early civilizations' epics and dramas. "Nobody can reconstruct the origins of literature, but students of drama have always been aware of its development from, or succession to, certain rituals devoted to promoting the food supply by verbal magic." This accords with farming societies' tendency to see nature as created for human use, as in *Genesis*, with magic as a way of controlling it.

Yet Frye slights the evolutionary implication that verbal art must originate with hunter-gatherers, who were less concerned with controlling nature and more with cooperating with it: following elk or waiting for salmon. Archaeologists once thought their cave art was meant to control nature by multiplying game and assisting hunting, but most of the animals they painted were not major food species. Rabbit and boar bones predominate in their middens, not mammoth and auroch ones. Although "nobody can reconstruct" its origins, their art, visual or verbal, probably was not so utilitarian. The often zoomorphic "gods and heroes" of hunter-gatherer mythologies, which are complex, suggest that magic rituals began as attempts to participate in natural processes as much as to control them. That participatory impulse must have contributed to later epics and dramas.

Thoreau expresses a proto-evolutionary viewpoint when-- belying his own complaint that English literature is "essentially tame and civilized" -- he writes in the same essay: "Our ancestors were savages. The story of Romulus and Remus being suckled by the wolf is not a meaningless fable. The founders of every state which has risen to eminence have drawn their nourishment and vigor from such a wild source. It was because the children of the Empire were not suckled by the wolf that they were conquered and displaced by the children of the northern forests who were."

The Anglo-Saxon language was the root that sprouted English literature when "children of the northern forests" overran Britain in the Dark Ages. Despite his "tame and civilized" complaint, Thoreau associates Shakespeare with that mythic root in "Walking" when he writes: "In literature it is only the wild that attracts us. Dullness is but another name for tameness. It is the uncivilized free and wild thinking in *Hamlet* and the *Iliad*, in all the scriptures and mythologies, not learned in schools, that delights us. As the wild duck is more swift and beautiful than the tame, so is the wild—the mallard—thought, which 'mid falling dews wings its way among the fens."

My association of Mooney's Woods with Ariel's Song suggested that there is more of mythic wildness in Shakespeare than the Whiggish Bard convention allows. Britain's wild lands resonated with the children of the northern forests as they displaced the Roman Empire, and remained a basic theme for them. It often was little valued, but it welled up in the liveliest writing, like Shakespeare's. I thought I might begin to understand his "otherness" through this. I decided to backtrack on my M.A. paper on wilderness in English literature and look for an inner-other Shakespeare, starting not in sixteenth century England, where he was born, but, in sixth century Britain, where English was born. What I found surprised me.

# Chapter Two

# Ground Water

---

The Angles, Saxons, Jutes, Frisians, and Danes who pushed the Romanized Celts to Britain's margins in the Dark Ages weren't Thoreau's "savages" anymore, although they were illiterate pagans. They were farmers and traders with a high regard for manufacturing. They also valued hunting, but above all they valued that most civilized of pursuits, war, whereby to get territory and property. Animal mythology remained from earlier totemic "savagery," however. Thanes wore magic "boar images" on their helmets: "the war-minded boar held guard over fierce men." Bards wove scavenging "beasts of battle" into their lays:

> No sound of harp shall waken the warriors,
> But the dark raven,
> Low over the dead, shall tell many tales,
> Say to the eagle how he fared at the feast
> When with the wolf he spoiled the slain...
> (*Beowulf*, XLI)

The Britain the barbarians overran wasn't so savage either. Archeology shows that hunter-gatherer "aborigines" had lived there but no historical record of them exists. A farming society began Stonehenge before Egypt built the Pyramids, and Neolithic population explosions deforested some areas. Many of Britain's historic moors and heaths were originally wooded, as logs still dug from bogs demonstrate. Later cultures further tamed the island and the Romans urbanized much of it. Towns dwindled after Roman rule ended in the fifth century, however, and Dark Age Britain was shaggier than it has been since. Boars, red deer, wolves, bears and lynx survived, perhaps other large species. Great forests and wetlands remained--wilderness.

The word wilderness is a combination of the Anglo-Saxon noun "wildeor," meaning "wild beast," with the suffix "ness": "state" or "condition." Much has changed in the way English-speakers regard it since the sixth century. Medieval Catholics listening to courtly epics saw it as ancient forest full of wolves and boars. Reformation Protestants reading the Old Testament saw it as "desert" with lions and other exotic beasts. Still, the basic meaning has persisted—places where wild beasts live, large ones. A farm woodlot's shrews and mice are as wild as wolves and boars, but we are relatively large animals ourselves and see the world accordingly.

English-speakers doubted from the start whether such places were acceptable. They associated them with death and destruction. Yet they liked to evoke them in art and literature as well as hunt in them. The earliest known Anglo-Saxon poem is about a Roman-Celtic city reverted to the wild:

> ...red arch twists tiles,
> Wryes from roof ridge, reaches groundward...
> ("The Ruin")

The reversion is a cause of regret. Judging from its literary persistence, however, it is also one of fascination with civilization's degenerative side and wilderness's regenerative one. Thirteen centuries after "The Ruin," D. H. Lawrence writes in one story of "the strange squalor of the primitive forest... of animals and their droppings" but in another of "the wild thing's courage to maintain itself alone and living in the midst of a diverse universe." Lawrence also contemplates a reversion: "And if we go on in that way, with everybody, intellectuals, artists, governments, industrialists, and workers all killing off the last human feeling," says the hero of *Lady Chatterley's Lover*, a gamekeeper who refuses to kill the owls and stoats that eat his

master's pheasants, "then ta tah! to the human species!
Goodbye! Darling! The serpent swallows itself and leaves a
void. Considerably messed up but not hopeless. Very nice!
When savage wild dogs bark in Wragby and savage wild pit-
ponies stamp at Tevershall bank!"

## Giant Walkers

The Anglo-Saxon epic, *Beowulf*, is set in ancestral
Scandinavia, but its glacier-scarred landscape would have been
dauntingly familiar to people in Britain. Population growth and
tribal conflict had driven them from the continent: poems like
"The Seafarer" eloquently describe displacement's miseries. The
new land with its strangely collapsing old civilization, sprawling
woodlands, trackless fens, and misty mountains to north and
west must have seemed full of threatening phantasmagoria.

> I have heard landsmen, my people,
> Hall-Counsellors, say they have seen
> Two giant walkers in wasteland
> Wandering the wild, unworldly wights.
> One of them, so far as they saw
> Was like a woman. The other wretch
> Trod exile's track with a man's mien
> But he was bigger than any human.
> Heathens in past days called him Grendel.
> They knew of no Father, as if in oldest times
> Some among dark spirits bore them.
> *(Beowulf* XX)

Yet there was more than simple dislike in their attitude to
wild land. Much settled country remained but pagan Anglo-
Saxon poetry rarely describes it, which suggests it is concerned
with qualities other than tame ones. It doesn't just describe its
wild settings, it invokes them, emphasizing the movement of

natural forces, as with the haunts of the "giant walkers," Grendel and his Mother:

> They hold to the secret land, wolf slopes, windy headlands,
> The perilous fen paths where the mountain rill
> Goes under hills' darkness, the flood under earth…
> Over it hoar woods hang, trees rooted fast over the water.
> There each night flares fire on the flood, a fearful wonder…
> From it surging waves heave up black to heaven
> When wind stirs storms until the air grows gloomy,
> The skies weep…
>
> *(Beowulf,* XX)

When Rome first encountered Germans, the historian Tacitus writes, they had neither temples nor gods in "the form of any human countenance," only sacred "woods and groves." *Beowulf* reflects this. The Icelandic Sagas' Odin pantheon is absent. The "giant walkers" seem older, and probably had been different before the Christian who transcribed the oral epic demonized them as cursed descendants of Cain. "Grendel" derives from an Anglo-Saxon word "grund" for earth or earth-water. Grendel and his Mother inhabit "the flood under the earth," the water table, where springs and streams begin.

Many Dark Age pagans had lost the sense of kinship with wild places implied by their ancestors' "woods and groves." Yet they still saw wilderness as a reservoir of vitality and an arena for testing and displaying it. Beowulf is a hero because he vanquishes the giants and gets their powers. And they certainly have powers, as when Grendel visits the local mead hall:

> The claws of the monster were like steel
> They said no hard thing could hurt him…
> Quickly the door fell, with forged bands fastened,
> When touched by his hands…

The foe stepped to the bright floor, advanced fiercely.
From his eyes came a light not fair, most like flame.
He saw many men in the hall, a band of kinsmen…
Then his heart laughed, fearsome fiend, he thought
That before light broke he would lift the life
From the flesh of each, for there had come
To him a hope of full-feasting…
(*Beowulf,* XI)

Beowulf drives Grendel away, tearing off the "strong arm" with his bare hands.  But he still must face the Mother's unexpected vengeance:

Then she came to Heorot where the Ring-Danes slept.
Then change came early to the earls therein…
(*Beowulf,* XXI)

When Beowulf repels the bloodthirsty Mother and leads the surviving earls in search of the "giant walkers," they find even older, stranger beings:

Her tracks were seen wide over the wood path
Where she had gone to ground, made her way
Forward over the dark moor…
He went before with a few wise men
To spy out the country, until suddenly
He found mountain trees over hoary stones,
A fell forest: water lay under, bloody and boiling…
Then they saw in the water many a snake shape,
Strong sea serpents exploring the mere
And water monsters lying on slopes of the shore
Such as those that in morning often attend
A dangerous sailing on the sea's strands …
(*Beowulf,* XXII)

This might seem the stuff of horror movies, but Grendel and his Mother are not just fantasy monsters to be destroyed before a happy ending. In a way, they are Beowulf's relatives, not so easy to get rid of. His name, Beowulf, "bee-wolf," is another totemic survival, and the giants are like "bee-wolves," brown bears, in their strength, fearlessness and potential for eating people. Bears are totemic ancestors and magical beings in aboriginal mythologies throughout their circumpolar range: one anthropologist calls them the major animals "in the history of metaphysics in the northern hemisphere." Bear skulls artfully arranged in Swiss Alps caves 80,000 years ago imply early mythological thinking. When James Boswell toured Switzerland in 1764, he remarked that the bear was "like the tutelary saint of this people." Such charisma was one reason why "baiting" imported ones with dogs continued in Britain after their eleventh century extirpation there.

A 9,000-year-old sculpture from the Balkans of a bear cradling her cub may be the earliest representation of motherhood. I once watched a grizzly with cubs in Alaska's Denali National Park, the youngsters tussling and sliding down snowfields as their mother lumbered over the steep ridges. Although they seemed small from a safe distance, their presence dominated a landscape overlooked by North America's highest peak, Mount McKinley. Cubs often remain with mothers awhile after reaching full size. In some old myths, an Earth/Water Mother has two sons who compete to create the world.

In *Beowulf*, a bear-man hero whose mother, like Grendel's, is unnamed, competes with a bear-man monster to secure a Dark Age world of farming, trade and war that the monster threatens to reclaim for the forest. Grendel eats dozens of men on each visit to the mead hall, and it is falling into ruin. Pursuing him into the "bloody and boiling" water, Beowulf beheads him and kills the Mother with "a victory blessed blade, a sword made by the giants" that he finds there. The blade melts as he does so, but he returns with the magic hilt and his mythic brother's head:

He flashed up through the water…
They flew to meet him, thanked God,
The strong band of thanes…
They bore the heavy head from the lake's bourn,
Hard for the hearty ones, four fought to carry
Grendel's great skull on spear-shafts to the gold- hall…
Then the gold hilt was handed
Unto the old one, the wizened war-chief…
Thus the Danes' Prince gained, after fiends' fall,
The work of wonder smiths…
(*Beowulf*, XXIII)

*Beowulf* is an exciting tale, but its solemn, graphic violence makes it a grim one. And it doesn't end well. The ominous serpents and melting sword in Grendel's lair foreshadow things to come after Bee-Wolf carves out his Dark Age kingdom and reigns over his people, the Geats, for fifty years. In coveting "the work of wonder smiths," they awaken an elemental power that even he cannot vanquish:

The Fire Dragon was dreadful with many colors,
Burnished by flames; he was fifty feet long…
He it is who must seek a hoard in the earth
To guard heathen gold, wise for his winters…
The lord of the Geats raised his hand, struck the hoary horror
So with his forged blade that the edge failed, bright on the bone,
Bit less surely than the folk-king had need…
The gold-friend of the Geats boasted no great victory…
(*Beowulf*, XL, XXXII, XXXV)

Perhaps the transition from a totemic, foraging life to a farmer, trader, and warrior one left an emotional void in Dark Age pagan life. The "strong bands of thanes" were self-regarding elites: lesser folk increasingly endured their wars without sharing their wealth. The folk included Anglo-Saxon bards, capriciously rewarded dependents. The world they evoke is so gloomy that the attempts of *Beowulf*'s transcriber to brighten it with references to "the Everlasting Lord" and the "Almighty's comfort and help" aren't convincing. It took later Christian attitudes to make Anglo-Saxon poetry less grim. But then it became less exciting.

A ninth century poem gives an idyllic cast to a holy hermit's forest life, which it describes more appealingly than the old epic:

> So that kindly saint, from man's joy severed
> Served the lord, and forsaking the world
> Found joy in wild things and beasts of the wood...
> (*The Life of Saint Guthlac*)

But Guthlac's wood lacks the vitality in elemental forces that infuses *Beowulf*. Saint Bartholomew had to exorcise that in the form of evil spirits before Guthlac could find joy there. Spiritual taming became physical. The monastic orders that the saints founded were major forest-clearers and wetland-drainers, partly because wood and marsh dwelling pagans were harder to convert than farmland ones:

> In God's safekeeping the meadows lay green
> A helper from heaven had driven out the fiend.

## Cockaigne

Wilderness persisted through the Middle Ages in gaps left by war, famine, and plague. It had few charms for the Middle English, who tersely called unpopulated areas "waste" and excluded animals from fantasies of earthly paradise except as roasts, hams, and cheeses. A poem by a young monk speaks for them:

> There is no serpent, wolf, nor fox,
> Horse nor sheep, cow nor ox;
> No pigs or goats does it enclose:
> There is no need there to hold your nose.
> ("The Land of Cockaigne")

According to Northrop Frye, the medieval cosmos had four levels: the celestial, which was good; the human, which was morally split; the wild, which was morally neutral; and the chthonic, which was bad. In practice, the four often were conflated into two, with the celestial and human against the wild and chthonic. In the Celto-Roman Arthurian legends that supplanted *Beowulf* in medieval English mythology, the chthonic monsters of Grendel's mere no longer hold even potential vitality. They just presage doom, as with King Arthur's dream before he dies in battle: "He saw on a scaffold a chair, and the chair was fast to a wheel, and on the chair sat Arthur in richest cloth of gold … And the King thought there was under him, far from him, a hideous deep black water, and therein was all manner of serpents and worms, and wild beasts foul and horrible. And suddenly the King thought that the wheel turned upside down, and he fell among the serpents, and every beast took him by a limb, and then the King cried as he lay in his bed, 'Help, help!'" (Malory, *Le Morte d'Arthur*)

Courtly poetry opposed persistent wilderness by reducing it to formal conventions. More detailed than Anglo-Saxon ones, Middle English descriptions of wild places have the mannered style of tapestries. A fourteenth century provincial dialect epic is typical in its account of an ancient forest through which its hero must pass.

> The Wilderness of Wirral—few were within
> That had great good will toward God or Man…
> Many a cliff must he climb in country wild;
> Far from all his friends, forlorn must he ride…
> So many were the wonders he wandered among

That to tell the tenth part would tax my wits.
Now with serpents he wars, now with savage wolves
Now with wild men of the woods, that watched from the rocks,
Both with bulls and with bears, and with boars besides,
And giants that came gibbering from the jagged steeps...
(*Sir Gawain and the Green Knight*)

The description is apt, but the bulls and bears and gibbering giants have a faded, decorative quality unlike the old Anglo Saxon poems, wherein wilderness thrusts itself into the human world. The Middle English poet doesn't enter the picture he makes: to do so would "tax his wits." Although such poems derived from pagan myths, their tapestry wilderness is not a real adversary anymore. It is static:

High hills on either hand, with hoar woods between
Oaks old and huge by the hundred together
The hazel and hawthorne were all intertwined
With rough raveled moss, that raggedly hung,
With many birds unblithe upon bare twigs
That peeped most piteously for pain of the cold...

*Gawain*'s real story begins after its hero has crossed Wirral and reached a settled demesne where woodlands are marginal to a tale of amorous temptation and feudal ethics-- everyday places where knights turn game into roasts and hams. *Beowulf*'s wilderness treasure hunting has become courtly pastime: its powerful monsters, mere beasts of the chase. And this is no faded tapestry: its graphic butchery verges on pornographic. Indoor venery spices outdoor as the scantily clad chatelaine tempts the hero— "My body is here at hand... Your servant to command" -- while her lord and his bowmen, spearmen, swordsmen, and hounds slaughter a boar:

With many a brave blast they boast of their prize

All hallooed with high glee…
He severs the savage head and sets it aloft,
Then rends the body roughly right down the spine…
Then he breaks out the brawn in fair broad flitches,
And the innards to be eaten in order he takes…
And so with the swine they set off for home;
The boar's head was borne before the same man
That had stabbed him… right through.

*Gawain*'s shift from truncated wilderness quest to extended courtly tale marks a medieval transition from itinerant bards who drew on oral tradition to literate poets who regaled sophisticated audiences with work based on classical and foreign sources. Their fourteenth century masterpiece, Chaucer's *Canterbury Tales*, lacks even a conventional wilderness element except for a parody of knightly romance, "The Tale of Sir Topas," which the poem's clerical and bourgeois characters dismiss as outdated.

Wilderness does thrust itself into some demotic poetry like the border ballads, as when "beasts of battle" divvy up a slain knight:

You'll sit on his white boned thighs
While I pick out his pretty blue eyes;
And with a lock of his gold hair
We'll mend our nest when it grows bare.
("The Two Ravens")

But more is in the Saint Guthlac tradition. As Thoreau complains, the Robin Hood ballads are tame: it is usually summer and the merry men--righteous if outlawed Saxons--feast on venison and resist Norman iniquity. Wild adversaries like wolves or boars are scarce. If not for the Normans, Sherwood Forest might be a backwoods Land of Cockaigne, where streams run ale and birds fly about cooked:

When he came to green wood,
In a merry morning,
There he heard the notes small
Of birds merrily singing.

It is far gone, said Robin
That I was last here;
Me lusts a little for to shoot
At the dun deer.

# Chapter Three

## Spring Water

---

Wilderness shrank further in the Renaissance as forest fell for ships and sheep. Thomas More includes no wild land in the 100,000 square-mile island of his *Utopia*. Tudor poetry receded further from real landscapes. *Gawain*'s mannered Wirral has verisimilitude: a real wilderness of that name existed where its author probably lived, in Chester near the Welsh border. Renaissance poets set pastoral allegories in "wilderness" concocted from courtly romances and travel tales. Such settings are as mannered as Wirral and less substantial. In Edmund Spenser's *Faerie Queen,* the knight errant wanders on a "plaine" from which groves and castles sprout arbitrarily. Forests are synthetic: aspen, palm, and cedar. Beasts are symbolic: lions, dragons, and unicorns.

Yet an old dynamism resurfaces in Shakespeare, who shows as much familiarity with wild places as the *Gawain* poet, also linked to courtly pursuits like hawking and hunting. Judging from his technical vocabulary and the ease with which he uses it, he is as versed in such things as the anonymous medieval poet. And his wilderness is more than a faded tapestry. It thrusts itself into his dramas, literally. The beasts that his knights hunt may hunt the knights, as with what is jokingly called "Shakespeare's most famous stage direction":

Mariner: "Make thou best haste, and go not too far i'th'land. 'Tis like to be loud weather. Besides, this place is famous for the creatures of prey that keep on't. "
Antigonus: "Go thou away. I'll follow instantly...

I never saw the heavens so dim by day. A savage clamour! Well
I may get aboard. This is the chase.
        I'm gone for ever!" *Exit, pursued by a bear...*
                (*The Winter's Tale,* 3, 3)


As a joke, "*Exit, pursued by a bear*" might have come
from a media hack, like a Vaudeville skit's punch line. One
critic accordingly calls it "a bringer of death to Antigonus but of
laughter to the theater audiences." Yet we don't really know if it
made contemporary audiences laugh. A description of a 1611
performance at the Globe Theater by an astrologer and physician
named Simon Forman mentions neither laughter nor bear.
Antigonus's quick exit leads into something different from
Vaudeville comedy, anyway. Shakespeare goes on to describe
the bear's attack and its elemental setting in gory detail through
witnesses, a shepherd and his son, called a "Clown," an archaic
term for a peasant:


Clown: I have seen two such sights, by sea and by land.
But I am not to say it is a sea, for now it is the sky. Betwixt the
firmament and it you cannot thrust a bodkin's point!
        Old Shepherd: Why, boy, how is it.
        Clown: I would you did but see how it chafes, how it
rages, how it takes up the shore. But that's not the point. O, the
most piteous cry of the poor souls! Sometimes to see 'em, and
not to see 'em; now the ship boring the moon with her mainmast;
and anon, swallowed with yeast and froth, as you'd thrust a cork
into a hogshead. And then for the land-service, to see how the
bear tore out his shoulder bone, how he cried to me for help, and
said his name was Antigonus, a nobleman! But to make an end
of the ship—to see how the sea flap-dragoned it! But first, how
the poor souls roared, and the sea mocked them, and how the
poor gentleman roared, and the bear mocked him, both louder
than the sea or weather...
                (*The Winter's Tale*, 3,3)

This is no joke. Jorge Luis Borges, who loved Anglo-Saxon poetry, remarked on the contrast between its settings and most sixteenth century literary wilderness: "The landscapes described in *Don Quixote* have nothing in common with the landscapes of Castile: they are conventional landscapes, full of meadows, streams, and copses that belong in an Italian novel. On the other hand, in *Beowulf*, we sense nature as something fearsome... what could be called sacred horror." And Borges added: "One often says, too hastily—because in addition to *Beowulf*, there is also Shakespeare—that this sentiment for nature is the same as the romantic sentiment."

The *Winter's Tale* bear attack is not "romantic sentiment" any more than it is "rousing melodrama." It is "sacred horror," and if this quality seems anomalous given the drift away from real wilderness, another aspect of the Renaissance was that it reached back past medieval versions of ancient mythologies to original sources, to Thoreau's "great dragon tree of the Western Isles." *The Winter's Tale*, one of Shakespeare's "late romances," is set in a mythologized classical era, but it is not a faded tapestry of medieval convention. Bear totems really were part of fifth century Athens: pubescent girls attended an ursine summer camp where they lived outside and imitated she bears as part of initiation into womanhood. The play's coast, "famous for the creatures of prey that keep on't," is classical Illyria, today's Balkans, where bears have always lived.

"In the tragedies, as in the comedies," writes Northrop Frye, "Shakespeare's settings are deliberately archaic. The form of society in them is closer to that of the *Iliad*, or of *Beowulf*, than it is to ours—or to his own." There is a sense of older things lurking behind the sparkling dialogue, gorgeous imagery, and snappy plots, although Shakespeare passes over the Anglo-Saxon Dark Ages, as if still feeling vaguely inferior to the 500-year-old Celtic-Roman civilization that came before.

His only play about northern barbarians, the "early revenge tragedy" *Titus Andronicus*, is set in a fanciful ancient Rome, and can seem just grisly melodrama. Tamora, Queen of the Goths, takes revenge on her Roman captor, Titus Andronicus, for ritually sacrificing her eldest son by inciting her younger sons to rape and mutilate his daughter, Lavinia. Titus takes revenge on Tamora by slaughtering *her* sons and serving them to her in a pie. Yet the play's relentless protagonist and savage antagonists echo the old *Beowulf* myth. Much of the action occurs around a "gaping hollow" in the forest, and Grendel resonates not only in Tamora's sons but in her lover, the "Moor" Aaron, who engineers her revenge. He has nothing but hatred for civilization: his only desire is to raise their son in the woods:

> Come on, you-thick lipped slave, I'll bear you hence…
> I'll make you feed on berries and on roots…
> And cabin in a cave…
> (*Titus Andronicus*, 4, 2)

## Fairies and Pucks

Shakespeare's other "early" plays generally transpire in more etherealized settings than *Titus*'s, like the "wood near Athens" of *A Midsummer Night's Dream*, which is mythic in Northrop Frye's sense of a realm created by humans, the anthropomorphic one of heroes and fairies. But even they have more sense of real places, flora and fauna, than typical Renaissance writing-- as with the fairy king Oberon's famous speech:

> "I know a bank where the wild thyme blows,
> Where oxlips and the nodding violet grows
> Quite overcanopied with luscious woodbine,
> With sweet musk roses, and with eglantine,
> There sleeps Titania sometime of the night
> Lulled in these flowers with dances and delight;
> And there the snake throws her enameled skin,
> Weed wide enough to wrap a fairy in…"
> (*A Midsummer Night's Dream*, 2,1)

It is elegantly described, but it is a real thicket, full of twigs and thorns as well as flowers, just the place to find a shed snakeskin. A folkloric ground water wells up through the fantasy, as with the *Dream*'s anomalous character of Puck or Robin Goodfellow. According to Northrop Frye, he is a figure of Anglo-Saxon folklore inserted into the play's Classical and Celtic matrix: "His propitiatory name 'Goodfellow,' indicates that he could be dangerous." He is wilder and more zoomorphic than the fairies:

> Sometimes a horse I'll be, sometime a hound,
> A hog, a headless bear, sometime a fire,
> And neigh, and bark, and grunt, and roar, and burn,
> Like horse, hound, hog, bear, fire at every turn.
> (3,1)

Oberon can't quite control the puck, who keeps scrambling the fairy king's orders and clearly likes doing it. He has his own realm, as when he appears-- after the story's romance and fantasy have ended in bridal beds and fairy dances-- to introduce a note of "sacred horror" that has a strange reality in my experience:

> Now the hungry lion roars,
> And the wolf howls the moon...
> While the screech-owl, screeching loud,
> Puts the wretch that lies in woe
> In remembrance of a shroud.
> (5, 2)

I gave no thought to legends that owls watch at deathbeds until I lived in a remote California town with many barn owls, also a British genus. Barn owls screech, and I heard them as they flew over the house most nights, although I only saw them when they perched on wires near streetlights. A neighbor across the street was in his nineties, and one evening an ambulance turned into his driveway. I heard a barn owl, and saw it perched on a wire nearby. Hours later, the ambulance was still there (the nearest hospital was fifty miles away) and the owl was still on the wire, screeching. I'd never seen one perch screeching in one place for so long. The man died that night.

## Vitality

Folkloric groundwater springs to the surface in Shakespeare's "later" plays like *The Winter's Tale*. The main action of *Cymbeline*, a "romance" set in Roman Britain, transpires in the Welsh border mountains, where a "wild-man" hero beheads a prince-villain and, in an echo of stone age burials, lays his torso in a cave beside the princess-heroine's apparently dead body:

> With fairest flowers
> Whilst summer lasts...
> I'll sweeten thy sad grave. Thou shalt not lack
> That flower that's like thy face, pale primrose, nor
> The azured harebell, like thy veins; no, nor
> Like the leaf of eglatine, whom not to slander
> Outsweetened not thy breath...
> *(Cymbeline, 4, 2)*

In the end, a zoomorphic god "descends in thunder and lightning" to save the protagonists:

> The holy eagle
> Stooped as to foot us. His ascension is
> More sweet than our blest fields.
> (5,5)

In Shakespeare's "last" romance, *The Tempest*, the magician Prospero's island is a *wildeor-ness,* as he reveals while scolding Ariel, a native spirit (a puck, judging from its unruly behavior) that he has bound to his service:

> .... Thou best know'st
> What torment did I find thee in. Thy groans
> Did make wolves howl, and penetrate the breasts
> Of ever-angry bears—it was a torment
> To lay upon the damned, which Sycorax
> Could not again undo. It was mine art.
> When I arrived and heard thee, that made gape
> The pine and let thee out.
> (The Tempest, 1, 2)

The island has a "wild man" along with its wolves and bears, Caliban, son of the Ariel-tormenting "blue-eyed hag," Sycorax. He seems a kind of dwarf Grendel as he protests to Prospero, who has enslaved him too:

> This island's mine, by Sycorax my mother,
> Which thou tak'st from me. When thou cam'st first,
> Thou strok'd me and made much of me...
> ... and then I loved thee,
> And showed thee all the qualities o' th' isle,
> The fresh springs, brine pits, barren places and fertile.
> Curst be that I did so! All the charms
> Of Sycorax, toads, beetles, bats, light on you...
> (The Tempest, 1, 2)

Although Shakespeare's "romances" describe their wild settings in less detail than *Gawain*'s Wirral, the vitality that characters draw from them is central. As Prospero says:

> Ye elves of hills, brooks, standing lakes and groves,
> And ye that on the sands with printless foot
> Do chase the ebbing Neptune, and do fly him
> When he comes back... by whose aim.

Weak masters though ye be—I have bedimm'd
The noontide sun, called forth the mutinous winds
And 'twixt the green sea and the azur'd vault,
Set roaring war...
(*The Tempest*, 5, 1)

## Sin and Redemption

Folkloric groundwater wells up darkly in Shakespeare's ancient British tragedies. *Macbeth*'s "witches" are not the pathetic village pariahs of Reformation jurisprudence: they are the Weird Sisters, who inhabit the blasted heath like early mythology's animal goddesses. Their equivocal prophecies set the tragedy in motion and move it through its murders and revenges. Lady Macbeth is their devotee, conjuring strength from elemental forces by invoking an Anglo-Saxon beast of battle:

The raven himself is hoarse
That croaks the fatal entrance of Duncan
Under my battlements.  Come, you spirits
That tend on mortal thoughts, unsex me here
And fill me, from the crown to the toe, top-full
Of direst cruelty! ...
(*Macbeth*, 1, 5)

When his enemies surround him at the play's end, Macbeth invokes the ultimate ancient British beast before they slaughter and behead him:

They have tied me to a stake; I cannot fly,
But bear-like I must fight the course.
(5,7)

King Lear's literally "heathen" invocations in the storm echo Anglo-Saxon "sacred horror" even more:

You cataracts and hurricanes, spout
Till you have drenched our steeples, drowned the cocks!
You sulph'rous and thought-executing fires,
Vaunt-couriers of oak-cleaving thunderbolts,
Singe my white head!  And thou, all shaking thunder,
Strike flat the thick rotundity o' the world,
Crack Nature's molds, all germens spill at once,
That makes ingrateful man!
(*King Lear,* 3, 2)

The Shakespeare tragedies' invocations have a big
difference from pagan ones, however.  Lear is not conjuring
elemental spirits to enhance his own power.  To do so would
bring on the evil that destroys the Macbeths.  Lear is calling
down divine retribution on human iniquity:

Let the great gods,
That keep this dreadful pudder o'er our heads.
Find out their enemies now.  Tremble, thou wretch,
Who hast within thee undivulged crimes
Unwhipped of justice...
(*King Lear,* 3,2)

Although Prospero does invoke nature spirits to gain
personal power in *The Tempest*, his motive is like Lear's and he
abjures his "rough magic" after he punishes his brother for
usurping his Dukedom.

Now my charms are all o'erthrown,
And what I have's mine own,
Which is most faint... Now I want
Spirits to enforce, art to enchant;
And my ending is despair
Unless I be relieved by prayer...
(*The Tempest,* "Epilogue")

The Christian concepts of sin, repentance, and redemption overlie Shakespeare's pagan side. Good women like Cordelia and Desdemona balance bad ones like Tamora and Lady Macbeth. Yet, although he portrays an attempt to gain personal power from wild nature as a potential evil, he doesn't see it as an absolute one as it had been seen since Christianity's inception. His writing is notably unlike the Humanists' in that it doesn't present Christianity as way *out* of wild nature--a mystical path to a higher spiritual reality. Shakespeare has no angelic virgin leading the way to heaven like Dante's Beatrice.

Shakespeare's tragedies depart from medieval Catholicism's basically "comedic" literature, of which *Gawain*'s happy ending is typical. The boar-slaughtering lord whose chatelaine tempts the hero turns out to be a Christ figure, the Green Knight, who absolves Gawain because he rose above that temptation. No Shakespeare character gets off so lightly: his "tragic" outlook seems a resurgence of *Beowulf*'s sense of *wyrd*, of earthly fate, a sense expressed throughout northern Europe as Catholicism's cloistered optimism faltered. Not even Shakespeare's happy-ending "late romances" (also called "tragicomedies") are "comedic" in the sense of opening a way to a heaven: they resolve earthly conflicts. Like Protestantism generally (and like *Beowulf*), his Christianity draws less from the New Testament than the Old, wherein sin, repentance, and redemption are in this world, with no institutional guarantees of salvation or clear ideas of immortality.

When Hamlet considers an afterlife, it is less reassuring to him than dreamless mortal sleep's oblivion:

> To be or not to be, that is the question…
>                    To die, to sleep—
> No more, and by a sleep to say we end
> The heartache and the thousand natural shocks
> That flesh is heir to— 'tis a consummation
> Devoutly to be wished. To die, to sleep.

To sleep, perchance to dream.  Aye, there's the
rub...

(*Hamlet*, 3, 1)


Earthly Being


Shakespeare's tragic outlook has a Puritan aspect.  While
Humanist poets fantasize airy allegorical wildernesses, he
presents uncomfortably real ones as places of recourse and trial,
as they were for Old Testament prophets.  Yet he likes life too
much to deny it in a Protestant way any more than a Catholic
one.  As his flora and fauna are real, his attention is focused on
their natural context:

Now my co-mates and brothers in exile,
 Hath not old custom made this life more sweet
Than that of painted pomp?  Are not these woods
More free from peril than the envious court?
Here feel we not the penalty of Adam,
The seasons' difference, as the icy fang
And churlish chiding of the winter's wind,
Which when it bites and blows upon my body
Even till I shrink with cold, I smile, and say
'This is no flattery.  These are counsellers
that feelingly persuade me what I am.'
Sweet are the uses of adversity
Which, like the toad, ugly and venomous,
Wears yet a precious jewel on his head;
And this our life exempt from public haunt
Finds tongues in trees, books in the running brooks
Sermons in stones, and good in everything.
(*As You Like It,* 2,1)


This speech by Duke Senior, leader of a group of
scholarly French nobles hiding from usurpers in wilderness,

brings up another Shakespeare influence, natural philosophy. Bears and storms are "sacred horror" to him, but they are also *interesting*. "With church authority crumbling," writes a twenty-first century philosopher, "Shakespeare held a view of man and the universe that has no established name... If I were to award him a single label, it would be 'naturalist,' in somewhat the same way one speaks of a student of natural history: he is a clear eyed observer and recorder, sensitive to the facts before his eyes..." It was a growing tendency. Unlike More's *Utopia*, Francis Bacon's *The New Atlantis* includes nature preserves of a sort: "We have great lakes, both salt and fresh, whereof we have use for the fish and fowl... We have also parks, and enclosures of all sorts, of beast and birds; which we use not only for view and rareness, but likewise for dissection and trials, that thereby we may take light what may be wrought on the body of man."

Still, Bacon's "parks" are more zoos and labs than wilderness, and their purpose is more utilitarian than naturalist—to understand nature in order to control it. Given Shakespeare's liking for old and wild things, his response to this is ambivalent—he is curious about what it might reveal, fearful of where it might lead. Sometimes he lampoons it, as when hard-boiled soldiers discuss Nile herpetology during a drinking bout:

> Lepidus: What manner of thing is your crocodile?
> Antony: It is shaped sir, like itself, and it is broad as it has breadth. It is just so
> high as it is, and moves with its own organs. It lives by that which nourisheth
> it, and the elements once out of it, it transmigrates.
> Lepidus: What color is it of?
> Antony: Of its own color, too.
> > (*Antony and Cleopatra*, 2,6)

Sometimes he affirms divine order, as when a commander rails against unruly troops:

The heavens themselves, the planets, and this centre,
Observe degree, priority, and place...
But when the planets
In evil mixture to disorder wander
What plagues and what portent, what mutiny?
(*Troilus and Cressida*, 1, 3)

In *King Lear*, natural philosophy's questioning of divine order fatally corrupts Edmund, the Duke of Gloucester's bastard son: "This is an excellent foppery of the world, that, when we are sick in fortune, often the surfeits of our own behavior, we make guilty of our disasters the sun, the moon, and stars; as if we were villains of necessity; fools by heavenly compulsion... An admirable evasion of whoremaster man, to lay his goatish disposition to the charge of a star!" (1, 2) Edmund's self-serving intellectualization of "natural law" turns him into a calculating usurper:

Thou, Nature, art my goddess; to thy law
My services are bound.  Wherefore should I
Stand in the plague of custom...
(1, 2)

In *Hamlet*, the Prince of Denmark's thoughts circle uneasily around new Copernican ideas of a heliocentric solar system and greatly expanded universe: "O God, I could be bounded in a nutshell and count myself king of infinite space, were it not that I have bad dreams..." (2,2) The new thinking doesn't make Hamlet a devotee of Bacon's progressive, utilitarian order.  He is introspective and pessimistic, hesitant to do his duty and purge the Danish court of his sluttish mother and treacherous stepfather: "This goodly frame the *earth* seems to me a sterile promontory, this excellent canopy, the *air*, look you, this brave o'er hanging firmament, this majestical roof fretted with golden *fire*, why, it appeareth nothing to me but a foul and pestilent congregation of vapors..." (2, 2)

Despite his unease, there is a sense of no return in Shakespeare's ambivalence. He may want the medieval heavens-down hierarchy, the Great Chain of Being, but he doubts it. Hamlet's "to be or not" is a basic statement of doubt. Poets like Dante never expressed, perhaps never conceived, the thought that human being might *depend* on earthly life. And if being depends on earthly life, wild beasts have a new significance, as a bankrupt nobleman turned forest hermit implies in the seldom-performed "late tragedy," *Timon of Athens*:

"If thou wert the lion, the fox would beguile thee. If thou wert the lamb, the fox would eat thee. If thou wert the fox, the lion would suspect thee when peradventure thou wert accused by the ass. If thou wert the ass, thy dullness would torment thee, and still thou lived'st but as breakfast to the wolf. If thou wert the wolf, thy greediness would afflict thee, and oft'st thou wouldst hazard thy life for thy dinner... What beast couldst thou be that were not subject to a beast?" (4, 3)

Shakespeare's sense of being can be surprisingly biological, as when he invokes the stomach's function in the circulatory and nervous systems as well as in digestion:

I send through the rivers of your blood
Even to the court, the heart, to th' seat of th' brain;
And through these cranks and offices of man
The strongest nerves and small inferior veins
From me receive their natural competency
Whereby they live...
        (*Coriolanus*, 1, 1)

Or geological, as when he invokes erosion's role in "deep time":

O God! That one might read the book of fate,
And see the revolution of the times
Make mountains level, and the continent,

Weary of solid firmness, melt itself
Into the sea…
> (2 *Henry IV* 3,1)

## Headstands

Shakespeare's uneasy mix of folklore, classicism, scripture, and natural philosophy evoked something new, a sense of integrity for wild places and their inhabitants, as expressed by the forest-dwelling exile, Duke Senior:

Come, shall we go and kill us venison?
And yet it irks me the poor dappled fools,
Being native burghers of this desert city,
Should in their own confines with forked heads
Have their round haunches gored…
> (*As You Like It,* 2,1)

In *The Winter's Tale*, the totemic bear-monster is not an agent of evil and death as in *Beowulf,* but of justice and life. Antigonus, the bear's prey, is a servile courtier of a Sicilian King, Leontes, who falsely believes that his queen, Hermione, has borne a girl child adulterously by his visiting friend Polixenes, king of Bohemia. Antigonus first tries to coax Leontes out of his jealous delusion by offering to "geld" his own three daughters if it is true. But when Leontes dismisses his objections and orders him, in classical Greek fashion, to expose the supposed bastard in wild Illyria, "the seacoast of Bohemia," he consents-- lugubriously but promptly:

I swear to do this, though a present death
Had been more merciful. Come on, poor babe,
Some powerful spirit instruct the kites and ravens
To be thy nurses. Wolves and bears, they say,
Casting their savageness aside, have done
Like office of pity…

*(The Winter's Tale, 3,1)*

Antigonus's self-absolving wish comes true in a way when the bear eats him instead of the infant as he exposes her on the shore. The "savage clamor" attracts the Old Shepherd and the Clown -- bear proxies who adopt the child, encouraged by the discovery of a purse of gold Antigonus has guiltily left with her. As I've said, we don't know if contemporary audiences took Antigonus's famous "exit" as a joke. But the Illyrian rustics' positive attitude to ursine manslaughter probably puzzled people for whom a bear's proper place was to be tortured for an afternoon's entertainment:

Old Shepherd: "Heavy matters. Heavy matters. But look thee here, boy. Now bless thyself. Thou met'st with things dying, I with things new born..."
Clown: "Go you the next way with your findings. I'll go see if the bear be gone from the gentleman and how much he hath eaten. They are never curst but when they are hungry. If there be any of him left I'll bury it."
Old Shepherd: "That's a good deed. If thou mayst discern by that which is left of him what he is, fetch me to th' sight of him."
Clown: "Marry will I; and you shall help to put him i'th' ground."
Shepherd: "'Tis a lucky day, boy, and we'll do good deeds on't."

*(The Winter's Tale, 3,3)*

Named Perdita, "the lost girl," the adopted infant grows up as part of the shaggy Illyrian coast, which is beautiful with spring wildflowers as well as dangerous with bears, as she proclaims to the Bohemian King Polixenes and his son, Florizel, when they eventually meet her:

daffodils,
That come before the swallow dares, and take

The winds of March with beauty; violets, dim,
But sweeter than the lids of Juno's eyes
Or Cytherea's breath; pale primroses,
That die unmarried ere they can behold
Bright Phoebus in his strength—a malady
Most incident to maids; bold oxlips, and
The crown imperial; lilies of all kinds
The fleur de luce being one...
(*The Winter's Tale,* 4, 4)

*The Winter's Tale* stands earlier English literature on its head. Rather than evil adversary, as in *Beowulf,* or a vestigial obstacle, as in *Gawain,* wilderness is a positive fulcrum of the drama as it fosters the survival of a female regenerative figure, Perdita. In *Beowulf,* the only active female is a bear-mother monster. In *Gawain,* the active females are ambiguous—the chatelaine who tempts the hero and a disguised witch who threatens him. The regenerative figure is the Christ-like Green Knight. In *The Winter's Tale,* the regenerative figure is a "bear-girl" whose reappearance, marriage to the Bohemian Prince Florizel, and return to the Sicilian court redeems her father by mysteriously bringing back to life her mother-- thought to have died sixteen years earlier from grief at her husband's accusations and her son's death.

When first confronted with rustic Perdita, the Bohemian King Polixenes makes her a conventional speech motivated by anxiety at Prince Florizel's obvious desire for the strange wild girl. He talks about horticulture, the art of grafting wild to domestic stock to improve usefulness:

You see sweet maid, we marry
A gentler scion with the wildest stock,
And make conceive a bark of baser kind
By bud of nobler race. This is an art
That does mend nature...

But Perdita doesn't like the implications of a wild plant being of "a baser kind," and rudely tells Polixenes what she thinks of "mended" flowers:

> I'll not put
> The dibble in earth to set one slip of them,
> No more than, were I painted, I would wish
> This youth should say 'twere well, and only therefore
> Desire to breed by me...

She hands Polixenes a bouquet of kitchen herbs and tells him that she believes "they are given to men of middle age." Then she tells young Florizel she wishes it were spring so she could give him native wildflowers:

> O, these I lack,
> To make a garland of, and my sweet friend,
> To strew him o'er and o'er...
> For love to lie and play on...
> (*The Winter's Tale* 4,4)

With this exchange, Shakespeare implicitly reaches back past millennia of sharp divisions between nature and culture. Perdita denies them, and Leontes's later redemption through the "animation" of a supposed funerary statue of Queen Hermione after Perdita's return embodies this, reversing the tag: "Ars longia; vita brevis." As her aging face shows, the "resurrected" Hermione has been alive all along: she has simply been waiting for the return of her lost one. "Nature provides the means for the regeneration of artifice," writes Northrop Fry, acknowledging the play's departure from convention. "[N]ature is associated, not with the credible, but with the incredible."

> Yet nature is made better by no mean
> But nature makes that mean; so, over that art,
> Which you say adds to nature, it is art

That nature makes.
(4, 4)


*The Winter's Tale* also stands Shakespeare's tragedies on their heads. In most, a hero dies because of evil women (Queen Gertrude, Lady Macbeth, Goneril and Regan) or because of what he thinks are evil women (Desdemona, Cordelia). In *The Winter's Tale*, good women redeem the evil-doing hero, Leontes, and do so in mythic three-fold form: as a maiden, Perdita; a mother, Hermione; and a crone, Paulina, who, although married to Leontes's infant-exposing toady Antigonus, eloquently denies the king's accusations of adultery against Hermione. When he threatens to burn her like a witch, she cries:

It is an heretic that makes the fire,
Not she that burns in't.
(3, 1)


Such upending had disturbing implications for conventional ideas of man's superiority. The problem of human nature—of origin and generation-- became a crucial one as ethnology's dawning knowledge of uncivilized people confronted *Genesis*. The "wild man" emerged from *Beowulf* and *Gawain*'s folkloric shadows into explorers' accounts like Thomas Hariot's *Brief and True Report of the New Found Land of Virginia*, published in 1588. Its description of Algonquian Indian mythology implied that humanity is much older than the Bible says. Shakespeare's Caliban is a token of this emergence. He may be called the "freckled whelp" of a witch and a pagan god named Setebos, but a civilized visitor who discovers him sees not a devil but a "natural curiosity," a potentially valuable one:
"What have we here, a man or a fish?... A strange fish! Were I in England now, as once I was, and but this fish painted, not a holiday fool there but would give a piece of silver. There would this monster make a man. When they will not give a doit

to relieve a lame beggar, they will lay out ten to see a dead
Indian." (2,2)

The implications were disturbing enough that convention
promptly placed Shakespeare in the innocuous role of a naive
rustic. In 1631, twenty-three-year-old John Milton, living on his
father's country estate, patronized him in his pastoral lyric,
*L'Allegro*, as "sweetest Shakespeare, fancy's child," warbling
"his native wood-notes wild" in contrast to "learned" Ben
Jonson. But Shakespeare's attitude to wild nature is far from
naïve although his refusal to render it as conventionally
decorative can make it seem so. That is one of the convincing
things about it.

# Chapter Four

# Downstream

---

Oliver Cromwell's revolution outlawed plays along with bear
baiting, which the Roundheads stopped—by shooting the
bears—because it was a kind of ritual drama as well as a source
of gambling and disorder. But the Puritans couldn't outlaw
Shakespeare's influence: many of their libraries contained his
poems and plays. His "sacred horror" penetrated to their
imaginations, which conceived an allegorical wilderness
stronger, if darker, than the Humanist one. Bunyan's *Pilgrim's
Progress* calls it the Valley of Death: "We also saw the
hobgoblins, satyrs, and dragons of the Pit... and over that valley
hangs the discouraging clouds of Confusion."

Massachusetts Bay colonists superimposed the Valley on
ancient forest –thus all the "Devil's Kingdoms" in New England
hills. Still, the Puritans couldn't fall into the Manichaean heresy
of saying that the Devil made wilderness, even if he inhabited it.
And it was not clear that he did inhabit it. The aged Milton of
*Paradise Lost* was more puritanical than the youth of *L'Allegro*
but he still prized Shakespeare's "wood notes." He surrounds his
Eden with a wilderness created to *repel* Satan:

> So on he fares, and to the border comes
> Of Eden, where Delicious Paradise
> Now nearer, crowns with her enclosure green,
> As with a rural mound, the Champaign head,
> Of a steep Wilderness, whose hairy sides
> With thicket overgrown, grotesque and wild,
> Access denied; and overhead up grew

> Insuperable height of loftiest shade
> Cedar, and Pine, and Fir, and branching Palm...
> (*Paradise Lost*, Book IV)

A gentleman Puritan, Milton is as eclectic about natural history as the Renaissance allegorists with his "Fir, and branching Palm." He has in mind corners of an estate left to natural vegetation, which landscapers had started calling wilderness. But the concept of even nominally wild places having a "use" was a departure from tradition, and Shakespeare's backwoods redemptions stood behind it. Daniel Defoe's Robinson Crusoe is a Puritan Prospero even though he uses prayer and industry instead of sorcery to "enchant" his desert island and wild man Friday.

The Restoration freed Shakespeare from the Puritan dungeon but by then he seemed too crude in the original. Francophile Stuart society continued to patronize his "wood notes" and saw his folkloric side as barbarism from which increasingly Whiggish society wanted to progress. *The Tempest*'s wild humanoid, Caliban, baffled the period's major poet, John Dryden, who describes him as "not in nature... a species of himself" although Caliban is *The Tempest*'s earthiest character, "smelling of horse piss." Dryden introduced his revival of the shaggy old play reverently but smoothed its edges to suit current taste:

> As, when a tree's cut down, the secret root
> Lives underground, and thence new branches shoot;
> So from old Shakespeare's honored dust, this day
> Springs up and buds a new reviving play...

The Grandest Imagination

When the Restoration merged into the Enlightenment, some writers began to regard the "wood notes" as more than naïvely rustic. "If any Author deserved the name of an *Original*," Alexander Pope writes in his 1725 edition of the plays, "it was *Shakespeare*. *Homer* himself drew not his art so immediately from the foundations of Nature." In his 1756 edition, Samuel Johnson expands on this: "The work of a correct and regular writer is a garden accurately formed and diligently planted, varied with shades, and scented with flowers; the composition of Shakespeare is a forest, in which the oaks extend their branches, and pines tower in the air, interspersed sometimes with weeds and brambles, and sometimes giving shelter to myrtles and to roses; filling the eye with awful pomp, and gratifying the mind with endless diversity."

Pope and Johnson also trimmed the "weeds and brambles." The Enlightenment focused on civilized Human Nature. When Jonathan Swift's rationalist knight-errant, Lemuel Gulliver, explores the globe he finds not bear-haunted wilds but fantastic cities. Even Swift's animals, the equine Houyhnnyms, are civilized although they have humanoid beasts of burden, the Yahoos, more of Caliban's literary offspring. Swift is not writing of a desert island's lone inhabitant, however, but of a crowded one's millions, the Romanized Celts degraded by horsey English landowners to "wild Irish": "the red-haired of both sexes are more libidinous and mischievous than the rest."

Shakespeare's anomalous Caliban still pointed back from there. Enlightenment writers who wanted a rational natural order either had to find a positive character in the wild man or conclude that he fell outside, "a species of himself," inconceivable if that order was the work of a rational providence. The ensuing search for him, noble or otherwise, failed. No real wild men remained: the "savages" all had technologies, languages, and mythologies. Gulliver distinguishes clearly between the bestial Yahoos and some Australian aborigines who shoot arrows at him. Yet the search increased interest in wild places. Late Enlightenment poetry describes real ones, albeit in artificial neoclassical diction:

All ether softening, Sober Evening takes
Her wonted station in the middle air
A thousand shadows at her beck…
(Thomson, *The Seasons*)

Writers still regarded large wild beasts with suspicion.
Gilbert White, a clergyman whose *Natural History of Selborne*
brought nature study to popular prose, was pleased when
frightened peasants killed moose or bison that nobles tried to
keep in their parks. He deplored even deer because they tempted
his parishioners to poach. Such writing entailed a shift of
convention, however. Writers always had valued pleasant,
useful nature— edible flora and fauna, cultivated landscape-- but
Shakespeare had stretched the limits of use, imbuing wild nature
with spiritual potential. Following on his evocations of ancient
worlds, poets began to prize "waste" and "vermin" for inducing
sentiments that they called "Sublime" because they combined
aesthetic pleasure with numinous awe. They began to sound like
genteel Lady Macbeths:

But cawing rooks, and kites that swim sublime
In still repeated circles, screaming loud
The jay, the pie, and even the boding owl
That hails the rising moon, have charms for me…"
(Cowper, *The Task*)

Although a product of the Enlightenment, the Sublime
led to a reaction against it. When, during his 1764 continental
tour, Boswell heard Voltaire call Shakespeare "a madman," he
defied the august *philosophe*, insisting that Britons revered the
Bard because they had the grandest imagination. Boswell exulted
in "immense mountains, some covered with frowning rocks,
others with clustering pines," and English poets soon followed
him, dropping Francophile neoclassicism for Anglo-Saxon
monosyllables and intimations of animism:

There is society where none intrudes
By the deep sea, and music in its roar…
(Byron, *Childe Harold*)

The Romantics positively embraced Shakespeare's old folkloric side. Prohibited to have a dog in his Cambridge rooms, Byron kept a bear. Walter Scott loaded his Elizabethan era novel, *Kenilworth*, with bear proxies, including an actor-turned-sorcerer's apprentice who lives under a ring of megaliths in a valley sacred to a Norse demigod. Baiting fascinated Scott: "There you may see the bear lying at guard with his red pinky eyes, watching the onset of the mastiff, like a wily captain…" A reference to box-office rivalry between it and theater ("the manly amusement of bear-baiting is falling into comparative neglect; since men would rather see rough players kill each other in jest…") features a walk-on by the Bard himself, called "Wild Will" and described not just as a deer poacher but as a seducer of gamekeepers' daughters.

Critics went from patronizing the wood notes to worshiping them. "O mighty poet!" writes Thomas de Quincy, foreshadowing Thoreau, "Thy works are not as those of other men, simply and merely great works of art; they are also like the phenomena of nature, like the sun and the sea, the stars and the flowers…" Where the Enlightenment had seen the Sublime as a complement to reason, the Romantics saw it as a challenge to supposedly enlightened reason's failure to improve society. Shakespeare morphed from a genial rustic to a rebellious one, and the Sublime became less of an enhancement to urban civilization and more of an alternative.

The Bard remained substantially Whiggish. For all their folkloric nostalgia, the Romantics clung to progress. Their rebel William stayed upward mobile, and although they liked imagining *Lear* and *Cymbeline*'s shaggy worlds, the reality was something else. Some projected the ancient world's savage side onto the modern city. The Puritans had fled Britain's sinful towns but still valued urbanism above wilderness: they wanted the City of God. The Lake Poets began to regard the industrial revolution's reeking mill towns with feelings like their ancestors' toward ancient forests: Wordsworth describes London as a "Parliament of monsters," a "monstrous anthill." His holy hermit lives:

> From crowded streets remote
> Far from the living and dead Wilderness
> Of the thronged world…
> (*The Recluse*)

Anyway, the romantics couldn't experience British wilderness: the period saw boar and wolf extirpation even from the Scottish Highlands. Wordsworth and his friends drew imagery from explorers' accounts like colonial naturalist William Bartram's colorful descriptions of Florida in his 1791 book, *Travels*, but getting to such places was beyond even the adventurous Byron. Most fled to settled countryside, which finally offered no alternative to the ills of progress. Whig mill owners eager to lower food prices and Tory land owners intent on raising rents held rustics in a vice.

## Jungle Law

Reacting against bucolic pieties, the Victorians reversed Wordsworth's urban metaphor in books like Darwin's *Voyage of the Beagle*. They began to sound like Duke Senior in *As You Like It*, describing wilderness as a "desert city" composed of complex competing hierarchies, with beasts "the native burghers." Except for anomalous Shakespeare, pre-Darwinian wilderness had been static and monolithic— beasts and devils united against God and man. Evolutionists saw it as a contest among all living beings, one that led to open-ended change. They began to sound like genteel Timons of Athens: "What beast couldst thou be that were not subject to a beast?"

This didn't necessarily improve wilderness's reputation, as with Tennyson's "nature red in tooth and claw." Yet breaking wild faunas into dynamic rivalries gave writers a new imaginative access to them. The expanding Empire let more of them see real wilderness, and it fascinated them:

> Now Chil the Kite brings home the night
> That Mang the Bat sets free—
> The herds are shut in byre and hut
> For loosed 'til dawn are we.
> This is the hour of pride and power,
> Talon, and tusk and claw.
> Oh hear the call! Good hunting all
> That keep the jungle law!
> (*The Jungle Books*)

As Shakespeare's bear girl escapes civilized evil in Illyrian forest, Kipling's wolf boy escapes it in Indian jungle. Kipling sees the jungle appreciatively from inside, with the lawful figures of Baloo the bear, Akela the wolf, and Bagheera the panther wisely ruling a society of weaker creatures and resisting outlaws like the lame tiger Shere Khan and invaders like the Red Dogs. The "Letting in The Jungle" chapter, wherein Mowgli summons the beasts to raze the hopelessly mean town that ruined his human foster parents, epitomizes the sense of regeneration that stretches from "The Ruin" to *Lady Chatterley's Lover*:

"They had no time to patch and plaster the rear walls of the empty byres that backed onto the Jungle; the wild pig trampled them down, and the knotty rooted vines hurried after and threw their elbows over the new won ground, and the coarse grass bristled behind the vines...

"A month later the place was a dimpled mound, covered with soft green stuff, and by the end of the Rains there was the roaring Jungle in full blast on the spot that had been under plow not six months before."

Kipling's beasts embody what Shakespeare sensed and Darwin showed: that mind is not imbued from above, but evolved from within neurons that we share with bears and wolves. Wild animals don't have human minds, but they have minds which we understand less than we do the moon. And although *The Jungle Book* can be read as an allegory of the British Raj, with Shere Khan as benighted Hindu civilization and the Red Dogs as invasive Russia, Baloo and Akela seem more grown-up, more "evolved," in their way than the progress-dazzled sahibs of Kipling's "adult fiction." They know their world better.

The nineteenth century's radical revision of the human-nature relationship raised the fraught possibility that humanity might prove impracticable. The twentieth century explored this in many practical ways, starting with the Great War, which brought Bunyan's Valley of Death to life in No Man's Land with its industrial beasts of battle, scavenging rats. As the war froze the expansion that had fueled British civilization since the Reformation, writers looked back in hope of learning what went wrong, involving more attempts to see past the Whiggish Bard's role as a naïve harbinger of progress.

Two Americans expressed the retrospective mood in *The Waste Land*, with its title parodying the medieval term for wilderness. T.S. Eliot and Ezra Pound fled an increasingly crass New World to recapture European high culture, but found it collapsing. The "waste" of their poem is not the unused land of Middle English but the used-up land of utilitarian Humanism, with its ruins and deforestation.

> A heap of broken images, where the sun beats,
> And the dead tree gives no shelter ...

*The Waste Land* echoes *Gawain*, but it is the moonscape of cultural exhaustion that opposes a regenerative quest, not beasts and monsters. In the fourteenth century poem, after enduring wilderness and earthly temptation, the hero finds the Christ-like Elf Knight in the ruined Green Chapel. In the twentieth century one, after enduring barren but crowded mountains, a nameless seeker finds only ruins:

> There is the empty chapel, only the wind's home.
> It has no windows and the door swings...

As the American poets rummaged through the heap of broken images, they looked back to ancient forests: "where the hermit thrush sings in the pine trees." The modernist epic that Eliot generated and Pound shaped gives a bird that sings North America's loveliest song an inviolate status opposite that of a mythic Eurasian counterpart. Evoking the story in Ovid's *Metamorphoses* of Philomel, a Greek princess changed into a nightingale after a Thracian king rapes her and cuts out her tongue to silence her, *The Waste Land* makes the Old World songbird an ironic embodiment of violation and, again, overuse, exhaustion:

> So rudely forced; yet there the nightingale
> Filled all the desert with inviolable voice...
> And other withered stumps of time
> Were told upon the walls...

In *Titus Andronicus*, after Tamora's sons rape Titus's daughter and cut off her tongue and hands to silence her, she exposes them by pointing with her stumps to Ovid's tale of Philomel. *The Waste Land* is full of such Shakespearean echoes, like "voices singing out of empty cisterns and exhausted wells," and nowhere more than when it parodies the speech just before *The Tempest* 's "Full Fathom Five." In the play, Prince Ferdinand of Naples rues his plight as the only apparent survivor of Prospero's magic storm, but Ariel's song leads him to a regenerative meeting with the mage's daughter, Miranda:

This music crept by me upon the waters,
Allaying both their fury and their passion
With its sweet air...
           (1, 2)

In *The Waste Land*, the "sweet air" leads to "the sounds of horns and motors" and a polluted Thames:

'This music crept by me upon the waters'
And along the Strand...
           The river sweats
           Oil and tar....

*The Waste Land*'s reaction against Whiggish utilitarianism set the tone for modernists like D. H. Lawrence. Despite his ambivalence, Lawrence idealizes wilderness vehemently at times: "The wild animal is at every moment intensely self-disciplined, poised in the tension of self-defense, self-preservation, and self-assertion." Like Thoreau, Lawrence places Shakespeare with Homer and the Bible as "the supreme old novels... Which means that in their wholeness they affect the whole man alive ... Man and the animals and the flowers all live within a strange and ever-surging chaos... Man fixes some wonderful erection of his own between himself and the wild chaos, and gradually grows bleached and stifled under his parasol. Then comes a poet, enemy of convention, and makes a slit in the umbrella; and lo! the glimpse of chaos is a vision ... Shakespeare made a big rent and saw emotional, wistful man outside in the chaos."

## A Painted Dome

The modernists' Shakespeare faded during the Great Depression as leftist utilitarians like W. H. Auden sought umbrellas against "strange and ever-surging chaos." The young Auden's "ideal landscape" was a prosperous coal-mining valley—what miner's son Lawrence had consigned to savage wild dogs. The Bard became proto-socialist-- his upward mobility an early form of class struggle, his wood notes again patronized. A rightist utilitarian, Wyndham Lewis, calls him "much more a Bolshevik... than a figure of conservative romance" and his "famous 'natural magic'" a "bag of tricks."

The Second World War "brought forth" the Shakespeare that congealed in my New England suburb. The heirs of Auschwitz and Hiroshima wanted not only umbrellas but what Lawrence called "a painted dome" against ever-surging chaos. Reverting to Anglican utilitarianism, the middle-aged Auden exhumed the medieval convention of wilderness as waste. "One must accept responsibility for making nature what it should be," he said in New York Shakespeare lectures. "I am continually shocked by the unhumanized nature of this country... One mustn't treat nature as morally responsible or we become superstitious... nature must be tamed."

Auden's lectures see the Bard as a Christian moralist (Tolstoy spins in his grave), his landscapes and beasts as symbols. *The Winter's Tale*'s Illyria is a figurative Eden, not a Balkan wilderness: "Man falls from the Garden of Eden and can only reach an earthly paradise again by a process of repentance and purgatorial suffering, as Leontes does." Interestingly, Auden calls the *"Exit, pursued by a bear"* scene "the most beautiful" in Shakespeare, which seems at odds with his *diktat* against treating nature as "morally responsible." The bear's eating Antigonus in lieu of the infant Perdita has moral implications. But Auden is vague: "In the middle of the desert near the scene, there is the storm, and there are beasts of prey, hunters hunting bears and bears hunting hunters... The scene has the archetypal symbols of death, rebirth, beasts of prey, luck."

Young postwar British writers, called "the Movement," hardly noticed wild nature in the 1950s economic boom. Critics called them "glad to be as comfortable as possible in a wicked, commercial, threatened world." Their leading poet, Philip Larkin, was attached to traditional countryside but deplored the

Empire's end as a fall into Third World savagery: "England is going down generally! It is shown now that one child in eight is born of immigrant parents. Cheerful outlook, isn't it? Another fifty years and it'll be like living in bloody India—tigers prowling about, elephants too, shouldn't wonder." Despite a liking for Lawrence, Larkin had no hope of wilderness regenerations. Like other Movement writers, he saw even Britain's cultivated landscape as finished:

> Before I snuff it, the whole
> Boiling will be bricked in
> Except for the tourist parts—
> First slum in Europe...
>     ("Going, Going")

Aside from imagery and elegy —butterflies, a hedgehog he accidentally dismembers with his power mower—Larkin writes of British wildlife symbolically:

> Ah, were I courageous enough
> To shout *Stuff your pension!*
> But I know, all too well, that's the stuff
> That dreams are made on:
> For something sufficiently toadlike
> Squats in me too...
>     ("The Toads")

Larkin's toads symbolize anxious dependence on secular civilization— his job as a university librarian. To him, Shakespeare's tragicomic redemptions are literally what "dreams are made on." Even democratized utilitarianism turned threatening as economic totalization brought unprecedented crowding and pollution, unnerving Auden, who fled humanized Britain and dithered in his New York Shakespeare lecture: "But we must not regard nature as having no rights and existing solely for our convenience, because nature will revenge itself."

Responding to anthropological studies that reveal "the savage mind" as more cultivated than had been thought, some writers looked back past Classics and Scriptures toward new relationships with wilderness's regenerative power. But how could they find them where wilderness had not existed for centuries? A country whose greatest writer saw an anomalous centrality in wilderness and that remains fascinated with it is among the few without any.

Writers set British wilderness in the past. Joseph Conrad's *Heart of Darkness* makes it a Roman Empire version of the African jungle that destroys his missionary anti-hero, Kurtz: "Think of a decent young citizen in a toga—perhaps too much dice, you know—coming out here… Land in a swamp, march through the woods, and in some inland post feel the savagery, the utter savagery, that had closed around him—all that mysterious life of the wilderness that stirs in the forest, in the jungles, in the hearts of wild men…" In Kipling's *Puck of Pook's Hill*, written years after *The Jungle Books*, "Puck" is not a wild shape-shifter but a quaint history tutor. Baloo and Akela's ancient British counterparts are mindless brutes, driven in chains to Roman circuses.

One postwar writer tried to imagine a kind of wilderness restoration. A library administrator like Larkin, Angus Wilson happened to like large wild animals. He also expected them to vanish, so his 1961 novel about them, *The Old Men at the Zoo*, is mainly about problems. The London Zoo's director wants to restore native species to a fenced tract and drive the public through in buses: "Stretches of pine forest provided the Historic British Reserve, soon to be closed to all but the guided and armed; for here in ten years we hoped for increase of deer that would maintain carefully limited packs of wolves and in the mountains that stretched beyond into Wales, golden eagles and brown bear." But the scheme founders as Common Market countries revert to Roman fascism and invade Britain. They plot to pit the zoo's bears and wolves against political prisoners in neo-gladiatorial displays.

Wilson's novel fails to address one problem: a scarcity of native ecosystems. Boars and bears need food trees like oak and beech but the medieval Wilderness of Wirral's probable location, Peak District National Park, now contains less than ten percent forest cover, much of it commercial softwood -- "stretches of pine forest." The rest of the park, England and Wales's fifth largest, has pastures, croplands, moors, and bogs. Convention resists wilderness in the Scottish Highlands, where sheep and semi-tame red deer prevent forest regeneration. Resistance is deep-seated even among nature lovers, as with *The Old Men at the Zoo*'s elitist, authoritarian fiat that the Historic British Reserve be closed to "all but the guided and armed."

Wilson's "reserve" is more like Bacon's "parks" than Shakespeare's forests and seacoasts. Restoring regenerative links between civilization and the biosphere's "strange and ever surging chaos" will need more than extended zoos. It will need basic cultural changes-- and what is more basic to utilitarian civilization than the Whiggish Bard? "But now, alas, the roof of our dome is simply painted over with Hamlets and Macbeths, the side walls too, and the order is fixed and complete. And this will go on until some terrific wind shivers the umbrella to ribbons... For chaos is always there, and will always be, no matter how we put up umbrellas of visions."

Yet the other-inner Shakespeare's big rent in the umbrella remains. He may seem Whiggish because he doesn't slight nature's dangers and discomforts:

> A barren detested vale you see it is;
> The trees, though summer, yet forlorn and lean,
> Overcome with moss and baleful mistletoe
> Here never shines the sun, here nothing breeds
> Unless the nightly owl or fatal raven...
> (*Titus Andronicus,* 2,3)

But the canon is a permanent reminder that wilderness comes first and last. The safety of palaces and castles destroys Shakespeare's tragic characters: the danger of forests, mountains, and desert islands redeems his tragicomic ones. And this is not just a genius hack's bag of tricks. "His love and understanding of the country are extraordinary," writes one prominent English historian, Hugh Trevor-Roper, "far deeper than that of the any other poet, even in England." The effects keep cropping up, as when Ariel's Song strangely validated my experience of Mooney's Woods. For all its sparseness, scattered through the canon, Shakespeare's wilderness remains a liberating force in a world of ever-growing walls:

> The birds chant melody on every bush,
> The snake lies rolled in the cheerful sun,
> The green leaves quiver with the cooling wind
> And make a chequered shadow on the ground.
> (*Titus Andronicus*, 2,3)

# II

# ANTHROPOLOGY

---

Since once I sat upon a promontory
And heard a mermaid on a dolphin's back...
That very time I saw...
Flying between the cold moon and earth
Cupid all armed...
Yet marked I where the bolt of Cupid fell
It fell upon a little western flower—
Before milk white; now, purple with love's wound...
(*A Midsummer Night's Dream*, 2,1)

# Chapter Five

## Two Dragons

———————

Tracing English literature's wilderness stream did connect with a mythic Shakespeare but it didn't explain my epiphany in response to Ariel's Song. Although Shakespeare's feeling for wild nature is unique among Elizabethan writers, his other concerns are not: love, honor, politics-- the everyday world. That world also comes into Ariel's song, which involves not just nature but the transformation of a basic authority figure. While I didn't feel that my attitude to my own father was part of my epiphany, I thought that it probably was, somehow. I wanted a mythic look at the canon's everyday world to understand Shakespeare's effect on me.

That proved elusive not only in biographies but in my reading on myth, although Joseph Campbell's four volume survey of world mythology *defines* it with a quote from *Hamlet*: "The first function of mythology is to reconcile waking consciousness with the *mysterium tremendum et fascinans* of this universe *as it is*: The second being to render an interpretive total image of the same, as known to contemporary consciousness. Shakespeare's definition of the function of his art, 'to hold, as 'twere, the mirror up to nature,' is thus equally a definition of mythology." Yet Campbell's massive survey has only passing references to the Shakespeare canon, as though it is not mythic enough. He concentrates on lofty savants like Dante and Goethe.

Shakespeare's mythic elusiveness was frustrating considering the Whiggish Bard's perennial popularity. A Stratford Festival I visited offered a "creative rejuvenation... enriched with more interpretive boldness" in its press release, but it seemed like the embalmed and dissected repertoire that TV's

*Slings and Arrows* satirizes: a modern dress "contemporary issues" tragedy, a "musical" comedy, a defanged "problem play." It was hard to see it as a branch of Thoreau's "great dragon tree."

Draughty Radiant Paradise

So I was intrigued when I chanced on the 524-page *Shakespeare and the Goddess of Complete Being* that Ted Hughes published in 1992. Poet Laureate from 1984 until his death in 1998, Hughes was the main postwar British exponent of restoring mythic relationships with wild nature. In a 1970 essay, he advocates them even more vehemently than Lawrence:

"The fundamental guiding ideas of our Western Civilization are... based on the assumption that the earth is a heap of raw materials given to man by God for his exclusive profit and use. The creepy-crawlies who infest it are devils of dirt and without a soul, also put there for his exclusive profit and use... Sure enough, when the modern mediumistic artist looks into his crystal, he sees always the same thing. He sees the last nightmare of mental disintegration and spiritual emptiness, under the superego of Moses, in its original or in some Totalitarian form, and the self-anesthetizing schizophrenia of St. Paul. This is the soul-state of our civilization. But he may see something else. He may see a vision of the real Eden, 'excellent as the first day,' the draughty radiant Paradise of the animals, which is the actual earth, in the actual universe."

"The draughty radiant Paradise of the animals" is an apt positive description of wilderness. Growing up in West Yorkshire, near the Brontes' moors, Hughes got an unusual intimacy with the landscape through hunting and fishing, initiated by an older brother. He loved "children's" books that imagine wild animal lives-- Kipling's jungle tales, Henry Williamson's *Tarka the Otter*-- and his own "children's" poems evoke strong kinship with non-human life. His first book of them-- *Meet My Folks!* -- drolly describes a crow sister and an octopus grandmother, then more serious relatives as a strange old woman introduces the narrator to a wood:

> They said: 'We are the oak trees and your own true
> family.
> We are chopped down, we are torn up, you do not blink
> an eye...
> When I came out of the oak wood, back to human
> company,
> My walk was the walk of a human child, but my heart
> was a tree.
> ("My Own True Family")

Hughes's sense of English goes back to the old folkloric bee-wolf:

> The bear is a well
> Too deep to glitter...
> (*Wodwo*, "The Bear")

In a 1971 essay on Shakespeare, he stresses: "The air of wild, home-made poetry which he manages to diffuse through a phenomenally complicated and intellectualized language, and which makes the work of almost any other poet seem artificial." He sees the canon as his own main influence. "In spite of its Elizabethan ruff, Shakespeare's language is somehow nearer to the vital life of English, still, than anything written down since."
Like Shakespeare's, his poetic animals tend to be real, alive in landscapes, whatever symbolic weight they carry:

> Cold, delicately as the dark snow,
> A fox's nose touches twig, leaf...
> ("The Thought Fox")

Hughes's "The Thought Fox" responds to the frustrations that Philip Larkin complains about in "The Toads" but it is also an incantation in support of Britain's tenacious wildlife link. It is anti-elegiac. "Long after I am gone, as long as a copy of the poem exists," he said when he read it on the BBC in 1961, "every time anyone reads it the fox will get up somewhere out in the darkness and come walking toward them…" With an anthropology degree, Hughes based his art on shamanism, wherein an initiate finds an identity and a way of expressing it through dreams and visions, often through time alone in wilderness. The pagan Anglo-Saxon sense of *wildeor-ness* as a source of power seems a remnant of this. Hughes's poetry evokes an old but resilient vitality:

> Against the rubber tongues of cows and the hoeing hands of men
> Thistles spike the summer air…
> ("Thistles")

## A Tragic Equation

*Shakespeare and the Goddess of Complete Being* is a search for a mythic Shakespeare that will affect the everyday world. Hughes interprets the canon as an attempt to resolve the psychic conflict that his 1970 essay expresses. He sees Shakespeare as a shamanic personality who evokes initiation dreams in his first published works, two narrative poems that appeared in 1593 and 1594: "It would be an interesting and not particularly difficult experiment to narrate the plots and details…to various primitive groups, or at least to groups that still hang on to their old ways of dealing with the supernatural… They would all recognize this… as a classic example of the dream of spontaneous shamanic initiation, the dream of 'the call.'"

Hughes sees Shakespeare as a "great shaman" whom "moments of breakdown or crisis" can evoke: "Throughout history, as countless precedents show, wherever a people, or a culture, or a social group, is threatened either with extinction or ultimate persecution and assimilation by the enemy, the great shaman tends to appear. The lesser shamans heal and solve problems with transcendental help. The great shaman, typically, gathers up the whole tradition of the despairing group, especially the very earliest mythic/religious traditions, with all the circumstances of their present sufferings, into a messianic, healing, redemptive vision on the spiritual plane."

"The Goddess of Complete Being" is Hughes's term for the Great Goddess, whom he considers the primal deity, life's source, now largely suppressed by the Great God, life's would-be controller, with a resultant alienation of instincts. Relicts of the Great Goddess lingered in Catholicism's Madonna, a bulwark of feudal stability against the Reformation's aggressive utilitarianism. But Puritanism's Great God threatened to annihilate her. In Tudor England, only the monarchy stood between the Puritans and the Great Goddess's vestiges: "Queen Elizabeth held off the explosion as long as she lived. Managing to keep herself from being too closely identified with the Satanic side of the old goddess, and encouraging her identification with the Heavenly Gloriana side, she held the balance of indecision right up to her death."

Hughes thinks Shakespeare attempted a ritual reconciliation of England's religious schism by creating a literary "Tragic Equation" first posed in the narrative poems, then "worked out" in the plays: "Somehow he had identified and appropriated the opposed archetypal forces of the Reformation, the two terrible brothers that Elizabeth had pushed down into her crucible, under the navel of England to fight there like the original two dragons of the island."

*Venus and Adonis*, the 1593 narrative, poses the Equation's first half through the ancient Mediterranean "myth of the Great Goddess and her sacrificed God." Shakespeare embodies them as the Roman Love Goddess, Venus, and the handsome young hunter Adonis who she passionately loves. But

Adonis resists Venus in favor of hunting, and talks like a Puritan prude:

> 'I know not love,' quoth he, 'nor will not know it,
> Unless it be a boar, and then I chase it;
> 'Tis much to borrow, and I will not owe it…
> For I have heard it is a life in death…'
> (*Venus and Adonis*, 409)

Venus begs the youth not to hunt the boar, but he does, and it kills him. Hughes interprets this psycho-mythically: "The dreamer, Adonis, is the uncomprehending, resisting ego, who simply wants to get on with his ordinary life." When Adonis resists the Goddess, "she appears in animal form, tears his ego-body to pieces, then reassembles it afresh as her obedient servant—the servant in the spirit world," symbolically changing him into a wildflower. The poem represents Shakespeare's "shamanic rebirth into the service of the Goddess, the dream form of the cataclysmic psychological event which was the source of his poetic inspiration. The Boar would thereafter be his shamanic animal, his link with the supernatural dimension of his vision—the animal form, as it were, of his visionary awareness."

But Hughes also sees Shakespeare in a role opposing his Goddess-servant one, observing that the narrative poem's version of the myth is the first in which Adonis *resists* Venus's love: "There is another shamanic type who rises not out of the defeat of some ancient, rooted culture, some humiliated nationalism, but out of a historically new spirit… His vision is an idealized renovation of society, a jolting re-adaptation, like the fault shift of an earthquake, to a fundamentally changed reality." Hughes sees Shakespeare's 1594 narrative, *Lucrece*, as a dream call from this opposing side. It continues the Tragic Equation as the boar-killed ego body of Adonis rebels against the Goddess's biotic imperatives and returns as an authoritarian Great God figure, a boorish Roman prince, Tarquin, who tries to conquer the

Goddess, embodied in his best friend's chaste wife, Lucrece, by raping her.

"Jolting re-adaptations" tend to fail, and Tarquin's fails prophetically. When Lucrece reveals the rape to her family and commits suicide, Rome rebels against his ruling dynasty and exiles them. Tarquin's crime has doomed him to "living death and pain perpetual."

> A captive victor that hath lost in gain;
> Bearing away the wound that nothing healeth...
> (*Lucrece,* 728)

The crime perpetuates a war of God against Goddess that goes back to the first civilizations: "As the shaman of Old Catholicism," Shakespeare "registered the suffering of the Goddess and raised a vision of her salvation. But as he dramatized the will, and the militant ferocity, of the Puritan God who attempts to overthrow the Goddess, and make a kingdom out of her ruins—exactly as in the primal combat of Marduk and Tiamat, or of Jehovah and the Goddess of the Temple—he was the prophet of the Puritan Ascendancy... Shakespeare demonstrates how the second myth grows out of the first. He shows just how the sacrificed god of the first poem is the larval form of the second's Goddess-destroying tyrant, and just how the female who has been overpowered in the second is the same figure as the Divine Love of the first.

"He was on both sides, simultaneously a major shaman of both types. His incarnation of the Goddess's suffering, and his incarnation of the Puritan that makes her suffer, but destroys himself in the process, are equal and entire. Both these demonic, vatic personalities fight to come to terms inside his head—and inside his heart, and throughout his nervous system... he understood their interconnection—the inexorable, as if natural, process that brought one out of the other and set them against each other, making a shadow play of that controlled historical explosion above which the English crown floated."

## Ritual Dramas

Hughes interprets fourteen of Shakespeare's "mature" plays, along with one "earlier" one, as an extended reworking of this basic story, "stripped of mythic frippery and 'secularized'." *As You Like It* is the "earlier" one, and its drama of usurped nobles retreating to forest wilderness serves as a shamanic "overture" to the sequence. Their retreat is a response to the "call" of the two narrative poems, and a preparation for the other plays' "initiation trials" wherein, again and again, Adonis resists the Goddess, falls victim to her sacred Boar, then becomes a Great God Tarquin-Boar, ravaging her and destroying himself.

It is not always "tragic." The first play of Hughes's sequence, the one that sets the basic pattern, is *All's Well That Ends Well*: on its surface, a bedroom farce. Its heroine, Helen, is a bourgeois doctor's daughter but she has goddess-like powers. She cures the French King of a deadly illness, and when he promises her a wish in return, she asks for the nobleman Bertram, her longed-for Adonis, as a husband. The King forces Bertram to marry her, but, insulted to be stuck with a commoner, Bertram becomes a Tarquin-Boar and runs away to Italy. Helen-Venus pursues him and makes him consummate their marriage with a "bed trick," substituting herself for another woman in the dark. Believed dead, like Lucrece, she reappears in France, pregnant, and the unsuspecting Bertram finally has to surrender his "ego body" to her biotic imperative.

"As the Tragic Equation demonstrates, this Boar returns, in some shape or other, to deliver the poetic *donnee*, the daemonic power charge, in every play that uses the tragic myth." But the myth is not simply that a bad Great God rebels against a good Great Goddess. *All's Well That Ends Well*'s Bertram is a callow snob, but he doesn't *choose* to be Helen's Adonis-Tarquin, and his befuddlement and final abject surrender are pathetic. God and Goddess have good and bad sides, and they can be hard to distinguish as roles shift. Othello worships his wife Desdemona as a good Great Goddess until his Evil Twin,

Iago, tricks him into seeing her as a bad one. Then he becomes a Tarquin-Boar and strangles her. But then, like Tarquin, he realizes his crime and, like Lucrece, stabs himself:

> 'Cold, cold, my girl,
> Even like thy chastity. O cursed, cursed slave!
> Whip me, ye devils,
> From the possession of thy heavenly sight...
> (*Othello* 5, 2)

Hughes thinks Shakespeare kept reworking the equation through the tragedies seeking a "solution": a hero who *doesn't* become a Great God Boar that ravages the Great Goddess after he has resisted her and suffered a symbolic death. The search starts with Hamlet, whose doubts restrain him from revenge until near the end, and it is a painful process as Othello and his counterparts—Troilus, Macbeth, Coriolanus-- wreak their havoc. When the solution finally begins, it is a biological accident. In *King Lear*, the hero is simply too old to take revenge after his daughters seem to embody the bad Great Goddess by first defying and then rejecting him. So he goes mad: "One inexorable law of the Equation, evidently, is that once the process had been triggered, then the old personality must die and a new one must be born. If Adonis's rebirth as Tarquin is blocked, he has to be born, says the Equation, in some other way.

"Another element of Lear's 'madness,' then, is a new and shattering kind of rebirth, an unprecedented and different kind of rebirth. Not the old kind, an easy leap into raving Tarquin, but a 'hard and bitter agony' into something else... And it delivers, after hideous labor, not a Tarquin, but the opposite of a Tarquin. Not a lustful purple flower springing through the blood of the mangled Adonis, but a crown of flowering, prickly weeds. Not a Jehovan Goddess-killing tyrant, but an infantile, frail, brainwashed idiot savant, the child of his daughter, the transfigured Lear..."

"What Shakespeare did at this point seems to have been unthinkable until he did it... The tragic error—the ego's rejection of the Divine Love of the Goddess—no longer ends in mythic sudden death... It lurches through into a prolonged consequence of intensifying agonies in which the hero is compelled to understand the full meaning of what he has done, while his whole mental and social universe comes crashing down and chaos erupts."

Lear's rebirth comes too late. But, in tragicomic romances like *The Winter's Tale*, there is a hope of redemption, although it comes slowly. When the sudden deaths of his heir and his Queen dispel the Sicilian King Leontes's delusion that she is guilty of adultery with his friend Polixenes, it seems too late. Yet he hasn't become the Tarquin-Boar and killed Hermione-Lucrece, so redemption finally comes sixteen years later when King Polixenes and his son Florizel find his lost daughter, Perdita, exposed by Antigonus and raised by the bear-proxy shepherds. As they all return to the Sicilian court, the supposedly long-dead Queen Hermione mysteriously returns to life and Leontes is saved— redeemed by the natural passing of time and by wild Illyria's vitality.

Finally, in *The Tempest*, a potential Tarquin becomes a new, shamanic hero, the enchanter Prospero. Although deposed from the Duchy of Milan by his bad brother, Antonio, he consciously resolves the Equation's vicious circle of rejection and revenge with the poetic magic of the wilderness island on which Antonio has marooned him for nearly sixteen years. When Ariel sings "Full Fathom Five" to Prince Ferdinand of Naples, shipwrecked by Prospero's magic along with Antonio and the Neapolitan court, the spell suspends the false authority that has divided God and Goddess. If Ferdinand's father, the King of Naples, were not "sea-changed," he and the usurper Antonio would hustle the prince off the island. But the suspension lets Prospero unite the prince, a potential Adonis-Tarquin, with his daughter Miranda, who combines the wild sensuality of Venus with the tame purity of Lucrece.

The song's image of a seabed strewn with skeletons and riches first appears much earlier in the canon on the Tragic Equation's infernal side. In *Richard III*, the Duke of Clarence dreams it just before his usurping brother Richard, a prototypical Tarquin-Boar who hates women because he is deformed, drowns him in a wine barrel:

> Methought I saw a thousand fearful wracks,
> A thousand men that fishes gnawed upon,
> Wedges of gold, great anchors, heaps of pearl,
> Inestimable stones, unvalued jewels,
> All scattered at the bottom of the sea:
> Some lay in dead man's skulls; and in those holes
> Where eyes did once inhabit, there were crept--
> As 'twere in scorn of eyes-- reflecting gems,
> Which wooed the slimy bottom of the deep
> And mocked the dead bones that lay scattered by.
> (*Richard III*, 1, 4)

In *The Tempest,* the old vision of sunken death becomes one of rebirth as Ariel's song transforms it to unite Ferdinand and Miranda. That union redeems the corrupt courtly world that had deposed Prospero. Instead of turning *him* into a bloody avenger, the Tarquin Boar enters the boorish, wild humanoid Caliban-- for Hughes the anomaly whereby the Tragic Equation is resolved: "But in *The Tempest* for the first time the situation is different. The text does not ritualize the invocation of the Boar into that triumphant Adonis-transforming, Tarquin-creating assault. Instead, it invokes the Boar—Caliban—to meet its match in the magically invulnerable Prospero, and to be not only stopped in mid-charge, not only arrested, as I said, in mid-air, but *sublimated* into its transcendent form."

"Shakespeare," Hughes writes, "is not one writer but two. Not simply and exclusively one of the greatest realists (like Tolstoy), but also, at the same time, the greatest of our mythic poets (like Keats). Which is exactly what Tolstoy didn't like about him.  Tolstoy hated… the musical dominance of the mythic substructure.  He called its effects (because he couldn't see the thing itself, either) 'depraved' and 'unnatural'.  They were the cause of what he regarded as hopelessly false characterization, ludicrously unreal situations and plots—the cause, in general, of the pervasive 'great evil' that he found throughout Shakespeare… My book simply traces the organized shape and working of the mythic complex in this other Shakespeare's head, and shows how it expresses itself through the work of the great realist… the mythic structure of Reformation Christianity and of the matrix of pre-Christian religions from which it issued, as they were mediated through his temperament."

# Chapter Six

# Bear People

---

Hughes is certainly right to see a religious conflict in the canon. The many plays sympathetically set in France and Italy imply that Shakespeare regarded Catholic Humanism as a source of motherly stability and compassion, qualities he apparently missed in his life. Bad mothers like *Hamlet*'s Gertrude outweigh good ones like *The Winter's Tale*'s Hermione, and good mothers have a bad time. But Shakespeare's "Madonna complex" contrasts with his lack of interest in the theology of Catholic Humanists like Dante. It is hard to imagine him touring *The Divine Comedy*'s purgatory and heaven, although hell might have appealed with Virgil as guide. As I've said, his Christianity was more of the Old Testament kind, focused on earthly life. So he was torn between a Catholic past and a Protestant future.

Hughes's idea of Shakespeare as a great shaman who invented a literary "algebra" to resolve the conflict is more problematic. We see shamanism as something that civilization has left behind as religion, medicine, science, and art have specialized. Joseph Campbell discusses it sympathetically, particularly bear-shamanism, in his survey's first volume, *Primitive Mythology,* but ignores it afterward. Campbell's notion of mythology was "progressive" in accord with twentieth century evolutionary ideas, looking outward and forward to globalization, high technology, space travel, and so forth. He writes: "Man, in contrast to the beasts, is endowed with a brain and nervous system not as stereotyped as theirs." But Shakespeare was less "exceptionalist." A pre-industrial man, he knew about non-human brains and nervous systems from experience, while Campbell mostly knew them second-hand, as scientific information.

Although he defines myth through Shakespeare in *Creative Mythology*, I think Campbell slights *Shakespeare's* "creative mythology" because, despite the Whiggish Bard convention, the Shakespeare canon really is *not* progressive. Instead, I would call Shakespeare's mythology "accretive," looking inward and backward (as well as outward and forward in its way) toward an Earth that civilization won't "transform." This happens to be congruent with a twenty-first century version of evolution that regards civilization's five thousand years not as a destined culmination of life's three billion, but as a contingency with both tragic and comedic potentials.

In a book about Hughes, the critic Diane Middlebrook tends toward such a "post-progressive" idea of creative mythology. She writes: "Eventually Hughes generalized this view of Shakespeare into a field theory of literary personhood. The idea is simple and clear. Hughes proposes that no single work of a writer's output stands alone, that a strong writer's work proceeds by accretion over time, unconsciously building a consistent, recognizable persona. The literary persona who enacts the poet's struggle can be glimpsed, always, in one early work that Hughes calls the 'first,' which contains, in a single image, 'a package of precisely folded, multiple meanings.'"

## Birnam Wood

According to an accretive mythology, a primal phenomenon like shamanism isn't left behind any more than bacteria and protozoa are. My experience leads me to see it that way. I've wondered why my feelings about nature were so different from my father's. One possibility was the influence of my nurse when I was a small child. She was an old colored woman from Albermarle County, Virginia, where I was born, who came to New England with my parents. We lived in the country until I was five, and she had an unusual attitude to it. Copperhead snakes lived in stone fences around our house but she wasn't afraid of them: she saw them as guardians, allies. When she told me bears lived around her home in Virginia, I wanted to go there. Her sense of wild animals and plants seemed magical, and it stayed with me after we moved to the 1950s suburbs.

My adolescent response to Ariel's song wasn't the only Shakespeare-induced state that seemed more a part of Mooneys' Woods than the everyday world. *As You Like It* had a similar effect. When I read the play in school, its forest had a radiance that, like the song, resonated in the Woods, which seemed vast in time if small in space. The play seemed truer to the Woods in that way than modern nature essays we read. Birnam Wood's advance on Dunsinane Castle in *Macbeth* also enchanted me. I walked to my school through the Woods because it was newly built on the adjacent upland where I had first seen deer. The school grounds were still raw clay from bulldozing, and I fantasized the Woods advancing to reclaim them. The trees and flowers seemed more than insentient "plants" to me, as when skunk cabbage buds came up through March snow, thick and resilient as claws. They were much more exciting than chasing balls in the dust.

Such associations faded in college, but then I started experiencing trance-like states not associated with anything more alive than the everyday world. This caused growing anxiety as I faced living in it. As the anxiety mounted, I began having colorful dreams about expanses of clear water inhabited by animals. The dreams seemed quite apart from the everyday world, with colors I'd never seen. Sometimes I watched from beaches or cliffs; sometimes I floated above the water, which might have radiant forests in its depths. This climaxed in dreams wherein the animals recognized my awareness of them and rose toward me, evoking a musical sense of exhilaration and reassurance that allayed the anxiety.

I went to the West Coast, where I discovered the public domain's wilderness areas. Their remote lakes, rivers, forests, meadows, and peaks seemed a realization of my dreams, as did their animals, particularly bears. Seeing them in the forest was like a fulfillment of my nurse's invitation. Exploring and writing about the wilderness in Thoreau's tradition seemed a way to resolve the anxious incongruity of dream-trance and everyday world that afflicted me. My dreams' depths were not just fantasy: they reflected evolutionary biodiversity. Writing about the inner and the outer wilderness seemed a way to oppose the everyday world's attempts to wreck it with logging, mines, dams, and roads, as it had wrecked places like Mooney's Woods with tracts and malls.

## Rattlesnake Meadow

The region that most attracted me, the Klamath Mountains in California and Oregon, has more than wilderness: it has giant lore. Huge hairy humanoids are said to inhabit its high country, raiding mining camps and logging operations, flinging equipment about and tearing buildings apart. They are said to cause great fear, albeit not as man-eaters like Grendel and his Mother. Collectively known as Bigfoot, the giants are, of course, a tabloid staple, although they seem less banal in wilderness than on supermarket magazine racks. They are an intriguing link to Anglo-Saxon myth, and to evolution, which sees humans as descended from hairy humanoids. And other giants, grizzly bears, inhabited the Klamaths into the twentieth century: they play a part in native lore as totemic ancestors and magical beings.

The giant lore seemed a way of evoking the region's evolutionary matrix, which, because the its coastal climate is milder than in most of the West, has retained unusual biodiversity, with plant species extinct elsewhere. It seemed a way into a fourth dimension, deep time, that counterbalances the everyday world.

But it wasn't that simple. I began experiencing worse anxiety than before, in wilderness. This was surprising because I'd spent time alone in wilderness without fear. And it seemed connected to bears, although grizzlies are extirpated from the Klamaths and I had no trouble with black bears. I'd found them asleep in sunny glades several times, one snoring, another still sleeping when I passed it again two hours later. But it seems there are bears… and bears.

One of the Klamaths' wildest areas is the High Siskiyou range inland from Redwood National Park. It is full of rare species: it is also rugged and heavily forested even for the region. When I ascended its Clear Creek Gorge in June of 1979, the trail was thick with flowering rhododendron, azalea, and orchids but scarily steep and faint. It took two days of backpacking to get near the summit. After spending a night at a place called Rattlesnake Meadow, I noticed that a large bear had walked in the tracks I'd made in a snowfield on the way up. Somehow, the sight of deep claw marks in my boot tracks unsettled me. I began to feel increasingly strange as I climbed down to camp on Clear Creek that evening.

I awoke at midnight afraid that I would die because my heart was beating so hard that it seemed it must stop, as though a large animal was attacking me. When I closed my eyes, angry faces appeared, mouthing at me, and the creek's murmur began to seem alarmingly articulate. This went on all night, and the only thing I could do about it was to imagine what others might have felt: "Audubon, feverish and vomiting from tainted turkey meat in the trackless Ohio forest; Thoreau dragging his tuberculosis to the Minnesota frontier… Taoist sages …Hebrew prophets …"

The next day I had a violent headache: the next night I dreamt vividly of death, evil, and decay. Tottering back down the Clear Creek trail, I told myself the strange sickness was a chance result of fatigue, altitude, sunstroke, or some microbe. But as I continued to explore the Klamaths, it came back. It came back in the Yolla Bolly Wilderness where a decade earlier I'd spent a month wandering around watching nocturnal wildlife without psychic upheavals. The anxiety got worse as I began to write the book. But I managed to publish it and the anxiety lessened after that.

The Klamath Mountains' native cultures regard parts of the High Siskiyous as places of shamanic initiation: they set a precedent for legal recognition of religious relationships to land when they stopped a U.S. Forest Service plan to build a "scenic highway" across the range. I had avoided sacred sites I'd heard about: I was trying to describe the region in eco-evolutionary terms and felt there were plenty to explore without intruding on native tradition. But my night on Clear Creek made me wonder. Eight years after my book came out, a traditionalist living on the region's Hoopa Valley Reservation, who described himself as "one of the bear people," wrote me about it. Referring to my Siskiyous experience, he wrote that I was the first "materialist" he knew of "to have been both 'called by Nature'... AND subsequently 'touched' by Nature..."

"Some touch," I thought at first: cowering in a sleeping bag. One of my fears had been that disgusted hikers would find my bloated corpse surrounded by backpacking gear. Death as littering. I'm not the only backpacker to have unexpected experiences with the Klamath Mountains, however. A few years after I was at Rattlesnake Meadow, a camper described a dream he had there: "In the moonlight I watched as a large animal with a lion's stout body and a glowing skull for a head approached my camp. I was momentarily frightened and stunned and incapable of movement. Then I understood the creature meant me no harm. It was aware of my presence but only vaguely interested. It paced about for a short while and then left the campsite to continue its rounds." He saw a bear there the next day.

I had stopped having aerial dreams for years: I started having ones wherein I could "swim" as well as float. The most memorable were of grizzly bears on California coastal hills. They were more somber than my original dreams: the colors were muted. But there was a similar sense of a reality deeper than the everyday world. I could see that night on Clear Creek as somehow being "tested" instead of a pointless anxiety attack. I had been "called" in a way: my book had reached an audience, as though readers somehow recognized my experience although I didn't describe it fully. It promoted wilderness protection by inspiring activists.

## An Instrument of Nature

Another thing about the experience that made sense was a resemblance to ethnological descriptions like one in the 1971 *Encyclopedia Britannica*: "A shaman is recognized as such only after a series of initiatory trials... as a rule the trials take place during an indefinite period of time in which the future shaman is sick and stays in his tent or wanders in the wilderness... But the 'chosen' one becomes a shaman only if he can interpret his pathological crisis as a religious experience and succeeds in curing himself. The serious crises that sometimes accompany the 'election' of the future shaman are to be regarded as initiatory trials. Every initiation involves the symbolic death and resurrection of the neophyte. In the dreams and hallucinations of the future shaman may be found the classical pattern of the initiation: he is tortured by demons, his body is cut in pieces, he descends to the netherworld or ascends to heaven and is finally resuscitated."

The description adds that some kind of performance follows successful initiation, whether healing or rituals and songs to affirm totemic values, or sometimes, as Hughes writes, "the gathering up of the whole tradition of the despairing group...into a messianic, healing, redemptive vision..." The Lakota shaman, Black Elk, is an example that Hughes cites in *Shakespeare and the Goddess*. Growing up as the U.S. was destroying the Great Plains tribes, he underwent such extreme trance states that he was sick for months, meanwhile having a "just and mighty" vision. Then he feared he would die if he didn't do something about it: "I could think of nothing but my vision. A terrible time began for me then... I could understand the birds when they sang, and they were always saying 'It is time!' 'It is time!'

"Time to do what? I did not know. Whenever I awoke before daybreak and went out of tepee because I was afraid of the stillness when everyone was sleeping, there were many low voice talking together in the east... Sometimes the crying of coyotes out in the cold made me so afraid that I would run out of one tepee into another, and I would do this until I was worn out and fell asleep. I wondered if I was only crazy...

"When the grasses were beginning to show their tender faces again, my father and mother asked an old medicine man named Black Road to come over and see what he could do... By now I was so afraid of being afraid of everything that I told him about my vision, and when I was through he looked long at me and said... 'Nephew, I know now what the trouble is! ... You must do your duty and perform this vision for your people upon earth... Then the fear will leave you...'"

Black Elk's description of that performance takes up a dozen pages with such an array of songs, dances, and tableaux that a Renaissance court masque comes to mind: "There were four black horses to represent the west; four white horses for the north; four sorrels for the east; four buckskins for the south. For all of these, young riders had been chosen. Also, there was a bay horse for me to ride on, as in my vision. Four of the most beautiful maidens in the village were ready to take their part; and there were six very old men for the Grandfathers.

"Now was the time to paint and dress for the dance. The four maidens and the sixteen horses all faced the sacred tepee. Black Roads and Bear Sings [another 'very old and wise' man] then sang a song, and all the others sang along with them, like this:

> 'Father, paint the earth on me...
> A nation I will make over.
> A two-legged nation I will make holy.
> Father, paint the earth on me.'"

Of course, sixteenth century England was a long way from the nineteenth century Dakota Territory. Shakespeare probably never heard the word "shaman," which means "knower" in the Tungusic languages of Siberia, where Russian explorers found it. Shamanic vestiges in Reformation Britain were slumped into disreputable practices like witchcraft and sorcery. They were also pervasive. As an Oxford scholar, Robert Burton, writes in his 1621 *Anatomy of Melancholy*: "Sorcerers are too common; cunning men, wizards, and white witches, as they call them, in every village, which, if they are sought unto, will help almost all the infirmities of body and mind." Sorcerers knew their natural surroundings: people thought they could influence weather, crops, and animals as well as human health. Their powers could be inherited, another trait of tribal shamanism.

The rise of public drama, transposing medieval mystery plays to secular subjects, seems a shamanic element in a new form, perhaps a less reputable one even than that of village sorcerers-- whose "health care system" was cheaper and often less harmful than sixteenth century physicians.' The new dramas often featured sorcery and witchcraft, more to thrill audiences than to ritually address spiritual conflicts, but some of the folkloric thrills have proved resonant. At the height of the rationalizing Enlightenment, Alexander Pope sensed a shamanic element in Shakespeare when he wrote that he "is not so much an Imitator as an Instrument of Nature; and 'tis not so just to say that he speaks from her as that she speaks thro' him".

# Chapter Seven

# Nothing Normal

---

Hughes's shamanic Shakespeare could explain my experience of Ariel's song as a kind of spell. Trance-like epiphanies in response to songs are typical of shamanism. Although described mainly among aboriginal people now, it probably was universal among early humans, with the shaman as the prototype of individuals who feel a "call" to work psychically for (or against) a community.

If Shakespeare had a shamanic personality, does it mean that his narrative poems "perform initiatory dream calls"? The canon has many dreams, like Bottom the Weaver's famous one in *A Midsummer Night's Dream*: "I have had a dream past the wit of man to say what dream it was…The eye of man hath not heard, the ear of man hath not seen, man's hand is not able to taste, his tongue to conceive, nor his heart to report what my dream was." (4,1). Bottom's dream that fairies turn him into a donkey beloved of their queen, Titania, is farcical. Yet its reversal of normal perception—hearing eyes, seeing ears--echoes the strangeness of shamanic dream calls.

Bottom's demotic prose is more like the terse vernacular of ethnological "informants" than the narratives poems' high-flown verse. Hughes's shamanic interpretation of them can seem far-fetched. Still, the narratives *are* dreamlike, although their eroticism can make them seem more like wet dreams than initiatory calls. They are not "imaginative fiction" anyway: they are cruder and more complex. They have little character or plot and proceed with dreams' peremptory irrationality. They do contain elements of mythic conflict that develop through the canon, wherein there is a sense of themes being reworked, and of artistic resolution. Shakespeare might have synthesized a complex of dreams in writing them. Shamanic dreams are like that, and they may involve sexual encounters that can be inspiring or frightening.

Although we barely associate the narrative poems with the canon today, the Elizabethans knew Shakespeare mainly from them. Most readers praised them without mentioning the plays and sonnets. They went through many editions, and other writers eagerly imitated them. But they fell from fashion in the seventeenth century, and modern critics often dismiss them as exercises in decorative rhetoric, Elizabethan retreads of the Roman poet Ovid, from whom the stories are taken. "The two long poems," writes one, "are pedantic studies of lust, without the least evidence of a dramatic gift—they are samples of good, sound but uninspired Elizabethan verse... a laborious effort to acquire... mastery of language."

Ovid's influence is clear, but the narratives don't seem like pedantic Ovid retreads to me, in fact, they seem quite different. The Roman poet, who lived when Augustus Caesar was consolidating the Empire, saw the old Homeric mythology, Thoreau's "great dragon tree," with his cosmopolitan era's irreverence, as postmodern sophisticates see Biblical mythology in *New Yorker* cartoons. Shakespeare's narratives are strange by comparison. Like his plays, they have a sense of what Borges calls "sacred horror" that seems older than Ovid, certainly older than Renaissance allegories like the *Faerie Queen*. "The beasts in "Venus and Adonis" are not allegorical, they are totemic others for Venus herself," writes a prominent historian, Gary Wills. "There is nothing normal in this poem."

Venus

Ovid's "mythic" characters can be normal to the point of banality: his irreverence was finally too much for Augustus, who banished him from Rome. In his *Metamorphoses*, Venus is more like a rich courtesan than the Homeric era's "foam-born Aphrodite," and Adonis is a handsome but dim young sportsman. When he catches her eye after her son Cupid accidentally pricks her with an arrow, she takes up hunting to please him although she fears the sun will ruin her complexion.

> ...she has always,
> Before this time, preferred the shadowy places,
> Preferred her ease, preferred to improve her beauty
> By careful tending, but now, across the ridges,
> Through woods, through rocky places thick with brambles,
> She goes, more like Diana than like Venus,
> Bare-kneed and robes tucked up. She cheers the hounds,
> Hunts animals, at least such timid creatures
> As deer and rabbits; no wild boars for her
> No wolves, no bears, no lions...
> (*Metamorphoses* 10, 239)

Ovid's Venus wants Adonis to hunt only harmless beasts because she especially hates dangerous ones. When he asks why, she explains with a chatty digression about two lovers, Atalanta and Hypomenes, who blame her for getting them turned into lions because of a sexual impiety, and want revenge. Adonis doesn't get it:

> ...But the young hunter
> Scorned all such warnings, and one day, it happened,
> His hounds, hard on the trail, roused a wild boar,
> And as he rushed from the wood, Adonis struck him
> A glancing blow, and the boar turned, and shaking
> The spear from his side, came charging at the hunter,
> Who feared, and ran, and fell, and the tusk entered
> Deep in the groin, and the youth lay dying...
> (*Metamorphoses*, 711)

It seems more an unlucky accident than a mythic tragedy, and although Venus-- interrupted while departing in her "swan-guided chariot" -- beats her breast and tears her hair, she ends by consoling herself almost casually, with a dash of Olympian one-upmanship:

> 'If Persephone
> Could change to fragrant mint the girl called Mentha,
> Cinyras' son, my hero, surely also
> Can be my flower.' Over the blood she sprinkl'd
> Sweet smelling nectar, and as bubbles rise
> In rainy weather, so it stirred and blossomed...
>    (*Metamorphoses*, 730)

Shakespeare's Venus doesn't wear tucked up robes—she doesn't wear anything. She doesn't try to please Adonis by going hunting with him: she just *wants* him, with a hormonal urgency. Under a Titian nude veneer (the Venetian artist painted the subject several times), she's a sweating biological female who grabs and claws at her lover. There's a touch of Grendel's man-eating Mother about her:

> Now quick desire hath caught the yielding prey,
> And glutton-like she feeds, yet never filleth.
> Her lips are conquerors, his lips obey,
> Paying what ransom the insulter willeth,
>  Whose vulture thought doth pitch the price so high
>  That she will draw his lips rich treasure dry...
>    (*Venus and Adonis,* 347)

Her warning to Adonis has nothing digressive about it. She tells him about dangerous beasts in graphic detail—no chatter about impious sex-- and then she mourns him for over 400 lines. It is not a boy toy's misfortune that concerns her. It is the death of an Orphic figure:

Alas, poor world, what treasure hast thou lost,
What face remains alive that's worth the viewing?
Whose tongue is music now? What canst thou boast
Of things long since, or anything ensuing? ...

When he beheld his shadow in the brook,
The fishes spread on it their golden gills.
When he was bye, the birds such pleasures took
That some would sing, some others in their bills
   Would bring him mulberries and ripe red cherries
   He fed them with his sight, they him with berries.

But this foul, grim, and urchin-snouted boar,
Whose eye still looketh for a grave,
Ne'er saw the beauteous livery that he wore:
Witness the entertainment that he gave...
     *(Venus and Adonis*, 1075)

And there's nothing casual about her remorse:

'But he is dead, and never did he bless
My youth with his, the more am I accursed.'
   With this she falleth in the place she stood,
   And stains her face with his congealed blood...

'Since thou art dead, lo, here do I prophecy
Sorrow on love hereafter shall attend,
It shall be waited on with jealousy
Find sweet beginning, but unsavory end...'
     *(Venus and Adonis*, 1120)

She doesn't just turn his blood into a flower: she picks it and keeps it between her breasts, forever:

Here in this hollow cradle take thy rest;

My throbbing heart shall rock thee day and night
There shall not be one minute in an hour
Wherein I will not kiss my sweet love's flower.
(*Venus and Adonis*, 1185)

## Lucrece

Ovid's *Fasti*, Shakespeare's source for the second
narrative, is less playful than his *Metamorphoses*, since it is a
history of Rome. But Ovid tells Lucrece's story in 150 lines as
opposed to Shakespeare's 1,850, and, again, his characters are
banal by comparison. Ovid's Tarquin is a callow bully; his
Lucrece is a proper housewife, first seen ordering her maids
about. When Tarquin gives her a choice of rape or a shameful
death in a stable groom's bed, she just lets him get on with it.
Then she worries about her reputation:

Without delay she stabbed her breast with the steel that
she had hidden
And weltering in her blood fell at her father's feet.
Even then in dying she took care to sink down decently:
That was her thought even as she fell...
(*Fasti*, 831)

There's nothing callow about Shakespeare's Tarquin:
he's an adult monster who knows how badly he's behaving. His
approach to his victim's bedroom brings Grendel's mead hall
visit to mind:

The locks between her chamber and his will,
Each one by him enforced, retires his ward;
But as they open, they all rate his ill,
Which drives the creeping thief to some regard.
The threshold grates the door to have him heard,
　　Night-wand'ring weasels shriek to see him there,
　　They fright him, yet still he pursues his fear.

(*Lucrece,* 302)

As the stanza's last lines show, Tarquin differs from Grendel in that he undergoes an agony of fear, guilt, and shame about his crime, although there's no doubt that he will commit it. And Shakespeare's Lucrece responds with elemental protests, what one would expect from a Great Goddess about to be desecrated:

> Mud not the fountain that gave drink to thee;
> Mar not the thing that cannot be amended;
> End thy ill aim before thy shoot be ended
>   He is no woodman that doth bend his bow
>   To strike a poor unseasonable doe...
>
> My sighs like whirlwinds labor hence to heave thee,
>   If ever man was moved by woman's moans,
>   Be moved by my sighs, my tears, my groans.
>
> All which together like a troubled ocean,
> Beat at thy rocky and wreck-threat'ning heart
> To soften it with their continual motion
> For stones dissolved to water do convert...
>                 (*Lucrece*, 578)

Shakespeare's Lucrece dies prophetically, not "decently." Her blood is a well of life, a Tarquin-polluted one:

> And bubbling from her breast it doth divide
> Into two slow rivers...
>   Some of her blood still pure and red remained
>   And some looked black, that false Tarquin-stained.
>
> About the mourning and congealed face
> Of that black blood a wat'ry rigol goes,

Which seems to weep upon the tainted place;
And ever since, as pitying Lucrece' woes,
Corrupted blood some wat'ry token shows...
(*Lucrece*, 1723)

Sexual pollution of a well of life is a big Shakespeare theme, as with Othello's response to Iago's innuendos on Desdemona's chastity:

The fountain from which my current runs
Or else dries up—to be discarded thence,
Or keep it as a cistern for foul toads
To knot and gender in!
(*Othello* 4,2)

One might see the strangeness of Shakespeare's narratives as an injection of Christian feelings into Ovid's etiolated paganism. Venus's constant love of Adonis; Adonis's rejection of her animal sexuality; Lucrece's sacrificial purity; Tarquin's guilty lust: all are earmarks of Christianity. But the narratives certainly aren't Christian by the standards of Thomas More or John Knox: they are far too carnal for the rationalized religion that emerged in Humanism and the Reformation. It's as though Shakespeare's poems try to do to conventional Christianity what Christianity itself tried to do at the end of Rome's Augustan age: to reach back--in an increasingly numbed everyday world-- toward deep feelings that a disintegrating old mythic framework could no longer evoke.

Hughes writes: "By modern secular definition, myth is something not be taken seriously. This is so rooted in the popular point of view, and that point of view has so thoroughly naturalized Shakespeare as a secular author, that it is almost impossible for a modern reader to consider the myth of Venus and Adonis, as Shakespeare adapts it, as anything more than a picturesque fable, a Renaissance ornamental fantasy... Forcibly desacralizing his poem in this way, we somehow exempt him, by a kind of arbitrary secular warrant, from the world of feeling in which he lived."

# Chapter Eight

## Doctor and Mrs. Fox

---

I think Hughes has something in his shamanic interpretation of Shakespeare's narratives, although it doesn't necessarily explain why they appealed to sixteenth century readers. Critics assume that the poems' eroticism was the reason, and much of the period's praise for it implies this. But Elizabethans didn't go in for literary analysis, and other poets wrote erotica to less effect. *Venus and Adonis* was popular with women as well as young blades: readers seem to have felt something deeper than decorative convention under the eroticism.

Another book I found on my parents' shelves in early adolescence was *Life's Picture History of Western Man*, a kind of illustrated primer of Whiggish history. I mainly liked the pictures, and one of my favorites was Titian's "Sacred and Profane Love," which showed two beautiful women sitting by a well, one of them sumptuously clothed, the other naked. I was surprised when the caption explained that the *naked* woman was sacred love: I'd assumed it was the other way around. But Shakespeare evidently agreed with Titian.

A verse published in 1600 by a man named John Lane implies a kind of Tragic Equation in the narratives, although it's a rudimentary one compared to the mythic dimensions Hughes sees in them:

> When chaste Adonis came to man's estate,
> Venus straight courted him with many a while;
> Lucrece once seen, straight Tarquin laid a bait,
> With foul incest her body to defile...

## The Moors

One thing *is* clear about Hughes's Shakespeare interpretation: that a Tragic Equation of his own influenced it. A full time poet-shaman who disliked literary criticism, he spent several of his last years obsessively writing his idiosyncratic version of it in *Shakespeare and the Goddess* because, I think, there was a personal echo in the story of a handsome young hunter who attracts a kind of goddess, who resists her to "get on with his ordinary life," whose "ego body" undergoes a "death in life" because of his resistance, and who finds himself "reborn," painfully and unwillingly, as a kind of goddess-destroying monster.

Hughes's life, starting with West Yorkshire, shows the difficulty of renewing the man-nature kinship that a Great Goddess embodies. Despite their remoteness, relentless exploitation had reduced the moors to a condition far from a "draughty, radiant Paradise of the animals." Their marginal farms, abandoned textile mills, and grimy towns would have seemed a literal "waste land" to Eliot and Pound. And life became less magical for seven-year-old Ted after his hunter brother left home and the family moved to more suburban South Yorkshire, where his father, a traumatized Great War veteran, kept a shop. Feeling bereft, Ted trapped mice and netted loaches for lack of larger game, and his "adult" poetry reflects this. It evokes a milieu where a relatively large beast like an otter lives "like a king in hiding" and dies "yanked above hounds."

In contrast to his "Thought Fox," some of Hughes's poetry presents wild animals in ways that seem Hobbesian and Cartesian—vicious, mechanical. In "Thrushes," songbirds feeding on a lawn are "terrifying... more coiled steel than living." In "Second Glance at a Jaguar," a zoo beast's crazed frustration seems robotic, his gait "a stump-legged waddle," his body "just an engine pushing it forward."

Critics have called this "a poetry of violence," and Hughes's vehemence against Judeo-Christianity in his 1970 "draughty, radiant Paradise" essay hints at a covert revulsion against nature's "fallen" qualities as well as his overt reaction against traditional utilitarianism. His search for the "spiritual" in life, including pursuits like astrology, implied animus toward the "bestial" and could supersede more direct perception of natural history. For all his love of wild things, his writing doesn't try to evoke British wilderness, past or future, as though the moors' wasted gloom has shaped his mind so strongly that imagining restored ancient forest with large beasts seems sentimental, or perhaps frightening.

Hughes devoted one book, *The Remains of Elmet*, to his childhood in West Yorkshire's Calder Valley. Its poems have vivid evocations of remnant wild places, but not much wildlife. D.H. Lawrence peoples his *Lady Chatterley's Lover* sketch of abandoned coal country with wild dogs and ponies. Hughes's main sign of non-human animal regeneration in Yorkshire is a trout in an abandoned millstream. Civilization has subdued the Calder Valley for so long that its wilderness state can be hard to imagine. As Diane Middlebrook writes: "The tumbled Pennine stone building blocks of factories and cottages, erected during centuries of settlement, were now reburying themselves in the lap of the valleys and the breast of the moors, to be reborn as mere stone."

Hughes's adult poem that tries most to enter imaginatively into non-human British life is a 1967 one titled after *Gawain*'s word for wild men. Its narrator is an otter-like being in a wild place, but detached, confused:

> What am I?  Nosing here, turning leaves over
> Following a faint stain on the air to the river's edge...
> ("Wodwo")

## Beautiful America

There is an element of blaming the victim in all this. "Bring up a child in the way that he will go and when he is a man he will not depart from it." Hughes didn't invent his grim native landscape: his poetry reflects the banality of traps, guns, poison, and road kills that industrialism takes for granted. He holds aloof from the hounded otter and caged jaguar because un-hounded, un-caged beasts have few places in Britain. Some critics take his Cartesian-Hobbesian side too literally, equating the predation in his poems with "mindless murderousness." But predation is a skilled livelihood, and a comparatively uncommon sight in wilderness. It is violently subdued lands that most generate "a poetry of violence."

Despite his ties to the moors, Hughes wasn't content with them, recalling: "everything in West Yorkshire is slightly unpleasant. Nothing ever quite escapes into happiness." He'd played with his brother at being an "American backwoodsmen," and he spent his youth trying to get away from drab postwar Britain, finally marrying an American poet, Sylvia Plath, and moving to New England with her. She'd had a similar childhood, first linked to an exciting place—the Massachusetts coast—then bereft after her charismatic zoologist father died and the family moved to inland suburbia. "My childhood landscape was not land but the end of the land—the cold, salt, running hills of the Atlantic."

Plath hadn't rebelled like Hughes: she'd mixed her literary aspirations with a compulsively ambitious academic career. But the repression that this required had led to severe depression, a breakdown and a nearly successful suicide attempt. Hughes's apparent freedom from repression thrilled her. She eagerly embraced his shamanic ethos, and wrote her mother gushy letters about the Yorkshire moors.

To Hughes, Plath embodied a wild, colorful escape, as he writes in *Birthday Letters,* the poem cycle on their marriage he published just before his death:

> You were a new world. My new world.
> So this America, I marveled.
> ("18 Rugby Street")

Thoreau's "Walking" might express Hughes's American hopes: "The West is preparing to add its fables to those of the East. The valleys of the Ganges, the Nile, and the Rhine have yielded their crop, it remains to be seen what the valleys of the Amazon, the Plate, the Orinoco, the St. Lawrence and the Mississippi will produce. Perchance, when, in the course of ages, American liberty has become a fiction of the past—as it is to some extent a fiction of the present—the poets of the world will be inspired by American mythology."

Yet Hughes failed to find a mythic new world in America. During two years there, he did relatively little outdoor exploring. Tight finances and Plath's emotional needs restricted him, but this lassitude contrasts surprisingly with his adventurous boyhood. He didn't visit Walden Pond while living nearby in Boston for a year, although he'd taught *Walden* at the University of Massachusetts. Maybe he felt that Thoreau just "isolated his own bit of locality and put it under a lens, to examine it," as D.H. Lawrence writes in his *Studies in Classic American Literature*. Although early American naturalists had the "sense of wonder" that his *Studies* calls "the *natural* religious sense," they didn't excite Lawrence like Fenimore Cooper's American backwoodsman, a childhood fantasy he shared with Hughes.

For both men, the backwoodsman fantasy evaporated in twentieth century America's mixture of megalopolis, agribusiness, and remnant wilderness. In *Birthday Letters*, Hughes's American impressions move from a sense of release at New World exoticism toward renewed alienation. Soon after he arrived:

> ... the chipmunk came
> Under the Cape Cod conifers, over roots
> A first scout of the continent's wild game...
> ("The Chipmunk")

But when they moved to Boston a year later, foreboding had set in. In "9 Willow Street," happiness looks in at their apartment window like a colorful American bird, a tanager or oriole, but it is "off course," gone before they can recognize it. "My emotional life has been like a dead man's here," Hughes wrote a friend. "I don't think its America. I think it's just me." When they spent the summer of 1959 touring the country, they stayed on the car-camping vacation circuit, and Hughes's Wild West memories in *Birthday Letters* are grim. Although the buffalo and antelope of "Home on the Range" roam North Dakota's Theodore Roosevelt National Park, a poem about it, "The Badlands," mentions neither. The only faintly encouraging animal in a landscape "staked out in the sun to die" is a "maniac midget" mouse, "hectic in a rickety thorn-bush."

When they encounter large beasts in Yellowstone National Park, guarded enthusiasm soon shifts to greater disquiet. The park's begging bears first seem a comically seductive promise of "marvelous abundance":

> We counted bears—as if all we wanted
> Were more bears. Yellowstone
> Folded us into its robe, its tepees
> of mountain and conifer.
> Mislaid Red Indian Mickey Mouse America...
> ("The 59th Bear")

But when they camp at night, the bears morph from Disneyland greeters into dangerous brutes, one of which fulfills Hughes's forebodings by ransacking their car. He describes it like the zoo jaguar, mechanistically:

> A bear's talons, which by human flesh
> Can be considered steel, braced on tendons
> Of steel hawser...
> ("The 59th Bear")

The poem's narrator seems unaware that the raid results less from innate rapacity than from decades of official folly that had created an unnaturally large and bold bear population by feeding them restaurant garbage so tourists could see them. The confrontation seems primal, and it reflects an increasingly troubled marriage, because Plath's goddess-like embodiment of "beautiful America" unnerved as well as exhilarated Hughes. She not only centered his shamanic identity—she had her own. Both their lives revolved around "initiatory" dreams.

## Two Dreams

Hughes dreamt that as he read English at Cambridge, a man-like fox with charred fur entered the room, spread a bleeding human hand on his page, and said: "Stop this, you are destroying us." Critics have seen the dream as a "call" because Hughes interpreted as such, with the fox as a spirit guide who told him to follow a shamanic path instead of an academic one.

Plath dreamt that as she hung in a helicopter over a huge lake, she saw "the real dragons" at the bottom, so deep she could barely discern them, and she was terrified: "Dream about these long enough and your feet and hands shrivel away." Critics haven't seen her dream as a "call," perhaps because, while she deems it her "dream of dreams" in a story, "Johnny Panic and the Bible of Dreams," she didn't interpret it as such.

It seems like one to me. They can be horrific as well as inspiring, as I found in the Siskiyou Wilderness. Plath's is horrific in a new way. Shamans traditionally fly or float free, but the helicopter divides her from the water where the dragons lurk, and they are not the root of her fear. The lake "bears no resemblance to those pure, sparkling-blue sources of drinking water the suburbs guard more jealously than the Hope diamond in the middle of pine woods… It's the sewage farm of the ages… It's into this lake that people's minds run at night…" It's an overcrowded everyday world lake. Its surface swarms with bloated corpses and bottled embryos, like "unfinished messages from the great I Am," with weirdly revolving "grains of dirt," and with "whole storehouses of hardware: knives, paper cutters, pistons and cogs and nutcrackers; the shiny fronts of cars, looming up, glass-eyed and evil-toothed."

Plath's dream calls her to witness not the pure flow of a Great Goddess's well of life but the filthy, stagnant wreckage of a great I Am's utilitarian subjection of it. It calls her, potentially, as a great shaman—a savior and prophet. Her "Bible of Dreams" narrator, "Assistant Secretary in the Adult Psychiatric Clinic," wants to save humanity from normality's polluted well with a "Johnny Panic gospel" of anxious *ab*normality: "I'm a wormy hermit in a country of prize pigs so corn-happy they can't see the slaughterhouse at the end of the track. I'm Jeremiah vision-bitten in the Land of Cockaigne."

In her journal, Plath calls writing a religious act. She identifies with the Apostles as a fisher of souls, "hauling up the pearl-eyed, horny, scaled and sea-bearded monsters sunk long, long ago in the Sargasso of my imagination." And she links her dream's savior-prophet role to Shakespeare: a formative childhood memory was of watching *The Tempest*. She considered calling her first poetry book *Full Fathom Five* because of "the background of *The Tempest*, the association of the sea, which is the central metaphor for my childhood … the pearls and corals…sea-changed from the ubiquitous grit of sorrow and dull routine."

In a poem from this period, she draws parallels between her dream and Shakespeare's, conflating Clarence's nightmare in *Richard III* with Ariel's song in *The Tempest*. Drowning brings a strange resuscitation:

> Your shelled bed I remember.
> Father, I would breath water…
>     ("Full Fathom Five")

Like her American goddess self, Plath's savior-prophet one both enthralled and unnerved Hughes. A voice warned him to "stay clear." After her successful 1963 suicide, he wrote: "Her poetry escapes ordinary analysis in the way clairvoyance and mediumship do: her psychic gifts, at almost any time, were strong enough to make her frequently wish to be free of them." Yet his own dream implied a call to be "like a guide dog, loyal to your stumblings," a fox-spirit witch doctor. He undertook to guide Plath to contact her shamanic self, as she began to do, he thought, in "Johnny Panic."

Plath's shamanic identity both abetted and rivaled Hughes's, so his guide role entailed dangerous ambiguities. Plath evokes this presciently in another story, "The Fifty-Ninth Bear," about a couple, Norton and Sadie, camping in Yellowstone. Norton sees himself as Sadie's guide: "Her sensuousness, her simple pagan enthusiasms... This was too flimsy, too gossamery a stuff to survive out from under the wings of his guardianship." But she is a risky acolyte. Among her "pagan enthusiasms" are the park's hot springs, suggestive of oracular powers but also of Plath's deathly dream call: "Her slender, vulnerable shape softened, wavered, as the mists thickened... The pool boiled up, right enough, a perfectly lovely shade of blue, but a freakish shift of wind flung the hot steam in her face..."

*Birthday Letters* narrates the failure-- and success-- of Hughes's guidance. He sees the attraction of her call, with its padded milieu where she can float and dream until "there's no point in any dreams at all." But he feels out of his depth:

> Your dreams were of a sea clogged with corpses...
> I hypnotized calm into you...
> Did it help? Each night you descended again...
> ("Dream Life")

A central poem, "Fishing Bridge," evokes a day they spent at Yellowstone Lake fishing for cutthroat trout that massed to spawn in the river that flows from it. By accompanying her to the National Park's unpolluted well of life, Hughes tries to guide Plath away from her dream well of death.  But he fails:

> Wandering off along the lake's fringe
> Towards the shag-headed wilderness
> In your bikini. There you nearly
> Stepped into America.  You turned back,
> And we turned away...

The American escape ends in a double bind.  Hughes's poetic ambitions combine with his guide role to make him follow Plath back into the "doorway, difficult and dark" of her dream call.  And she understands this: "He did not see, or did not care to see, how her submissiveness moved and drew him..." A *Birthday Letters* poem, "Epiphany," about their post-Yellowstone return to England, confirms the marriage's failure when he can't accept his own spirit guide's offer of help in the form of a fox cub strangely for sale on a London street.

His guidance succeeds, tragically, when the failure unveils Plath's savior-prophet self in the *Ariel* poems that made Robert Lowell describe her as "something imaginary, newly, wildly and subtly created—hardly a person at all, or a woman, certainly not another 'poetess,' but one of the super-real, hypnotic, great classical heroines."

## A Tragic Explosion

*Birthday Letters* enacts a Shakespearean Tragic Equation in their marriage.  At first, Hughes is a modern Adonis chosen by a modern Venus, the wild, promiscuous, bleached-blond, red-lipstick co-ed Plath, as in the passage wherein the goddess offers the young hunter her naked body:

> 'Fondling,' she saith, 'since I have hemmed thee here
> Within the circuit of this ivory pale,
> I'll be a park, and thou shalt be my deer;

Feed where thou wilt, on mountain or in dale;
Graze on my lips, and if those hills be dry,
Stray lower, where the pleasant fountains lie...'
(*Venus and Adonis,* 229)

For all its eroticism, the passage also reflects Plath's dream of dreams. Venus's "pleasant fountains" are the female organs, and the clinical metaphor stands out starkly from the poem's lush background. The pagan breasts and vulva that she offers the skittish young hunter are wells of life but also—in the process—of menses, urine, and glandular secretions at best, and of infections, tumors, and stillbirths at worst. Puritans abhor them as a source of ritual pollution unless controlled through wedded childbearing. Adonis replies:

'I hate not love, but your device in love.
That lends embracements unto every stranger,
    You do it for increase: O strange excuse,
    When reason is the bawd to lust's abuse!...
Call it not love, for Love to heaven is fled,
Since sweating Lust on earth usurp'd his name...'
*(Venus and Adonis* 789)

As the bottled embryos in her dream lake imply, the puritanical sense of menstruation as "the curse" haunted Plath. Her lake is a well of frigidity and sterility as well as decay and death. Anxiety overwhelmed her as her will to autonomy struggled with a conviction that—even in an overcrowded, polluted world—wedded motherhood defines womanhood. Her anxiety fed on Hughes's sense of emotional deadness in America, which she felt as loss of love for her, and burst out in "hysteria" that clashed with his own puritanical, egotistical side.

"A liar and a vain smiler," she calls him in her pre-Yellowstone journal. "The late comings home, my vision, while brushing my hair, of a black-horned grinning wolf all came clear, fused, and I gagged at what I saw." Gazing in her mirror, a

jealous American Venus invokes a beast to punish a faithless
Adonis. Her "Fifty-Ninth Bear" is a surprisingly open
expression of this anger, ending as Norton falls fatally afoul of a
bear that ransacks their car while Sadie, having goaded him to
repel it, waits in their tent:

"At any moment, the bear should break and run. 'Get
out…' But there was another will working, a will stronger, even,
than his.

"The darkness fisted and struck."

Plath calls the trip "the experience of our lives" in a letter
to her mother about the bear incident. Her account mingles
sacred horror with vicarious gratification. The bear smashing the
rear window wakes her from a dream of the car exploding:
"There in the blue weird light of the moon, not ten feet away, a
huge dark bear shape hunched, guzzling at a tin." It incites her to
the "mediumship" that enthralled and unnerved Hughes. She lists
the tin's banal contents, Ritz crackers, Oreo cookies and
postcards, then draws a kind of divination from them:

"I found the postcards the next day, lying among the
rubble, the top card of moose antlers turned down and *face up*
the card of a large bear with an actual bear paw-print in it."
Venus solves the equation posed in her mirror: "black-horned"
deer plus "grinning wolf" equals "huge dark bear."

It enters the dark hole of the head…
The page is printed.
("The Thought Fox")

In *Birthday Letters*, Hughes reflects on the real bear's
ransacking of their car, and on her story:

I had not understood
How the death hurtling to and fro
Inside your head, had to alight somewhere…
("The 59th Bear)

Destroyed by the Venus-Bear, Hughes's Adonis self becomes a boorish modern Tarquin-Boar who destroys a modern Lucrece, the tame, chaste, natural brunette wife and mother, Plath—and destroys her through sexual pollution—adultery with a dark woman who, in the poem "Dreamers," is garishly dressed and "slightly filthy with erotic mystery."

Hughes writes of Shakespeare's narratives: "these two long poems (which eventually combine to make the Equation) become basically two terrible howls from the Female: the first, of the undivided Divine Love's baffled passion, the second, of the sacred and true love's mortal injury. And in each case, the reason for her outcry is blindingly clear. For length, mythic scope, and intensity of Woman's grievance, one would have to look a long way in subsequent literature to find anything remotely like these."

In Shakespeare's narrative, Lucrece cries:

Why should the worm intrude the maiden bud...
   Or tyrant folly lurk in gentle breasts,
   Or kings be breakers of their own behests?
   (*Lucrece*, 848)

In Plath's *Ariel*, "Lucrece" cries:

Pure? What does it mean?
The tongues of hell are dull...
Greasing the bodies of adulterers...
    ("Fever 103")

First mythically destroyed by Plath, then her mythic destroyer, Hughes receives "a wound that never healeth." The union of Miranda and Ferdinand that completes *The Tempest* is what Hughes and Plath had, then lost. Hughes explicitly links this to Shakespeare with a *Birthday Letters* poem wherein their modern Tragic Explosion unravels the play's tragicomic solution. Plath begins as Venus-Miranda and ends as Lucrece, a self-immolated victim; Hughes begins as Adonis-Ferdinand and ends as Tarquin, an outlawed fugitive:

> 'Who has dismembered us?' I crawled
> Under a gabardine, hugging tight
> All I could of me, hearing the cry
> Now of hounds.
> ("Setebos")

# III

# PSYCHOLOGY

---

If but as well I other accents borrow
That can my speech diffuse, my good intent
May carry through itself to that full issue
For which I razed my likeness…
(*King Lear*, 1, 4)

# Chapter Nine

# Squire Crow

―――――――――

Hughes conjectures that Shakespeare underwent a personal Tragic Equation: a "knot of obsessions" around "a sexual dilemma of a particularly black and ugly sort." Given the severity of his own Tragic Explosion, this might be a projection. Yet Hughes's tragedy, while extreme, is not unique. Many relationships undergo some kind of Venus and Adonis, Tarquin and Lucrece, conflict. In her journal, Plath calls human life "a great, stark, bloody play acting itself out over and over again behind the sunny facade of our daily rituals, birth, marriage, death, behind parents and schools and beds and tables of food: the dark, cruel, murderous shades, the demon-animals, the Hungers."

Hughes generalizes his own "sexual dilemma" in an appendix to *The Goddess*: "That division of the loved and loathed woman in the one body, which precipitates the Tragic Equation, is projected on to her (involving her in its real consequences) by the man. And he projects it on to her in so far as his rationality is separated from nature, is therefore insecure, is therefore autocratically jealous of power and fearful of what he suppresses: i.e. in so far as he fights against her maternal control, fears her reproductive mystery and is jealous of her solidarity with the natural world."

Plath's *Ariel* is a "terrible howl" from the dilemma's other side:

> The blood jet is poetry
> There is no stopping it.

("Kindness")

In his *Goddess* Introduction, Hughes paraphrases Plath when he writes that the "blood jet autobiographical truth" is what decides the value of a "truly mythic work." What, then, is the blood jet truth about Shakespeare? Did he experience trance states, initiatory dreams, visions of death and rebirth, anxieties that drove him to performance?

Documents

Baptism records show that William was born in 1564 to middle class parents in Stratford, a town on the Avon River in Warwickshire north of London. His father, John, did well enough as a glove maker and wool broker to be an alderman; his mother Mary, *nee* Arden, was from a landed family. John's status would have entitled William to attend Stratford grammar school, but no records of it survive. The next record of him is marriage in 1582 to Anne Hathaway, who was twenty-six. She came from a local family but documents say little about her: the discrepancy in their ages has raised questions but no answers.

Anne was pregnant when they married, which has added to the confusion. The diocesan register records that a "wm Shaxper" got a license to marry an "Anna whateley de Temple Grafton," a nearby hamlet, the day before two men posted a marriage bond for "willm Shagspere" and "Anne hathwey" on November 28. Most historians think a clerk misspelled Anne Hathaway's name on the license; some conjecture sexual double-dealing that led to a "pitchfork" wedding, but the wedding itself is not recorded. Whatever happened, Anne bore a daughter, Susan, six months later. Baptism records show the birth of twins, Hamnet and Judith, to the couple in 1585.

William's life again went undocumented for seven years except for his name on a property dispute. His father had fallen into debt and run afoul of the law: William may have left Stratford because of that. From 1592 until a few years before his death, documents show his presence in London, where he had various lodgings, belonged consecutively to two acting companies, held shares in the Globe and Blackfriars theaters, and invested in loans and property. They also show his presence in Stratford, where he added land, tithe leases, and commodities to his investments.

Many of the documents about William are tax and court records: he was slow to pay taxes, quick to sue defaulting debtors. A 1596 London docket cites him and three others, two of them women, for threatening a man named William Wayte, presumably about theater business, bolstering an impression of astute, aggressive personality. A 1612 court deposition suggests a more empathetic side, naming him as a witness in a lawsuit about a London family he'd lodged with from 1602 to 1604. He had encouraged a match between the daughter and an apprentice: when the apprentice sued for a dowry he said he'd been promised, William traveled from Stratford to testify although he couldn't swear to the case because he'd forgotten the details.

William prospered quickly given an inauspicious start, buying a large Stratford house in 1597 and acquiring a coat of arms, a status symbol that had eluded his family. He became a small town squire, a gentleman, although his acting and money lending, along with speculative grain hoarding, skirted disrepute. But the authorities never fined him as they had his father. When James I succeeded Queen Elizabeth and sponsored his company, changing its name from the Lord Chamberlain's Men to the King's Men, he was listed as a "groom of the chamber" along with the other members. His will left substantial assets, mostly to his older daughter and her husband, along with token, interlineated bequests to three London actors, Richard Burbage, Henry Condell, and John Heminge.

Biographers think William lived mainly in London from the late 1580s or early 1590s until retiring to Stratford sometime in the early 1600s, but the exact chronology is unclear. His 1616 death in his early fifties from an unknown cause may reflect a stressful life. The loss of his son Hamnet in 1596 would have been a blow although his reaction to it is unknown. His marriage may have deteriorated. He refused to pay a debt Anne had incurred and left her nothing in his will except his "second best bed." William was not particularly short-lived for the times, however. He outlasted six of seven siblings, including a younger brother who was an actor in London.

## Soule of the Age!

In 1592, a playwright named Henry Chettle published a pamphlet by another playwright, Robert Greene, which warns three other, unnamed playwrights against actor-impresarios who exploit writers. Entitled *Greene's Groat's Worth of Wit*, it particularly denounces "an upstart Crow, beautified with our feathers, that with his *Tiger's heart wrapped in a Player's hide*, supposes he is as well able to bombast out a blank verse as the best of you, and being an absolute *Johannes fac totum*, is in his own conceit the only Shake-scene in a country."

"*Tiger's heart wrapped in a Player's hide*" paraphrases from a play published anonymously in 1595, *The True Tragedy of Richard Duke of York*. Since Shakespeare's *Henry VI* part 3 is a revised version of that play, biographers see the pamphlet as a jealous rival's attack on William as a playwright, although it doesn't call the "upstart Crow" one. But a number of contemporary commentators did call William Shakespeare a writer, including Henry Willobie (1594), William Camden (1605), and Francis Beaumont (1615). The best known reference, in Francis Mere's 1598 book, *Palladis Tamia*, attributes a dozen plays to him and describes him as "mellifluous and honey-tongued" like a reincarnation of Ovid's "sweet witty soul."

Many Shakespeare poems and plays were published during William's life, beginning with the two narratives in 1593 and 1594, both of which carry signed dedications to a major nobleman, the Earl of Southampton. Quartos, small books printed with single plays, started to appear anonymously in 1594 and began to bear the Shakespeare name in 1598. In 1609, a publisher named Thomas Thorpe brought out a book of "Shake-speare's Sonnets," although authorities soon suppressed it, probably because it contained love poems to a handsome young man. None of these publications described or pictured the author, but that was not unusual for the times. Most biographers think the narratives' dedications to the Earl of Southampton shows that he was William's patron, then a common literary relationship. Some think they imply that the Earl, a handsome young man, was William's lover.

Two posthumous developments cemented William's literary reputation-- the Stratford Monument and the First Folio of the plays. Both identify the Shakespeare canon with a whiskered, balding man portrayed in the monument's bust by sculptor Gerard Janssen and in the folio's engraving by Martin Droeshout. The Monument in Stratford's Trinity Church evidently came first since a poem in the First Folio by a scholar named Leonard Digges mentions it:

> *Shake-speare, at length thy pious fellowes give*
> *The world thy Workes; thy Workes, by which, out-live*
> *Thy Tombe, thy name must: when that stone is rent,*
> *And Time dissolves thy Stratford Moniment,*
> *Here we alive shall view thee still.*

A syndicate led by William Jaggard, a printer who already had published Shakespeare quartos and poems, brought out the First Folio in 1623, with "epistles" signed by two of the actors mentioned in William's will, John Heminge and Henry Condell. The actors say that they collected the plays and arranged for their publication "cured and perfected in their limbs... as he conceived them," and praise Shakespeare as a "happy imitator of nature" whose "mind and hand went together" in producing his works. Verses facing the portrait engraving-- initialed B.I. – also laud him. Ben Jonson presumably wrote them, since he signed a longer eulogy that calls Shakespeare "Sweet Swan of *Avon*":

> *...Soule of the age!*
> *The applause! delight! the wonder of our Stage!*

Neither Digges's eulogy nor Jonson's describes Shakespeare's life and personality, although Jonson's implies that he may have lacked classical learning:

> *And though thou hadst small* Latine, *and lesse* Greek,
> *From thence to honour thee, I would not seeke*
> *For names; but call forth thund'ring* Aeschilus,
> Euripides, *and* Sophocles, *to us...*

Jonson elsewhere claimed personal knowledge of Shakespeare as a good if erratic writer. In a 1618 chat with a Scottish poet, William Drummond, he said that he "wanted art" and made mistakes like setting a play on the "Seacoast of Bohemia," believed a landlocked kingdom. Manuscript notes found in his lodgings after Jonson's death in 1637 say that "*Shakespeare*" was "honest, and of an open, and free nature; had an excellent *phantasie*; brave notions, and gentle expressions: wherein he flow'd with that facility, that sometimes it was necessary he should be stopped," and that he "loved the man, and do honor his memory (on this side idolatry) as much as any."

## An Urbane Rustic

For later writers like Milton, the Monument and Folio identified the canon with a small town William "warbling his wood notes wild," and the breezy Shakespeare of my parents' red leather volume "sprang up." A 1662 book by a historian, Thomas Fuller, describes him breezily: "Many were the *wit-combates* betwixt him and *Ben Jonson*, which two I behold like a *Spanish great Gallion* and an *English man of War... Shake-*

*spear*, with the *English-man of War*, lesser in *bulk*, but lighter in *sailing*, could turn with all tides, tack about and take advantage of all winds, by the quickness of his Wit and Invention." The diary of John Ward, Vicar of Stratford from 1662 to 1681, gives a like impression, repeating local hearsay that "Mr. Shakspeare was a natural witt, without any art at all," and that he'd died of a fever after a "merrie meeting" with Jonson and another playwright, Michael Drayton.

Around 1680, an antiquarian named John Aubrey wrote the first "biography" in a compendium called *Brief Lives of Eminent Men*. A modern editor describes him as "excited" about "a new culture of invention, profit, and control," and *Brief Lives'* two-page Bard is accordingly Whiggish. Aubrey writes that Shakespeare was a Stratford butcher's son who made speeches "in a high style" while slaughtering calves, that he "understood Latine pretty well: for he had been in his younger yeares a Schoolmaster in the Countrey," that he "came to London, I guesse, about eighteen," and that he "began early to make essayes at Dramatique Poetry, which at that time was very lowe; and his Plays took well." He describes him as "a handsome well shap't man: very good company, and a very readie and pleasant smooth Witte," who was "wont to say that he never blotted out a line in his life."

Aubrey's sketch is mostly hearsay, like Ward's diary, and came from sources such as the son of an actor who briefly had apprenticed with the King's Men in the early 1600s. Anthony a Wood, an Oxford Fellow who employed the impecunious Aubrey to do legwork for an official tome entitled *Athenae Oxoniense*, called him "roving and magotie–headed." The *Brief Lives* manuscript is such a scribbled mess, in fact, that it stayed unpublished for over a century.

In 1709 an actor-impresario named Nicholas Rowe got William's life into print with longer account in his edition of the plays. It adds more hearsay about youthful deer poaching and hobnobbing with gentry, and parallels Aubrey's in presenting a Bard both naïve and urbane, "a good-natured Man of great sweetness in his manners, and an agreeable companion" who "had no knowledge of the Writings of the Antient Poets" because his works had "no traces of anything that looks like imitation of 'em." This still only filled a few pages, so Rowe expanded his account with what would become Shakespeare biography's mainstay: he drew from the canon for a sense of William's identity. Rowe's forty odd pages are thus mostly about the plays.

William's reputation burgeoned in mid-century, especially after the famous actor-impresario, David Garrick, held the first "Shakespeare Festival" at Stratford in 1769. "Bardolatry" became a cult with relics and shrines, including what Thoreau would call "Shakespeare's house," although it was not William's big one, demolished in 1759, but a nearby tenement deemed his birthplace. During the next century, impelled by Bardolatry, the first Shakespeare scholars compiled the genuine documents and dispelled many of the hearsays, leaving the slim dossier.

This austerity might have discouraged biographers: on the contrary, it inspired them, like a blank canvas. Every generation since has produced an abundant crop of lives, few of them brief. They vacillate between dressing up the dossier in new conjectures and stripping it down to documents again, but the basic approach remains like Rowe's in 1709: drawing from the canon for a sense of William's identity.

## Chapter Ten

## The Nest in the Redwood

---

When I moved into a Berkeley, California, neighborhood in 1989, no crows lived here. Crows were farmland birds, and there isn't much around Berkeley, although there is wooded open space. But crows were uncommon there too, and they were getting uncommon in farmland as agribusiness got more efficient. Then something happened. Crows began turning up in suburbs nationwide, as though news had spread of a land of opportunity. By the 2000s, they were common Berkeley birds, picking through gutters and lawns for earthworms, mobbing hawks, scavenging road-killed squirrels.

A pair nests in a big redwood next door, using twigs broken from a sycamore on another lot. It's interesting to see them craftily circling the tree when they bring food so as to not give away the nest's exact location. Birders suspect crows of eating garden chickadees and hummingbirds but I haven't seen this. I've never seen a crow in my garden, although they forage on the street in front of the house every day. They seem to have a sense of public space as opposed to private, or perhaps they're just wary of enclosed places.

Their cawing has a resonance as deep, in its way, as the thrush song I tried to locate in Mooney's Woods half a century ago. Their suburban invasion is not so surprising from a mythic viewpoint. Crows are prominent among creatures that embody "The Trickster," a major figure of creation myths. When Earth/Water Woman has twin sons in some old tales, one of them is often The Trickster, a clever, energetic being who is also so greedy and devious that his main contributions to creation are doubts and dilemmas. It helps to explain why life is so erratic. Coming out of nowhere, putting on airs, grabbing goodies, and getting away with it: The Trickster lives on in rustic-urbane crows.

## Soule of the Age?

Robert Greene's "upstart Crow" pamphlet has raised doubts and dilemmas about Shakespeare. When two of the playwrights that the pamphlet warns objected to it, Henry Chettle, the publisher, made an apology to one, and some biographers think William was that playwright. But this implies that the pamphlet was warning William the exploited writer against William the exploiting actor-impresario—against himself. Some historians doubt that the "upstart Crow" passage is about William: they think its target was another actor-impresario. Some doubt that Greene wrote it: he was a diseased alcoholic who died some weeks before its publication. They suspect from its style that Chettle did, thus further confusing its motive. If Chettle wrote the pamphlet to attack William as an upstart, it seems incongruous with verses he wrote after Queen Elizabeth's death in 1603, which address Shakespeare respectfully while lamenting his failure to elegize her:

> Nor doth the silver-tongued Melicert
> Drop from his honeyed muse one sable tear,
> To mourn her death that graced his desert
> And to his lays opened her royal ear.
> Shepherd, remember our Elizabeth,
> And sing her Rape, done by that Tarquin, Death.
> (*England's Mourning Garment*)

The pamphlet is not the sole contemporary source of doubts and dilemmas about William: a dubious undertow ran through his life, and beyond. Several Elizabethan commentators said equivocal things about Shakespeare's identity, including Gabriel Harvey (1593), Thomas Nashe (1597), and John Marston (1598). Several plays, including Shakespeare ones, portray unliterary Squire Crow-like characters who come out of nowhere and put on airs. Ben Jonson's *Every Man out of His Humor* features a parvenu named Sogliardo who brags of a newly acquired coat of arms, whereupon another character suggests that its motto be: "Not Without Mustard." William's motto was: "Not Without Right." *As You Like It* has a walk-on by a rustic named William who says "Faith sir, so-so," when asked if he is "rich," "Aye, sir, I have a pretty wit," when asked if he is "wise," and, "No sir," when asked if he is "learned." His interlocutor, Touchstone, an ex-courtier who acts as "fool" to the heroine, Rosalind, replies:

"Then learn this of me. To have is to have. For it is a figure in Rhetoric that drink being pour'd out of a cup into a glass, by filling the one, doth empty the other. For all your writers do consent, that *ipse* is he: now you are not *ipse*, for I am he." (5,1)

Historians have found no letters, journals, or other personal writings by William. No manuscripts of definite Shakespeare works survive, although scholars liken some handwritten pages of a collaborative play, *Sir Thomas More*, to William's signatures, six of which survive. The signatures are inconsistent scrawls, however, and, as with most documents about him, they are variants of "William Shakspere," presumably pronounced with a short "a" unlike the long "a" in Shakespeare. A very few of the plays published in William's lifetime give the author's name as "Shak-speare" but most give it as "Shake-speare" or "Shakespeare."

Despite the many literary mentions of Shakespeare, no known records from William's lifetime describe a London theater shareholder and Stratford squire as a writer. An impresario named Philip Henslowe who staged some "early" Shakespeare plays in his Rose Theater kept a log of payments to playwrights from 1590 to 1604: it doesn't mention William. Thomas Thorpe published his 1609 edition of *Shake-speare's Sonnets* without recorded payment to William.

Biographers explain the payment hiatus by saying that William wrote the narrative poems to establish his reputation and get the Earl of Southampton's patronage; the plays for his share of profits from the Globe and Blackfriars theaters; and the sonnets to please himself and his literary friends. Yet no other record links him with Southampton; other theaters like the Rose staged Shakespeare plays; and, despite legends of Mermaid Tavern revelry, no record from William's lifetime shows that he had literary friends. (Aubrey's *Brief Lives* says that he "wouldn't be debauched.") His will only mentions actors and Stratford businessmen, and it doesn't mention books, costly items often bequeathed to friends or family in the days before public libraries. His death entry in the parish register just calls him "gent," and no writers published eulogies in the years just after he died, which was unusual.

The playwright Michael Drayton, alleged in Reverend Ward's diary to have been with Jonson at William's fatal drinking bout, was also a Warwickshire native. Yet, although he was a patient of William's son-in-law, Dr. John Hall, Drayton's poetry rarely refers to Shakespeare, and then only briefly and impersonally. Even Hall, who called Drayton "an excellent poet," never mentioned William as a writer.

Nobody knows how the Stratford Monument got there. Such edifices usually honored clerics and burghers. Ben Jonson's grave marker covers eighteen square inches on Westminster Abbey's floor: when workmen raised it during repairs, they found leg bones sticking from the sand. He'd been buried on his head to save space. Anyway, the Stratford Monument doesn't call William a playwright, and what it says is puzzling. A Latin inscription likens him to the classical worthies Nestor, Socrates, and Virgil, but only Virgil was a writer, while Shakespeare's *Troilus and Cressida* (5,4,) calls Nestor, a Greek

leader in the Trojan War, a "stale old moth eaten dry cheese."
The inscription concludes: "Terra tegit. Populus maeret.
Olympus habet": "The earth encloses. The people grieve.
Olympus holds." Parnassus was dead poets' usual destination,
and William was buried without record of public grief.

An English inscription tells visitors to read "whom
envious death hath plast with in this monument Shakspeare."
William is "plast" in the tomb. Then it says that his name "doth
deck y tombe" although the gravestone carries only the famous
curse against moving his bones. It concludes: "Sieh all y hath
writt, leaves living art, but page, to serve his witt." Biographers
assume "sieh all y hath writt" refers to the canon, although the
only "writ" visitors can "sieh" is the gravestone verse. What "but
page, to serve his witt" means is anyone's guess.

It's unclear where Gerard Janssen got the likeness for the
Monument's bust. Many consider the "Chandos" painting of a
raffish-looking man wearing an earring a life portrait of William
but it is unlike the present bust, although that may differ from
Janssen's original. A crude 1634 sketch of the bust shows a
lanky man with a drooping moustache resting empty hands on a
bulky cushion or sack. The bust now shows a pudgy man with
Van dyke whiskers writing with a quill pen on a flat cushion.

Ben Jonson's First Folio eulogy says something
incongruous after calling Shakespeare "*Soule of the age!*":

> *My* Shakespeare *rise!*...
> *Thou art a Moniment, without a tombe!*

The Folio has other incongruities. About half of its thirty-
six plays were previously unpublished: some were, as far as is
known, unperformed. This apparent level of failure seems
contrary to William's later reputation as a theatrical and fiscal
superman. Despite what Heminge and Condelle say, the Folio
plays are not "perfected…as he conceived them." The book has
many errors and is organized by genre, not chronologically. And

it's unclear where two actors got the influence for the lavish enterprise. Like William's, their education is a blank except that Heminge, who moonlighted as a publican, was apprenticed to a grocer. Jonson probably wrote their epistles. They dedicate the Folio to two men who did have influence, the earls of Montgomery and Pembroke, but the earls don't take credit.

I.B.'s verses facing the Folio engraving tell readers to pay more attention to Shakespeare's works than his "figure," which is unprepossessing. Despite a solemn expression, William's face has a louche five o'clock shadow and his costume's proportions are so odd that some commentators liken it to a clown suit. The engraving lacks the symbolism-- laurels, Muses, books or scrolls—that was usual in author's portraits. An engraving of Jonson is from an authenticated life painting and shows him caped and laurel-crowned, with books by his hand.

The Monument and Folio cemented over the skeptical undertow, but they didn't stop it. In 1628, a critic named Thomas Vicars published a book that lists other authors by name but refers only to "that famous poet who takes his name from shaking and spear." In 1640, the last pre-Civil War Shakespeare publication made striking forays into Trickster territory. Entitled *Poems Written by Wil. Shake-speare, Gent*, it includes most of the sonnets, which had been out of print since the authorities suppressed Thorpe's 1609 edition for its homoerotic content. The 1640 book dodges that problem by changing male pronouns to female: other aspects of it are even trickier.

It has a portrait engraving based on the First Folio's but it alters the original and shows William to the waist, as on the Stratford Monument. Instead of writing with his right hand, the 1640 William hides it under a cape, while his left grasps what looks like an olive branch. A paraphrase from Jonson's First Folio eulogy under it has punctuation that looks like a "reverse" of the Folio's laudatory exclamation marks: *"This shadowe is renowned Shakespear's? Soule of th'age The applause? delight? the wonder of the Stage."*

An introductory note is initialed "I.B," the reverse of the Folio introduction's "B.I." The initials evidently are those of a "John Benson," named as the book's seller. A possible implication of this is that, whereas "I.B." is selling the 1640 version of Shakespeare, "B.I." had been "selling" the 1623 one. The book also has a eulogy by Leonard Digges, the scholar whose First Folio eulogy refers to Shakespeare's "Stratford Moniment." Digges was another Warwickshire native, like William and Michael Drayton, but although his 1640 eulogy is much longer than his Folio one, it still says nothing about Shakespeare's personal identity.

The Puritans' Shakespeare moratorium checked the skeptical undertow, but it flowed again as Bardolatry sprang up. When in 1747 a Stratford cleric named Joseph Greene found a copy of William's will, he called it "absolutely void of the least particle of that spirit which animated our great poet." In 1769, a physician named Herbert Lawrence published an "allegory" which describes "Shakespear" as a thief. When an Oxford fellow named James Wilmot moved near Stratford to study William's life in the 1780s, he found so little pertinent information that he gave up. In 1786, an anonymous novel entitled *The Story of the Learned Pig* appeared, the eponymous narrator of which "transmigrates" from Italy to Elizabethan England. There he becomes an "ostler" called "Pimping Billy" and meets "the immortal Shakespeare," who turns out to be a philandering plagiarist whose thefts include five of the Learned Pig's own plays: *Hamlet, Othello, As You Like It, The Tempest,* and *A Midsummer Night's Dream.*

As Shakespeare scholarship developed, some of William's admirers tried to compensate for his shrinking dossier with forgeries. Incited by his father's Bardolatry, a youth named William Henry Ireland faked letters, deeds, and manuscripts so crudely that cultists' delighted embrace of them surprised him. Ireland also produced a "new" Shakespeare play, which was his undoing when Edmond Malone, an early scholarly biographer, published a book debunking his frauds. In the mid-nineteenth century, another leading Shakespeare scholar, a journalist named John Payne Collier, may have practiced forgery more subtly, interpolating his frauds into real documents in ways that were hard to detect. Yet Collier's twentieth century biographer maintains that he was innocent, implying that others committed the forgeries, and thus increasing the confusion. Some frauds may remain undetected.

## Experience and Language

As scholars dispelled hearsay and forgeries in the late nineteenth century, it had the tricky side-effect of allowing the skeptical undertow to surface. It came up with some big names. Walt Whitman remarked: "It is my final belief that the Shakespearean plays were written by another hand than Shakspere's." Mark Twain (a.k.a. Samuel Clemens) devoted a caustic booklet to his doubts, singling out the Monument's "emotionless bust, with the dandy moustache" for special derision. Henry James, "haunted by the conviction that the divine William is the biggest and most successful fraud ever practiced on a patient world," published a story based on testimony of a former Shakespeare Birthplace custodian that the "traditions and legends of the place" were an "abomination." Sigmund Freud mused: "The name 'William Shakespeare' is probably a pseudonym behind which there lurks a great unknown."

William's current advocates, "Stratfordians," mostly ignore or downplay the skeptics. Stephen Greenblatt, an American academic, doesn't mention them in the "new narrative" biography I quoted earlier, *Will in the World*. Peter Ackroyd's *Shakespeare: The Biography* gives William's fictive funeral more space. Others dismiss them. Northrop Frye, a Canadian, writes that "so-called controversies" about authorship "are not serious issues." Another American, Gary Taylor, writes: "The theory that Shakespeare did not write Shakespeare's works belongs to the class of propositions that have no meaning, because they cannot under any circumstances be disproved." An English academic, Jonathan Bate, writes: "There is a mystery about the identity of William Shakespeare. The mystery is this: why should anyone doubt that he was William Shakespeare, the actor from Stratford-upon-Avon?"

Whitman, Twain, James, and Freud are not easily dismissed. Another American professor, Harold Bloom, has to pooh-pooh Freud's skepticism twice in a doorstop opus, *Shakespeare: The Invention of the Human*, while a journalist, Ron Rosenbaum, dismisses the skeptics nine times in *The Shakespeare Wars*, a book about intra-Stratfordian squabbles. Some Stratfordians argue with the skeptics, claiming that the canon fits a well-read genius educated at Stratford grammar school and that slim Elizabethan dossiers are normal. The first claim is moot for lack of evidence, but they have a point with the second. Skeptics reply that Shakespeare's popularity in his time makes William's slim dossier suspect. Stratfordians say that we know as much or more about his career as other early modern writers. Skeptics reply that we know more about others' *literary* careers, and they have a point.

A 2001 book, Diana Price's *Shakespeare's Unorthodox Biography*, examines over twenty Elizabethan "name authors" for contemporary records in ten career categories including education, correspondence, payments, patronage, manuscripts, book ownership, and obituaries. Most attended university, such as a coterie called the "university wits" that included Robert Greene of the "upstart Crow" pamphlet, Thomas Lodge, John Lyly, Thomas Nashe, and Christopher Marlowe. Two who didn't-- Ben Jonson and Thomas Kyd—went to grammar schools. Six, including Anthony Munday, George Chapman and Michael Drayton, left no evidence of formal education but were recorded as writing for pay. Price finds one name yielding no contemporary evidence of professional writing—William's.

Stratfordians claim that incongruities between William and the canon are irrelevant since Elizabethan writing manifests little authorial personality or experience. "The 'experience' argument," writes Northrop Frye, "is based on the amateur's notion that you don't write but only 'write up' something you've already been exposed to." The claim is suspect in that William's biographers routinely use Shakespeare quotes about rustics, theater, and business to support their version of the author as a rustic turned theatrical businessman. Still, they have a point in that most Elizabethan professional writing is conventional and derivative, as in all eras.

But major congruities exist in the unusually original work of Marlowe and Jonson. Marlowe was a freethinker who boasted of a fondness for boys, also a government spy, counterfeiter, and possible traitor: his conduct led to his murder at age 29. His plays portray an atheist scholar in *Doctor Faustus*, a sodomite monarch in *Edward II*, and a Machiavellian terrorist in *The Jew of Malta*. Jonson was an autodidact classical scholar who worked as a bricklayer and soldier before getting into theater through acting. Witty and quarrelsome, he escaped hanging for killing a man in a duel by pleading benefit of clergy—proving literacy. He lived past sixty, rare for Elizabethan writers, and left a library as well as manuscripts. His plays display his erudition in wordy tragedies like *Sejanus*, his pugnacity in now obscure lampoons like *Poetaster*, and his wit in still popular comedies like *The Alchemist*.

In another manuscript, Jonson writes: "Language most shows the man: speak that I may see thee. It springs out of the most retired and innermost parts of us, and is the image of the parent of it, the mind." Judging from Shakespeare's language, which includes around 20,000 words, four times modern college-level vocabularies, skeptics see in the canon a knowledge of many things that seem incongruous with William-- not only hunting and hawking but upper class pursuits in general as well as classical and foreign languages, philosophy, law, warfare, medicine, history, and geography. They profile the author as well traveled, erudite and aware of the latest natural philosophy, but with conflicted religious feelings, strong class prejudices, and neurotic fixations with political treachery, sexual jealousy, insanity, and the occult. They infer a life as turbulent as Marlowe and Jonson's.

"Conceived out of the fullest heat and pulse of European feudalism," writes Walt Whitman in an 1884 essay, "personifying in unparalleled ways the medieval aristocracy-- its towering spirit of ruthless and gigantic caste, with its own peculiar air and arrogance (no mere imitation)—only one of the 'wolfish earls' so plenteous in the plays themselves, or some born descendant and knower might seem to be the author of those amazing works…"

Stratfordians sometimes show anxiety by charging headlong against such ideas. To quote the 1957 Folger Library editors again: "Most anti-Shakespeareans betray an obvious snobbery. The author of their favorite plays, they imply, must have a college diploma… The anti-Shakespeareans talk darkly about a plot of vested interests … Nobody has any vested interest in Shakespeare, but every scholar is interested in the truth, and in the quality of evidence advanced by special pleaders who set forth hypotheses in place of facts… it is incredible that anyone should be so naïve or ignorant as to doubt the reality of Shakespeare as the author… the effort to prove him a myth [is] one of the most absurd in the history of human perversity."

When a 2005 *New York Times* essay suggested including the skeptics in school curriculums, Stephen Greenblatt likened them to Biblical creationists in a letter to the editor: "The idea that William Shakespeare's authorship of his plays and poems is a matter of conjecture and the idea that the 'authorship controversy' be taught in the classroom are the exact equivalent of current arguments that 'intelligent design' be taught alongside evolution. In both cases, an overwhelming scholarly consensus, based on serious assessment of hard evidence is challenged by passionately held fantasies whose adherents demand equal time."

Greenblatt's analogy is shaky in that his *Will in the World* devotes much more space to his own conjectures about

William's writing-- in effect, "passionately held fantasies" -- than to the hard evidence of the business documents. It is also shaky on creationism's relationship to science. An "overwhelming scholarly consensus, based on serious assessment of hard evidence" *against* evolution prevailed for most of the modern era. And evidence *for* it was inconclusive: fossils suggested that life had changed, but professional experts like Richard Owen and Baron Cuvier saw no sign it had changed through what was then called "transmutation of species." Ralph Waldo Emerson (a mild Shakespeare skeptic) observed that Owen "indemnified himself in the good opinion of his countrymen, by... abusing without mercy... these poor transmutationists." Academics cited scripture as further proof that a "designing intelligence" created life, while a few amateurs like Darwin cited a scarcity of other proof and evidence implying other origins.

Similarly, Shakespeare skeptics were hard-put to propose alternative candidates when experts cited the Monument and First Folio as proof of William's authorship. Like the "transmutationists," the "anti-Shakespeareans" faced an old established orthodoxy. Even some Stratfordians seem uncomfortable with identifying them with creationists. Ron Rosenbaum, *The Shakespeare Wars* author, quips in a 2011 online article that the identification is "not fair to the creationists."

The canon's incongruities with William's dossier remain evident enough that Stratfordians sometimes acknowledge them. In *Will in the World*, Greenblatt writes of other Shakespeare biographies: "After examining even the best of them and patiently sifting through the available sources, readers rarely feel closer to understanding how the poet's achievement's came about. If anything, Shakespeare often seems a drabber, duller person, and the inward springs of his art seem more obscure than ever." In *Soul of the Age: A Biography of the Mind of William Shakespeare*, Jonathan Bate writes: "The elusiveness of both his face and his hand is in keeping with the process whereby he made himself invisible through absorption in his works."

But why would a man of William's recorded fiscal acumen and status consciousness want to be invisible as the author of brilliant, popular works? One might say that his money lending, tax evasion, and commodity hoarding dictated a low profile. But, if so, why would a successful poet, patronized by nobility and royalty, persist in them?

# Chapter Eleven

# Desire and Will

---

If William's dossier is vague on a literary identity, it is vaguer on a shamanic one. Its main evidence of thoughts and feelings aside from teenage sex, fiscal shrewdness and social ambition is the will that slights his wife and younger daughter. If William experienced visions, initiatory dreams, and compulsive anxieties driving him to artistic performance, the reader has to look for them in the canon. That is what Ted Hughes does in *Shakespeare and the Goddess*.

Hughes acknowledges incongruities between the canon and the dossier: "It is not too difficult to show how solidly Shakespeare belonged to his times. Or rather, it is comparatively easy to find links between his words and current tradition of the historical record. But it is not so easy to say anything about just what gave his inner illumination that peculiar, not to say extraordinary, power, scope and depth, or just why it expressed itself in poetry, or why his poetic, dramatic activity was of that particular quality. And his creative activity not only resurrected ancient patterns of vision and understanding into urgent, familiar life, and embodied the climactic struggle of the day, it was, as I say, also prophetic. This cannot be discussed in any but the psycho-biological terms of his individuality, of which, it might be thought, we know nothing."

Yet Hughes expresses no doubts about William, adding: "But we do know what he told us." In his introduction, he portrays the Bard as the media hack genius that the Folger Library editors described in 1957, with the Tragic Equation as a crowd-pleasing stage device: "The immediate practical function of the equation is simply to produce, with unfailing success, an inexhaustibly interesting dramatic action. From *Hamlet* onwards it produces, as I say, tragic action, and from *Cymbeline* onwards, the redemption of tragic action. In this way, it works as a basic flexible formula, a prototype plot model.

"Would Shakespeare descend to such a device? Every reader will answer differently, according to what they know of modern instruction manuals for professional writers or of the actual working habits of professional writers harnessed to a demanding production line (whether in Athens's great, competitive century or in the modern TV drama and pulp fiction markets), or perhaps according to their sense of Shakespeare's attitude to his trade. He was, after all, part theater owner, part manager, part worker, part supplier of raw materials, and full time entrepreneur in a precarious yet fiercely demanding industry. Whether it was an old play rejigged or a new piece, it had to work. Maybe, under those pressures, it was inevitable that he would do as other hack professionals have always done, and develop one or two basic reliable kits of the dynamics that make a story move on stage...

"In the end, of course, this is all speculation. But the circumstances of Shakespeare's working life, in the thirty-year boom of the Elizabethan/Jacobean drama, and the way he manipulated and developed the various factors of his Equation from play to play, suggest that he knew exactly what a successful piece of stage equipment he had invented, and what a useful skeleton key, also, to his own deepest resources (such as every writer dreams of finding)."

## Obsessive Private Experience

Hughes's unfailingly successful hack professional *is* all speculation: roughly half of the fourteen plays in the Tragic Equation went unperformed and/or unpublished in William's lifetime. As I've said, Hughes further speculates that "some obsessive private experience" of William's engendered the Tragic Equation at a deeper level than stage devices, but he doesn't go beyond standard academic conjectures in this, attributing the Great Goddess shamanist role to hidden Catholicism in his family, the vivid nature imagery to a rustic youth, the sonnets' aura of shame and guilt to a provincial's discomfort with urban wits, and the Tragic Equation to William's sex life:

"According to his received biography, Shakespeare probably left Stratford and his wife in about 1585, and did not return to live with her permanently until she was fifty-four... One thing that cannot be imagined is that he was unaware, when he came to plot *All's Well that Ends Well,* just how closely the story tracked his own domestic life, and particularly that most decisive move he ever made—his first flight from his wife (for whatever reason). And he continued to stay away, except for those visits.

"If he had happened to scribble on some (surviving) page of a notebook an account of being pursued by an infatuated woman, forced into marrying her by her powerful guardian, and then, after having escaped from her again, and thinking himself free, finding her in his arms when he was, as he thought, enjoying some adulterous conquest, it can be imagined what volumes of speculation would have been written about it."

Hughes refers here to the confusion about "wm Shaxper" getting a license to marry "Anna whateley" the day before a marriage bond was posted for "willm Shagspere" and "Anne hathwey." This provides no real evidence of a pitchfork wedding or bedroom chicanery, however. It is possible that William worshiped Anne as a rustic goddess, then spurned her and fled. But what little is known of her suggests neither a lusty Venus nor a ravaged Lucrece. She seems as practical as William, whom she outlived by seven years. One recent book, Germaine Greer's *Shakespeare's Wife*, conjectures her running his business while he's in London. And while Robert Greene of the "upstart Crow" pamphlet notoriously had a London mistress as well as a country wife, there's no record that William had any such arrangements. Aside from his marriage, his recorded sex life is blank except for a rumor in a 1602 playgoer's diary about his tricking Richard Burbage out of a tryst with a woman fan. Some historians suspect this is a John Payne Collier forgery. Anyway, it speaks little to the canon's complex sexuality:

> Down from the waist
> They're centaurs, though women all above.
> But to the girdle do the gods inherit,
> Beneath is all the fiend's. There's hell, there's darkness
> There is the sulphurous pit, burning, scalding, stench...
> *(King Lear, 4, 5)*

The part of the book wherein Hughes tries hardest to link dossier and canon is his first chapter, with the narrative poems' dedications: "By the time he emerged into history—announced in typically English fashion, by a howl of indignation from an older writer (Greene's diatribe against the 'upstart Crow')— Shakespeare had written the *Henry VI* trilogy, *Titus Andronicus*, and two or three successful comedies. His foothold on the stage, as can be seen now in hindsight, was firm... But he must have been aware that at any time the stage itself could founder. In that autumn of 1592, when an unusually severe outbreak of plague had closed all the theaters since summer, it could well have seemed they would never open again.

"During these times of plague, it was customary for the lordly patrons to carry their poets off to their country houses. On this occasion, perhaps, the precocious young Henry Wriothsley, third earl of Southampton, seized the opportunity to carry off Shakespeare. However it happened, by April 1593 Wriothsley had become Shakespeare's patron.

"Throughout his life, notoriously, the money-lending, corn-chandlering, property speculating, wheeling and dealing dramatist displayed a flexible opportunism, nimbly attuned to market forces. Perhaps at this point Shakespeare had a shrewd premonition of the gap in income that lay ahead. Anyway, Wriothsley presented a new kind of opportunity, which he took. As if he had put the stage firmly behind him, during this winter of 1592-3 Shakespeare made a determined bid (denying any earlier offspring of his pen, and describing this as the 'first heir' of his invention) to establish an alternative career as a respectable poet of the classical, high court culture, with his long narrative poem (as long as a play) *Venus and Adonis*, dedicated to Wriothsley and published in 1593."

From this, and from the fact that Shakespeare also dedicated *Lucrece* to Wriothsley, Hughes infers that William and Henry had a relationship, expressed in the sonnets with an older man's avowals of love for a younger one. Yet the name on the dedications is the only evidence for this. Shakespeare wasn't Wriothsley's only literary admirer. Thomas Nashe dedicated a 1594 novel, *The Unfortunate Traveler*, to "the Right Honorable Lord," declaring: "My reverent, dutiful thoughts, even from their infancy, have been retainers to your glory." The *Venus and Adonis* dedication is similar: "Right Honorable, I know not how I shall offend in dedicating my unpolished lines to your lordship..."

Shakespeare's dedication in *Lucrece* is less conventional: "The love I dedicate to your Lordship is without end ... What I have done is yours, what I have to do is yours, being part of all I have, devoted yours..." This suggests familiarity, but whether it was between an actor-businessman and a young nobleman is not clear. At his father's death, Wriothsley had become a ward of Queen Elizabeth's chief minister, William Cecil, who held a tight rein on his household and took a dim view of theater. When, as Hughes conjectures, Henry "carried off" the twenty-nine-year-old William to his "country house," he was twenty.

Anyway, the narratives' dedications have little relevance to Hughes's ideas of shamanic identity and a Tragic Equation. His opening the book with them seems an attempt to lend substance to a historically vague writer before he sets out to interpret him. He might have invoked the common rationale that the writing matters, not the biography.  As his introduction's portrait of a media hack genius shows, he doesn't hesitate to identify with Shakespeare as a writer, expounding confidently on the canon's techniques and meanings.  But critics who ignore the man behind the work are not trying to transform an academic monolith into a living mythos as Hughes's book is.

## Actual Life

Thoreau says something else about Shakespeare's identity in his 1857 journal that at first seems an example of his sometimes clownish contrariety: "The real facts of a poet's life would be of more value to us than any work of his art.  I mean that the very scheme and form of his poetry (so called) is adapted at the sacrifice of vital truth and poetry... But we want the basis of fact, of an actual life, to complete our Shakespeare, as much as a statue wants its pedestal.  A poet's life with its broad actual basis would be as superior to Shakespeare's as a lichen, with its base or thallus, is superior in the order of being to a fungus."

Of course, Shakespeare's actual life would mean no more to us than those of a million forgotten Elizabethans if he hadn't written the canon.  Thoreau doesn't explain how "the very scheme and form of his poetry (so called) is adapted at the sacrifice of vital truth and poetry." *Hamlet* is "so called" poetry? Emerson called this Thoreau's "habit of antagonism": "He praised wild mountains and winter forests for their domestic air, in snow and ice he found sultriness, and commended the wilderness for resembling Rome and Paris."  Yet, as often with Thoreau, there's truth under the clowning, because the actual life does come before the poetry.  Shakespeare wouldn't have written anything if he hadn't had a life, and we can't interpret his writing as well as we might if we don't know "the real facts" of that.

And, rustic origins aside, William's known life doesn't fit easily with *Shakespeare and The Goddess*.  Even the nature imagery is a conjectural link.  Small towns regard nature lovers as impractical idlers, but William's contemporaries didn't see him that way. George Greenwood, among the first scholarly skeptics to examine authorship in depth, devotes a chapter of a 1908 book, *The Shakespeare Problem Restated*, to challenging the "orthodox conception" that "except when he was cramming himself with Latin at the Free School" William "was wandering through the fields and woods of Stratford, and along the banks of the Avon, observing the birds and beasts…" In fact, the canon is set in forests, mountains, and seacoasts much more than the tame countryside of "barnes, stables, orchards, gardens, landes, tenements and herediments" William mentions in his will.

In a "Postcript," Hughes acknowledges the incongruity between the dossier and the plays' focus on "misfits" like the hunchback Richard III, the Jew Shylock, the Moor Othello, the sorcerer Prospero, and the savage Caliban: "Even more ominously than Goethe's Mephistopheles, or the vengeful, pitiless, lonely hatred behind Dante's *Inferno*, Shakespeare's misfit, in its elemental otherness and ferocity, suggests an almost pathological psychic alienation from the culture within which his plays triumphed, a radical estrangement that sits oddly with the traditional idea of the 'gentle Shakespeare,' the benign senior citizen of an English country town."

What is known of William's "actual life" gives no evidence of "radical estrangement." No proof exists that he acquired "otherness" by traveling and learning foreign languages, or that he manifested "ferocity" by slaughtering calves and poaching deer. William does have a mythic side in his "upstart Crow" Trickster role, "the money-lending, corn-chandlering, property speculating, wheeling and dealing figure" who "displayed a flexible opportunism, nimbly attuned to market forces." With a fox spirit guide, Hughes knew The Trickster well, calling him "nothing really but an all-out commitment to salvaging life against the odds… turning everything to his advantage, or trying to." *Shakespeare and the Goddess* might have been livelier if he could have brought more of William's "loan shark" side into it. But The Trickster comes before the

Tragic Equation of civilized sex, as Hughes points out in *Crow*, a
1970 poem cycle on the myth:

> God tried to teach Crow how to talk,
> "Love," said God. "Say Love."
> Crow gaped and the white shark crashed into the sea…
> ("Crow's First Lesson")

Oasis and Mirage

Hughes's "Postscript" tries to resolve the incongruities by
referring them back to the mythic ramifications of his previous
five hundred pages. The misfit might sit oddly with William:
"But not when the Boar is translated, according to the Equation,
back into its true being. As he embodies the rejected Divine
Love, and as he strives to recombine with its lost light and its
fallen consort, and as he is the power unit and vital protagonist of
Shakespeare's entire dramatic, tragic, transcendental, poetic
creation, this Blackamoor, alias the boar with the Flower in its
mouth, can be translated, word for word, like the last lines of
Dante's *Paradiso*:

> Already my Desire and Will are rolled—
> Even as a wheel that moveth equally—
> By the Love that moves the sun and other stars."

The passage provides a sonorous finale to the book but
not much sense that William had such qualities. The incongruity
weighs on *Shakespeare and the Goddess*. The first hundred
pages, which apply the shamanic personality and Tragic
Equation to the narratives, are the liveliest. Much of the rest sets
play summaries in a matrix of stylistic analysis, mythological
exposition, and psycho-linguistic theory that can verge on the
incomprehensible. As another poet puts it, Hughes had a
penchant for "brandishing a fistful of resonant but opaque

abstractions, to which the resounding proper names give only an illusory glow of substance."

Hughes feared that the stress of writing *The Goddess* had brought on the cancer that killed him, bringing to mind Mr. Casaubon in George Eliot's *Middlemarch*, who dies trying to write a "key to all mythology." It is stressful just to read pages-long *Goddess* passages that begin like this: "Of the Irish Lyr's ancestry in Greece and Egypt, the Egyptian is the best known and more fully developed, and it is here that the full story behind the Welsh Lyr and Creidyllad and the British King Lear and Cordelia becomes clear, as well as its close family link to the myth of the Goddess and her sacrificed god, and in particular to the myth of Adonis. This is relevant to the poetic and dramatic life of Shakespeare's King Lear in that he was not only aware of this rich Egyptian matrix, from which his Tragic Equation and Rival Brothers emerge so strongly, but seems to have found it especially fascinating...."

Biographical references are like oases in such dry stretches, or like oasis mirages, since William's shamanic identity tends to dissolve on approach. A later Hughes study of Coleridge shows how William's vagueness desiccates his Shakespeare interpretation. He also sees Coleridge as a shamanic personality who tried to reconcile a Great Goddess vision with Puritanism, but although his interpretation is complex it isn't arid because there is ample documentation of Coleridge's life. It shows that he knew of shamanism from early ethnology, and that visions of animal spirits and elemental beings inspired him. It shows that he knowingly underwent initiatory dreams and anxieties related to artistic performance. "From the epic of Gilgamesh onwards, literature is full of mythicized and poetically adapted forms of such flights. But so far as I'm aware Coleridge is the first poet in English to refer to the shaman's flight as technically such, and to make use of it."

...the Greenland Wizard in a strange trance

Pierces the untraveled realms of Ocean's bed
Over the abysm, even to that utmost cave…
Where dwells the Fury Form…
("The Destiny of Nations")

The poem's "Fury Form," according to Coleridge's notes, is "a nameless female; she dwells under the sea in a great house, where she can retain in captivity all the animals of the ocean by her magic power. When a dearth befalls the Greenlanders, an Angekok or magician must undertake a journey thither. He passes through the kingdom of souls, over a horrible abyss into the Palace of this Phantom, and by his enchantment causes the captive creatures to ascend directly to the surface of the ocean."

Hughes also sees Coleridge as caught in a Tragic Equation of attraction and repulsion to women, from an adored mother who favored his siblings through a failed marriage and unrequited loves to a nervous collapse and puritanical reaction that finally smothered his poetry: "The Christian Self was the one he wanted to be—from the time he was the youngest child of the Vicar (and Headmaster) of Ottery St Mary, from the time he was the ferociously eloquent and informed eight-year-old-prodigy, to the time he all but accepted the salaried post of Unitarian Minister in Shrewsbury (in the middle of writing 'The Ancient Mariner'), to the time he increasingly filled his published writing, notebooks and letters with his Christian preoccupations: increasingly and intensifyingly Christian-Philosophical up to the day of his death: One Christian Self.

"On the other hand—'that 'unleavened *Self*'. What happened to him? Lying there, immune to Christ's love under the kiss of the serpent—refusing to pray or to take any part in the Christian Coleridge's efforts to speak, as Wordsworth did (or as Wordsworth almost did), with 'the language of the whole man.' There in the pious boy. Still there in the fifty-three-year-old Christian ruins of a man.

"What was he up to all those years?

"The unleavened *Self*, refusing to have anything to do with Christianity or its moralizing intelligence, wrapped with a great snake, who constantly kissed him.

"Two selves."

*Shakespeare and the Goddess* would be livelier if Hughes could have used similar material. That is too bad since Shakespeare is so much more central to the ultimate Tragic Equation as civilization's Great God keeps trampling the planet's Great Goddess. It was the trampling as well as the personal implications of a Renaissance attempt to balance religion and instinct that motivated Hughes to reinterpret the canon. Like Plath in her "dream of dreams" and the writing she drew from it, he saw that the present's environmental disasters arise from the past's mental ones. In his "draughty, radiant paradise" essay, he writes: "The subtly apotheosized misogyny of Reformed Christianity is proportionate to the fanatic rejection of Nature, and the result has been to exile man from Mother Nature—from both inner and outer nature."

# Chapter Twelve

# Lord Boar

———————

When Hughes was writing *Shakespeare and the Goddess*, a case that someone else wrote the canon was getting renewed attention. I ran across recent accounts of it in my biographical reading: Joseph Sobran's 1997 *Alias Shakespeare* and Mark Anderson's 2005 *Shakespeare by Another Name*. It began when an English schoolmaster named J. Thomas Looney (pronounced "Loney") who had taught Shakespeare for years decided that William's dossier just didn't fit. "We must," he concluded, "free the problem from illogical entanglements and miraculous assumptions, and look for a scientific relationship between cause and effect." He started combing Elizabethan documents for a dossier that he thought did fit, and found one that he describes in a book, *"Shakespeare" Identified*, published in 1920.

According to a novelist and critic named William McFee, Looney's book gave Shakespeare skepticism what *The Origin of Species* gave "transmutation": a testable theory with evidence to support it. "In my opinion after several readings, *Shakespeare Identified* is destined to occupy in modern Shakespeare studies the place Darwin's great work occupies in evolutionary theory… All modern discussions of the plays and poems will stem from it."

Of course, that hasn't happened since McFee predicted it in his introduction to a 1949 edition of *"Shakespeare" Identified*. Academic resistance has continued to marginalize Looney's theory. But it has not disproved it, which does not make the theory "meaningless" as Garry Wells says. It has gained supporters, including prominent Darwinians like Freud, and evidence for it has grown.

## More Documents

*"Shakespeare" Identified* argues that a man named Edward de Vere had the motive, means, and opportunity to write the canon; that it reflects his life and personality; and that he thus probably wrote it. Born in 1550, de Vere belonged to an originally Danish family that was granted the earldom of Oxford after they supported the Norman Conquest. Famous ancestors included Robert de Vere, the ninth earl, a favorite of King Richard II, and John de Vere, the thirteenth earl, a supporter of King Henry VII. The two typified the family's sociopolitical ups and downs. John was a stalwart soldier, instrumental in defeating Richard III and placing Henry Tudor on the throne. Robert was an effete intriguer, partly responsible for Richard II's unpopularity and deposition. He fled to the continent, where a wild boar was said to have killed him.

The family had legendary links with that animal: their heraldic emblem was a blue boar, *Verres* in Latin. Edward's father John, the sixteenth earl, was said to have killed a charging boar with a fencing rapier in France, amazing his hosts by telling them it was a common way of killing boars in England. There is reason to doubt that. Hunters had to use heavy spears with cross bars behind the head because a speared boar might still have strength enough to push its way up an unbarred shaft and gore the hunter. John's feat sounds fictive, like the knight's in *Sir Gawain*, who "stabbed him ...with his strong arm...right through":

> Sights well the slot, slips in the blade,
> Shoves it in to the hilt, and the heart shattered...

Whatever Earl John's hunting skills, his political ones were adroit: he continued a family tradition of exploiting social change. He figured at Henry VIII and Edward VI's increasingly Protestant courts and held vast estates augmented by Crown redistribution of Church lands. At his main one, Castle Hedingham, he maintained a company of actors who performed plays meant to promote Protestantism, a practice that Thomas Cromwell had begun. During Mary Tudor's brief Counter-Reformation, John supported the Crown but otherwise kept a low profile, boarding Edward, his only son, with a rustic scholar, Sir Thomas Smith. After Elizabeth acceded in 1558, he returned to prominence, enrolling Edward at Cambridge and entertaining the Queen at Hedingham, where he continued to maintain an acting company.

John died unexpectedly in 1562, and Edward's mother, Margaret, *nee* Golding, soon married a man of lower rank and withdrew from her son's life, while Elizabeth's favorite, Robert Dudley, took custodial possession of much de Vere property. The Queen placed the adolescent seventeenth earl in the household of William Cecil, the magnate who later warded the Shakespeare narratives' dedicatee, Henry Wriothsley. Cecil was a brilliant statesman, and highly cultivated despite his puritanical dislike of theater. He was also devious in support of the wealth and power he enjoyed through the Queen: he didn't mind using plays to influence the public. Edward benefited from Cecil's cultivation, getting a classical education from mentors like his uncle, Arthur Golding, whose translations from Latin, including Ovid's *Metamorphoses*, were highly regarded. Cambridge and Oxford granted him degrees in his teens. Those were honorary titles, but Edward became unusually literary.

Edward's privileged, emotionally conflicted situation flawed his behavior, however. In 1567, Cecil shielded him from punishment after, for unknown reasons, he stabbed a household under-cook in the thigh. The cook bled to death, but the court ruled that he had run on the sword himself. Despite several years of law study at Gray's Inn, Edward began to behave semi-criminally, rather like *Henry IV*'s Prince Hal, associating with riffraff and sending them on raids against real or perceived enemies. He tried to channel his aggressions into war, beginning with service against a northern rebellion in 1570, but he proved too erratic for military glory.

In 1571 Edward married Cecil's fifteen-year-old daughter Anne, a useful link to the nobility for her father, who had become Baron Burghley a few months earlier. Anne was pretty, popular for kindness and generosity, admired for scholarship and piety. Her love for Edward was constant: some of her affectionate letters to him survive. Court gossip said she pursued him more than he did her. Edward's feelings about Anne are less clear since none of his letters to her survive. Cecil had wanted her to marry Philip Sidney, a protégé of Dudley's, but she preferred Edward to the teenaged Philip, so Cecil agreed to the match, apparently respecting de Vere despite his misbehavior. "There is much more in him of understanding," he wrote a friend, "than a stranger would think." Indeed, Cecil might have done more than agree to the match. He might have tempted the free-spending young earl with a dowry or threatened him in his role as warder, which gave him the power to fine Edward heavily if he refused an approved match. He would later fine Henry Wriothsley five thousand pounds for doing so.

De Vere soon began to resist having a child bride emotionally tied to a domineering father. He lived apart, squandered money, flirted with the middle-aged Queen, who called him "my Turk," squabbled with Dudley and Elizabeth's other chief favorite, Christopher Hatton, and in 1574 absconded briefly to the Netherlands, annoying the Queen, who required his quick return. The next year, he got her permission to go on a continental tour, leaving his wife behind. This was much against his father-in-law's wishes. Cecil later wrote: "Suffer not thy sons to cross the Alps, for they shall learn nothing there but pride, blasphemy, and atheism."

A copy of a portrait painted in Paris shows a fashion plate in a fancy hat. But de Vere was athletic despite dandyism-- he excelled at horsemanship and jousting--and proved a good traveler. With eight retainers, he went via northern France,

Germany and Switzerland to Italy, probably traversing the Saint Gothard Pass into Lombardy. "After passing the falls at Basel, the shores of Lake Constance, and the deep gorges of the Alps," writes Mark Anderson, "de Vere's train at last looked up toward the stream tracing to the Rhine's glacial source, Lake Toma. For a youth whose idea of mountains was the rolling northland hills he had seen in 1570, the Alps must have been a visual feast. As de Vere's retinue pulled into Andermatt, in what is now Switzerland, and he gazed up at the 10,400-foot peak of Pizzo Rotondo, words may have failed-- at least for the moment."

De Vere's letters to England don't complain of mountain hardships, and he crossed the Alps again on his return, probably via the Mont Cenis Pass into southern France, terrain even steeper than the Saint Gothard. He must have felt accomplished. The "grand tour" wasn't yet a banal diversion, and there was no question of closing carriage curtains against the peaks' fearsome sight like later tourists. No carriages crossed the Saint Gothard or Mont Cenis passes: travelers unwilling to walk or ride horseback hired litters. A 1607 play by George Chapman, *Bussy d'Ambois*, suggests that Edward crossed in good shape:

> I overtook, coming from Italy,
> ... the most goodly-fashion'd man
> I ever saw...
> He was beside of spirit passing great,
> Valiant and learned, and liberal as the sun...
> And 'twas the Earl of Oxford...
> (3,1)

Alpine crossings may not have been the tour's only wilderness adventures. When de Vere was in Paris, the French king, Henri III, gave him letters of introduction to the Turkish court, and he wrote Cecil that he planned to "bestow two or three months to see Constantinople and some part of Greece." Mark Anderson conjectures that he spent an undocumented period in the middle to late summer of 1575 sailing in a Venetian galley down the east Adriatic coast, the one called "famous for the creatures of prey that keep on't" in *The Winter's Tale*, where a central European realm extended to the shore—a Seacoast of Bohemia.

"Upon leaving Venetian waters, within its first twenty-four hours under sail, the galley would have passed along a thirty-five miles stretch of Hungarian coastline, the seafaring end of a kingdom then ruled by Rudolph II, King of Bohemia… The Venetian galley would then most likely have followed the currents south down what is now the Croatian coastline, snaking its way past an Adriatic archipelago and shores belonging almost entirely to the Turks. These were dangerous waters, with pirates aplenty on the seas and unwelcoming ports on shore." Anderson further speculates that the voyage reached Greece before turning west to Sicily, where Edward's presence is documented.

De Vere spent most of his tour in the Italian city-states, which impressed him with their splendors, if not unreservedly. He wrote Cecil: "For my liking of Italy, my Lord, I am glad I have seen it, and care not ever to see it any more, unless it be to serve my Prince and country." Unfortunately, his tour didn't help him to do that. Too impulsive for the calculation that empowered Cecil and Dudley, he was also unlucky. He injured his knee on a Venetian galley, and had "fever" while in Venice in the fall of 1575. On his Channel voyage home, Dutch pirates kidnapped and robbed him. So his confidence was shaky. After Anne gave birth to a girl during his tour, he heeded rumors that the child wasn't his or that he'd been tricked into impregnating her. He rejected her, and the disgrace may have curdled Cecil's disapproval into covert hatred. Although their relations stayed civil, de Vere never gained the preferment of lower-ranking courtiers like Hatton and Walter Raleigh.

Raised as a Protestant under Edward VI, as a pseudo-Catholic under Mary, then as a Protestant again under Elizabeth, de Vere was conflicted about religion. Although he had served against Catholic rebels in the 1570 campaign, he nursed Papist sympathies and his Italian stay encouraged them. On his return, he professed the "old faith" and started intriguing against Dudley's Protestant faction in Elizabeth's court. He also seduced one of her maids, a black-haired, sharp-tongued teenager named Anne Vavasour. In 1580, as Catholic plots to kill the Queen proliferated, he either had a change of heart or panicked. He confessed to Elizabeth and accused his fellow intriguers, Henry Howard, Charles Arundell, and Francis Southwell, of treason. They retaliated by accusing him of murder, atheism, heresy, sorcery, drunkenness, pederasty, and bestiality as well as treason. The Queen didn't act on their accusations, but when she learned that Vavasour had delivered his son, she threw him in the Tower of London along with the girl and her newborn. She released them after a few months, but kept Edward under house arrest for longer and banished him from court for several years.

Edward proved resilient as well as wayward. He reconciled with his wife, who bore him two other girls who survived childhood and a boy who didn't. He expanded his literary pursuits at a London theater district mansion called "Fisher's Folly" that he owned until 1588, associating with writers like Lyly, Munday, Greene, Lodge, and Nashe, and sponsoring acting troupes. George Chapman, who describes him "coming out of Italy" in *Bussy d'Amboise*, has a de Vere-like character in another play, *Monsier d'Olive*, say: "I'll have my chamber the rendezvous of all good wits, the shop of good words... critics, essayists, linguists, and other professors of that faculty of wit, shall at certain hours i'th' day resort thither. It shall be a second Sorbonne, where all doubts or differences of learning, honor, duellism, criticism, and poetry shall be disputed." (1,1) Writers dedicated dozens of works to him, although Cecil deplored these "lewd friends," who "ruled" his son-in-law "by flattery."

Edward continued to be unlucky. After his release from house arrest, he fought with a Vavasour relative named Thomas Knyvet and received a wound that may have lamed him. Fights between de Vere and Knyvet gangs continued for over a year, causing more bloodshed, and Anne Vavasour's brother challenged Edward to a duel that he had the nascent maturity to ignore. Finally restored to court, he went to serve in a campaign against Spain in the Netherlands in 1585, but Dudley edged him out, Elizabeth again required his return, and pirates again robbed him in the Channel.

All this cost a lot. Along with his grand tour, theatrical ventures, and military misadventures, de Vere lost thousands on failed schemes of a promoter named Michael Lok to find a Northwest Passage and mine gold on Hudson's Bay. Within a decade, he had spent one of England's great fortunes and fallen deep in debt. A 1586 portrait by a Dutch artist, Marcus Gheeraedts, shows an "Earl of Oxford" fingering a blue boar pendant, dressed in clothes so old-fashioned that he might be costumed for a play. He has a feral look so different from the Paris portrait's that they hardly seem the same man.

Surprisingly, given her notorious stinginess, Elizabeth saved him that year by granting him a lifelong pension of a thousand pounds a year, worth hundreds of thousands today. This encouraged him to behave, and he sat on the commission that condemned Mary Stuart for treason. In 1588, the year his long-suffering wife died, he outfitted a ship, the *Edward Bonaventure*, to fight the Spanish Armada and took part in the initial engagement as the Spanish fleet appeared off Plymouth:

> De Vere, whose fame and loyalty hath pierced
> The Tuscan clime, and through the Belgike lands
> By Winged Fame for valour is rehearsed,
> Like warlike Mars upon the hatches stands.
> His tusked Boar 'gan foam with inward ire,
> While Pallas filled his breast with warlike fire.

Erratic behavior and bad luck stopped him from commanding the ship in the main battle. After a squabble with Dudley over reassignment to land duty, he quit in a pique before the Armada's final defeat across the Channel. With typical resilience, however, he accompanied the Queen in the victory parade three months later and presented a play to her that evening.

Failing health further subdued de Vere. His main political pursuits through the 1590s were vain bids for trade monopolies and administrative posts. In 1591, he made over Castle Hedingham in trust to his daughters and married another of the Queen's ladies, Elizabeth Trentham, who bore him an heir. He also supported a campaign to marry his and Anne's first daughter, Elizabeth, to Cecil's ward, Henry Wriothsley. But Henry rejected the match and incurred the five thousand pound fine, perhaps just as well for Edward who in 1601 had to sit on the tribunal that convicted Wriothsley and Robert Devereux, Earl of Essex, of trying to depose the Queen.

Her death in 1603 crushed him. In a letter to Cecil's brilliant, devious son Robert, he wrote: "I cannot but find a great grief in myself to remember the mistress which we have lost—under whom both you and myself from our greenest years have been in a manner brought up… In this common shipwreck, mine is above all the rest, who least regarded though often comforted, of all her followers, she hath left to try my fortune among the alterations of time and chance."

King James I didn't hold Edward's past against him, renewing his annuity and restoring some property. He died in 1604, however, and, compared to his notorious life, his death was obscure. Its cause is unclear, no will survives, and no record of a funeral exists, although suggestive things occurred afterward. On the day he died, June 24, the King had Henry Wriothsley, who he'd recently freed from Elizabeth's life sentence, arrested along with several of his followers, then released them the next day. At the end of the year, James had a number of Shakespeare plays performed at court to celebrate the marriage of Edward's youngest daughter, Susan, to Phillip Herbert, future Earl of Montgomery and Shakespeare folio dedicatee.

De Vere has neither a monument nor a tomb. A relative, Percival Golding, said in a brief eulogy that he was interred at Westminster Abbey, but no other mention of this exists. His second wife asked in her will that she be buried with him in a church in the London suburb of Hackney where they lived after 1597, and an old record tells of a "table monument" with armorial crests defaced by Oliver Cromwell's soldiers. But the church was rebuilt in the eighteenth century and no trace of a grave remains.

The seventeenth earl of Oxford faded from history. A 1911 book on Renaissance travel mentions Raleigh, Sidney, Spenser, Nashe, and Chapman but not de Vere, despite Chapman's reference to him "coming out of Italy." When the book's author touches on "Shakespeare's knowledge about Italy," he concludes: "no deduction can be made from all this as to whether Shakespeare ever left England or the reverse, because his capacity for using second hand-knowledge was so unique."

## Circumstances

De Vere was a prominent writer in his time, and *"Shakespeare" Identified* brought this to light: signed poems, prose, and letters survive, in manuscript and published. The known poems seem youthful work, and scholars disagree as to their number and quality. But his reputation grew during his lifetime and for decades afterward, implying that it wasn't based just on early work.

In 1578, Gabriel Harvey, a Cambridge Fellow, praised his writing during a royal progress at the University. In 1586, the critic William Webbe called him the "most excellent" poet at Elizabeth's court. The anonymous *Arte of English Poesie*, published in 1589, cites "The Earl of Oxford" among aristocratic poets who have "written excellently" in comedy and "interludes," other kinds of plays. It places de Vere "first" in a "crew of courtly makers, noblemen and gentlemen of her Majesty's own servants, who have written commendably well—

as it would appear if their doings could be found out and made public with the rest." Francis Meres's 1598 book, *Palladis Tamia*, also praises him, along with Shakespeare, as a poet and dramatist. A list of Elizabethan poets in *The Compleat Gentleman*, a 1622 book by a scholar named Henry Peacham, rates the Earl of Oxford first without mentioning Shakespeare.

Bernard M. Ward, who uncovered the document proclaiming Elizabeth's thousand-pound annuity and published the first book-length de Vere biography in 1928, writes that Edward and Philip Sidney were rival leaders of the "two great literary factions" at court: "Oxford headed the newly arisen Euphuist movement, which aimed at refining and enriching the English language. It was the magic of words and the imagery of sentences that appealed to him and to his lieutenants, John Lyly and Anthony Munday. Sidney was the leader of the Romanticists. Their object was to reclothe the old stories of knighthood and chivalry so as to render them more vivid and applicable to their own times."

The "movement" began with a popular novel, *Euphues: The Anatomy of Wit*, that Lyly published in 1579. It is set in Naples and its eponymous hero is a rich young Athenian who has various witty conversations (*euphues* is Greek for "well-proportioned" or "clever"), including one with a puritanical old man who tells him to behave in a more civilized way. Euphues replies: "Do you not know... that nature will have its course after kind? ... Doth not Cicero conclude and allow that if we follow and obey nature we shall never err? ... Nature was had in such estimation and admiration among the heathen people that she was reputed for the only goddess in heaven."

Most historians see Lyly and Munday as the "euphuist" leaders, with "Oxford" as a dilettante patron. There's no doubt about the rivalry with Sidney, anyway: it may have dated from their competition for Anne Cecil's hand. (Sidney was one of those bright young men who charm old men sooner than young women: his later suit for the Earl of Essex's daughter, Penelope Devereux, failed although he wrote a famous sonnet sequence,

*Astrophil and Stella*, to her.) Historians most often mention Edward in regard to a "tennis court quarrel" they had at Greenwich Palace in 1579, when he climaxed a shouting match over court precedence by calling Philip a "puppy." Tweedledee and Tweedledum agreed to have a battle, although it's unclear exactly why, but the Red Queen sat on that by ordering Philip to defer to Edward's rank. Sidney went away mad, but he won in the end by dying gallantly in the Netherlands campaign after Dudley had packed de Vere home, becoming a soldier-poet national hero in a lavish Westminster Abbey funeral that happened to coincide with Mary Stuart's execution.

Of course, de Vere's literary reputation doesn't prove he wrote the Shakespeare canon. Although he'd been mentioned as a possible authorship candidate by an earlier skeptic, Delia Bacon, Looney's book was the first to link him explicitly with the canon. And although *Shakespeare Identified* inspired his de Vere biography, Bernard Ward "refrained from comment on what the conservative element among literary critics is wont to stigmatize as a 'fantastic theory'." Evidence for Edward's authorship is largely circumstantial, although in the 1990s a researcher, Roger Stritmatter, found correlations between various Shakespeare passages and markings in a "Geneva Bible" that de Vere owned. Most scholars see the Geneva Bible as a Shakespeare influence.

De Vere's advocates, called Oxfordians, cite a lot of circumstantial evidence. The canon emerged after he withdrew from public life, beginning with the narrative poems' publication. Both poems concern subjects popular with artists and poets when de Vere visited Italy. Both describe paintings by Julio Romano, an early sixteenth century artist whose work decorates places de Vere probably visited. *Venus and Adonis* also has suggestive similarities to a painting that was in Titian's Venice studio in 1575: in both, a sprawling naked Venus clutches at a disdainful Adonis, who wears a fancy hat.

Books about Shakespeare and Italy are a genre in themselves and present strong evidence that whoever wrote the canon was there. A 2011 one, Richard Roe's *The Shakespeare Guide to Italy*, argues convincingly that the author knew many of its settings first-hand—from canals and rivers linking inland cities like Milan and Verona, whereon protagonists travel, to still extant houses wherein they live. Roe even finds, in Verona, a "sycamore" grove like one that "westward rooteth from the city's side" wherein Romeo mopes in Act I of Shakespeare's most popular play. Oxfordians generally see similarities between anonymous Italianate dramas from the 1570s and 80s and Shakespeare plays like *The Taming of the Shrew* and *The Two Gentlemen of Verona* as well as *Romeo and Juliet*.

Other Shakespeare plays, including *King John, Henry IV, Henry V, Henry VI, Richard III* and *King Lear* also resemble anonymous versions performed in the 1580s by a troupe called the Queen's Men. Oxfordians think de Vere wrote them, perhaps collaborating with Munday, Lyly, Nashe, and others. They think the Folio contains de Vere's revised versions of these early plays along with later ones. And they think the plays reflect his life in many ways.

They think the comedies and romances reflect his travels and affairs: fleeing to Italy to escape an arranged marriage as in *All's Well That Ends Well*, dallying along the way as in *As You Like It* and *Much Ado About Nothing*, coasting the Balkans as in *Twelfth Night* and *The Winter's Tale*, trying to marry his daughter to a rich young nobleman as in *The Tempest*. They think the histories and tragedies reflect his lonely, fearful courtier's career: rebelling against the establishment as in *Henry IV*, suspecting a virtuous wife as in *Othello*, plotting against a friendly monarch as in *Macbeth*, consorting with an illicit lover as in *Anthony and Cleopatra*, caught in a frustrating military expedition as in *Troilus and Cressida*, humiliated by family conflicts as in *King Lear*.

They see the most parallels in the most famous play, *Hamlet*. De Vere's father died suddenly, like Hamlet's, and his mother soon remarried, like Hamlet's. He then acquired epically troubling "foster parents": Queen Elizabeth, who, Gertrude-like, behaved seductively as well as maternally; Dudley who, Claudius-like, acted as Elizabeth's *de facto* consort; and Cecil, who, along with other Polonius-like behavior, oversaw Edward's courtship of his Ophelia-like daughter Anne. Polonius's famous advice to his departing son Laertes ("neither a borrower nor a lender be… to thine own self be true…") closely resembles Cecil's written "precepts" to his sons. Like Hamlet, Edward fled the court and fell afoul of pirates. Like Hamlet, he returned with a vengeful attitude linked to half-baked intrigues and court theatricals.

Hamlet's conflicted behavior to Ophelia is a theme that recurs through the canon. Oxfordians conjecture that Hamlet's feelings when he returns from England and finds Ophelia dead reflect de Vere's when he returned from the Armada campaign to find Anne dead. *Othello*, *Much Ado about Nothing*, *The Winter's Tale*, and *Cymbeline* all center on husbands or lovers who reject innocent women out of jealousy and suspicion and then deeply regret their loss, a regret vicariously transcended in the latter three plays when the supposedly dead women return to life.

Oxfordians see circumstantial evidence in the plays' publishing history as well as their content. They ask why the ambitious William would have tolerated the authorial hiatus that prevailed for years as anonymous quartos flooded the market before the "Shakespeare" label appeared on the plays. They conjecture that Edward was revising plays and releasing them first anonymously, then pseudonymously, because public authorship was beneath his rank. "Among the nobility or gentry… and especially in making poesie," says *The Art of English Poesie*, "it is so come to pass that they have no courage to write and if they have are loath to be known of their skill." There was good reason for this. When Cambridge fellow Gabriel Harvey praised de Vere's writing in 1578, for example, it was as a pretext for exhorting (in effect, shaming) him, as a "hero worthy of renown," to "throw away bloodless books and writings that serve no useful purpose… and to handle the great engines of war." Plays were a waste of time, "unconsidered trifles."

Oxfordians note that publication of Shakespeare plays stopped for several years after 1604, implying that the source was defunct, and they maintain that the plays' topical references and source materials date no later than 1604, further implying a dead author. They observe that although, as a member of the King's Men, William was appointed a groom of the chamber on James's accession, Shakespeare never commemorated Stuart royal occasions as did Jonson and many other poets.

The sonnets, the canon's most problematic works, offer Oxfordians many suggestive circumstances. They think the narrator's image of himself as aging, lame and disgraced is more congruent with Edward in the 1590s than William. They think de Vere wrote early ones to Henry Wriothsley as part of Cecil's matchmaking with his daughter Elizabeth Vere: homilies on the need to procreate abound in them, as they do in the early stanzas of *Venus and Adonis*, dedicated to Wriothsley. They note that Thomas Thorpe, the sonnets' 1609 publisher, described their author as "ever-living," a term applied to dead, thus "immortal," authors.

Oxfordians think that Edward masked his identity because of the canon's personal and political implications as well as his social rank. In *Shakespeare Identified*, Looney maintains that his portrayals of his in-laws and enemies compelled him to publish pseudonymously. Oxfordians aren't the only ones who liken *Hamlet*'s Polonius to William Cecil, and some see his younger son Robert, an intriguer with a twisted spine, as a model for *Richard III*'s devious anti-hero.

Oxfordians think the plays lampoon other powerful de Vere enemies and rivals such as Dudley, Raleigh, Hatton, and Sidney. Soon after his tennis court quarrel with de Vere, Sidney wrote a book, *An Apology for Poetry*, which "subdivides" poems into "the heroic, lyric, tragic, comic, satiric, iambic, elegiac, pastoral" and "certain other" denominations. It deplores contemporary plays for not observing Aristotle's dramatic unities of time and place. In *Hamlet,* which sprawls over many times and places, pompous Polonius "subdivides" plays into "tragedy, comedy, history, pastoral, pastoral-comical, historical-pastoral, tragical-historical, tragical-comical-historical-pastoral, scene-individable or poem unlimited." (2,2)

Sidney's *Apology* declares: "Nature never set forth the earth in such tapestry as divers poets have done; neither with so pleasant rivers, fruitful trees, sweet-smelling flowers, nor whatsoever else may make the too much loved earth more lovely. Her world is brazen, the poets only deliver the golden." This exaltation of artificiality seems the antithesis of Shakespeare's love of wildness:

> Yet nature is made better by no mean
> But nature makes that mean. So over that art
> Which you say adds to nature is an art
> That nature makes.

In his conflicted familial ties, his sexual misbehavior, his enmities with other courtiers, his wanderings, his involvement with the disreputable public theatre, his heedless extravagance, not to mention the intrigues and violence for which a less privileged man could have hanged, de Vere fits Ted Hughes's concept of Shakespeare as an "elemental misfit." His enemies at court called him "the boar."

# Chapter Thirteen

# The Trap at the Spring

Hunters introduced wild boars to California in the 1920s, and they've adapted so well to its oak woodlands that authorities now try to get rid of them. In Mount Diablo State Park, wire mesh cages set with trap doors lie along trails. One hot July morning, I happened on a trap at a spring where a female with young had come to drink. The piglets were investigating the trap, which would have ended badly for them because it was set. That wasn't right for a 95 F day. The State paid trappers to remove boars, not torture them. I sprung the trap and scared them off.

They seemed, as nineteenth century naturalist John Muir wrote of the then-outlawed coyote, to lead a "brave life" there. The spring was no "Paradise," a muddy patch of rushes between a chaparral gulch and a grassy ridge, yet they gave it a "draughty, radiant" feeling. A woman who helped to start Costa Rica's national parks once told me that a reason she did so was because the creatures that wandered through her *finca* "seemed so happy." The boar family struck me that way, and they asked little enough of life-- spring water, nuts, berries, roots-- the odd gopher snake or turkey egg.

Some exotic organisms have advocates here: attempts to clear Australian eucalyptus from parks because of fire danger meet vehement opposition. One might think boars would have a few supporters. The prolific immigrant species would be a more apt mascot for crowded twenty-first century California than the slow-breeding, extirpated grizzly. But I don't know of any.

Biologists and land managers despise them as they did coyotes a century ago, although they've filled the absent grizzly's niche as rooters and mast-eaters, one that large mammals have occupied since the dinosaurs and that, along with unsightly digging, cycles plant propagules and symbiotic fungi through the ecosystem.

Anyway, more boars keep coming as they remove trapped ones. When I walked by the trap at the Mount Diablo spring a year later, I found two adults there, a male and a female. It wasn't set, but it was freshly baited with a plastic cylinder of pheromone-soaked corn. They had opened it and were happily eating the bait. Adam and Eve.

I think California's disdain for boars is more cultural than ecological, reflecting civilization's penchant for control. The twenty-first century can afford to be *laissez-faire* about many things because technology has given it so much control. Tranquillizer darts and radio collars make wolves and bears into political pawns. But some things are harder to control, like wild boars, so we put them outside the pale: dirty pigs, stinking swine, greedy hogs, ravening boars, fat sows.

Wire Mesh

Entering the Shakespeare debate at about the same time wild boars arrived in California, Edward de Vere was another unruly interloper. The academic establishment dislikes Lord Boar even more than the other main authorship candidates, Francis Bacon and Christopher Marlowe. This is partly because the circumstantial evidence for him is better. Bacon died three years after the First Folio's avowedly posthumous publication. Marlowe died years before some of the First Folio plays' likely completion: *As You Like It* apparently refers to his murder in a tavern bedroom when the "fool" Touchstone says that, if a writer's work is not understood, it strikes him "more dead than a great reckoning in a small room." (3,3) De Vere's feral quality also rankles. With his zoos and labs, Bacon would make as good a Whiggish bard as William. Marlowe, for all his delinquency, was an academic. Shakespeare's Venus runs around the woods naked. Marlowe's narrative heroine is a shop mannequin:

> The outside of her garments were of lawn,
> The lining purple silk, with gilt stars drawn...
> Upon her head she wore a myrtle wreath,
> From whence her veil went to the ground beneath...
> (*Hero and Leander* 16-20)

Even passing historical references to de Vere tend to hostility. In *Kenilworth*, Walter Scott dismisses him as an effete "young unthrift." A 1958 biography of Elizabeth calls him "spoiled and ruthless," "bitter and preposterous," with an "exceptionally disagreeable temper" and a "pathological selfishness." Like Scott's novel, it ignores his literary reputation, although it does say that "he was one of those who, like Hamlet, are so impressed with the importance of their own sufferings, they are completely indifferent to the pain they themselves give to other people." A 2004 Marlowe biography calls him a mediocre poet and a rich libertine, "the only titled Elizabethan to be charged with sodomy." It deems his 1580 co-conspirators' accusations of general depravity "quite believable," and infers from them that Marlowe got his naughty ideas at Fisher's Folly:

"Oxford's remark that the Bible was 'only to hold men to obedience, and [was] man's device' anticipated Marlowe's observation 'That the first beginning of Religion was to keep men in awe' ... Where Oxford claimed 'that he could make a better and more orderly Scripture in six days,' Marlowe asserted 'That if he were put to write a new religion, he would undertake both a more Excellent and Admirable method'... Where Oxford declared 'that after this life we should all be as we had never been and the rest was devised but to make us afraid like babes and children of our shadows,' Marlowe persuaded 'men to Atheism, willing them not to be afeard of bugbears and hobgoblins'...These remarks sketch out a carnal philosophy of religion."

Some of the malice is "magotie-headed." According to a 2003 biography of Elizabeth: "There were many instances of her mischievous turn of mind, the most famous perhaps being on the return to court of Earl of Oxford after seven years of self-imposed exile, having embarrassed himself in front of the Queen. Elizabeth's merry words of greeting were: 'My Lord, we had forgot the fart!'"

The story, somewhat embroidered, comes from John Aubrey's *Brief Lives*, which then "roves" to a scholar named Nicholas Hill whom Aubrey deems "so eminent for knowledge that he was the favourite of the great Earle of Oxford, who had him to accompanie him on his travells (he was his Steward) which were so splendid and sumptuous, that he lived in Florence in more grandeur than the Duke of Tuscany." Born around 1570, Hill was a toddler when de Vere was in Italy: he may have worked as his secretary in the late 1590s. Aubrey also fails to mention de Vere's literary reputation, although his employer, Anthony a Wood, calls Edward "an excellent poet and comedian" in his *Athenae Oxonienses*.

## Conspiracy

There are smelly things about de Vere's candidacy. Why, in 1593, should he start using a pseudonym like a young actor-impresario's name? Oxfordians say he'd been using "Will Shake-Speare" as an expression of literary identity before William came to London. At the 1578 royal progress in Cambridge where he ambiguously praised his writing, Gabriel Harvey characterized de Vere thus: "Thine eyes flash fire, thy countenance shakes speares... Pallas striking her shield with her spear shaft will attend thee ..." One de Vere heraldic emblem shows a lion shaking a spear. In 1591, when Edward withdrew from public life, Edmund Spenser (who partly dedicated *The Faerie Queene* to him, calling him "beloved of the Muses") wrote of a poet who was withdrawing from public life:

And he, the man whom Nature self had made
To mock her selfe, and truth to imitate,
With kindly counter under mimick shade,
Our pleasant Willy, ah! Is dead of late...

But that same gentle spirit, from whose pen
Large streams of honnie and sweete nectar flowe,
Scorning the boldness of such base-born men
Which dare their follies forth to rashly show;
Doth rather choose to sit in idle cell
Than so himselfe to mockerie to sell.
(*The Tears of the Muses*)

But why would a provincial also identified as "Shaksper," "Shagspere" or "Shaxper" get credit for a wolfish earl's work? The question implies conspiracy theory, sometimes the end of verifiable history. This has led to books like Charles Beauclerk's *Shakespeare's Lost Kingdom*, which says de Vere used a pseudonym not just because of his rank and lampoons of rivals, but because he was Queen Elizabeth's son by her stepfather, Thomas Seymour, and the father, with Queen Elizabeth, of Henry Wriothsley. Whatever its historical merits, I think this overcomplicates the authorship question.

Still, conspiracies happen. Oxfordians think Elizabeth granted her thousand-pound annuity to de Vere in 1586 to fund patriotic propaganda as well as to coax a troublesome grandee into line. She was never generous without expecting something in return, and plays did have a propaganda function. In 1586, the Venetian ambassador to Spain reported of King Phillip II: "What has enraged him much more than all else, and has caused him to show a resentment such as he has never displayed in all his life, is the account of the masquerades and comedies which the Queen of England orders to be acted at his expense." For example, the villain of *Much Ado About Nothing*, Don John the Bastard, seems like a lampoon of Phillip's illegitimate half-brother, Don Juan, who plotted in the 1570s to become King of England with Mary Stuart as his queen.

De Vere's main literary associates, Munday and Lyly, were both Protestant partisans. Munday served as a government spy in Rome in the late 1570s, posing as a Catholic convert to lure English Jesuits to capture back home. In the 1580s, Munday and Lyly both joined in a "pamphlet war" defending the Church of England from Puritan attacks. In 1592 another associate, Thomas Nashe, published an anti-Puritan pamphlet, *Pierce Penniless*, that defended a "Policy of Plays" as a way of encouraging patriotism. Half a century later, Stratford Vicar John Ward reported hearsay to the effect that: "Mr. Shakespeare... supplied the stage with two plays every year, and for that had an allowance so large that he spent at the rate of one thousand pounds a year." William wasn't *that* prosperous, and nobody says he "supplied the stage" with "masquerades and comedies" in 1586.

Walt Whitman found it "impossible to grasp" the plays "without thinking of them as, in a free sense, the result of *essentially controlling plan.*" Like Whitman, Oxfordians see the plays' patriotism as reflecting de Vere's aristocratic outlook. They note that while *Richard II* ignores the naughty ninth Earl of Oxford, possibly the king's lover, *Richard III* gives the doughty thirteenth Earl a ringing pair of lines just before Richard's defeat at Bosworth Field:

> Every man's conscience is a thousand swords,
> To fight against this guilty homicide.
> (4,5)

Yet a conspiracy to produce patriotic plays still doesn't explain why William would get credit. Some Oxfordians think Edward and/or associates paid him to front for the plays, shielding him from retaliation for the lampoons. Nicholas Rowe's 1709 biography alleges that "the Earl of Southampton" gave him a thousand pounds to "buy property." William didn't suffer the hardships that plagued many writers. Greene, Jonson, Marlowe, and Nashe accumulated mainly debts. William accumulated hundreds of pounds. Chapman, Jonson, Marlowe, Marston, and Nashe spent time in jail. William didn't, even after his company agreed to stage *Richard II*, wherein a monarch is deposed, just before Wriothsley and Devereux's attempt to depose Elizabeth.

"I am Richard II. Know ye not that?" said the Queen to a historian named William Lambarde some months after Devereux's execution.

On the other hand, since no document from his lifetime proves that William was an author, some Oxfordians think his immunity just shows that nobody considered him one. They think conspirators who wanted to disassociate de Vere from the canon waited until William and most of Edward's enemies were dead to install the monument and publish the Folio, paying Ben Jonson to orchestrate the ruse. As I've said, Jonson hinted at inside knowledge. In *Every Man out of His Humor*, the social-climbing Sogliardo's coat of arms-- for which the burlesque motto "Not Without Mustard" is suggested-- has a "boar without a head, rampant" as its crest. Another character remarks: "I commend the herald's wit. He has deciphered him well; a swine without a head, without brain, wit, anything indeed, ramping to gentility." (3,1)

Oxfordians think the Folio conspirators included the earls of Montgomery and Pembroke, to whom it is dedicated. Both were de Vere associates. Montgomery, Philip Herbert, married Edward's youngest daughter, Susan, as I've said; and Pembroke, William Herbert, tried to marry his second daughter, Bridget. (His eldest daughter, Elizabeth, married William Stanley, Earl of Derby, described in 1599 as "busied only in penning comedies for the common players.") Appointed Lord Chamberlain in 1615, William Herbert arranged to pay Jonson a pension of 66 pounds a year: in 1621, he temporarily raised it to 200. Oxfordians find it significant that, although the narrative poems were Shakespeare's best-known works and the sonnets were published, the First Folio fails even to mention them. Jonson's own folio includes his poems as well as his plays. They think the Shakespeare conspirators excluded the poems because of their scandalous links to Henry Wriothsley, still living in 1623.

## Snubs and Snaps

Stratfordians often cut Oxfordians dead by ignoring de Vere's candidacy. Stephen Greenblatt's *Will in the World* indexes "Oxford, Earl of" about the tennis court quarrel. Jonathan Bate's *Soul of the Age* indexes "de Vere, Edmund" about aristocratic education by tutors (implying that Edward would have lacked "the exact knowledge of Elizabethan grammar school methods" that Bate finds in the plays). Some dismiss it. "It seems to me," writes Northrop Frye, "that a critic practically has to maintain that the Earl of Oxford wrote the plays of Shakespeare before he can be clearly recognized as making pseudo-critical statements." Most who do consider the de Vere case soon conclude that Edward didn't write well enough, know the theater well enough, or live at the right time to write the canon.

James Shapiro examines it at more length in a 2010 book: *Contested Will: Who Wrote Shakespeare?* He makes good points: that impresarios like Philip Henslowe prospered without fronting for earls, and that personal biases motivate skeptics. Yet Shapiro starts from a firm belief in William: his book really should be titled: *Contested Will, Who Wrote Shakespeare!* In his earlier *1599: A Year in the Life of Shakespeare*, he writes that we know "more than enough" about William's "career as a writer" to "persuade a reasonable skeptic that he wrote his plays himself," and dismisses unreasonable skeptics' "latest candidate, the Earl of Oxford" because "there's no evidence" that he was part of "a tight-knit group of practicing playwrights."

*Contested Will* considers Oxfordians' biases more than their arguments, focusing on Looney's "neo-medievalist" bias that a lofty nobleman wrote the canon and on Freud's "self-deceiving" one that *Hamlet* supports his Oedipus complex theory. But it was the many congruities between de Vere and the canon that mainly convinced them. As Freud wrote the novelist Arnold Zweig: "I do not know what still attracts you to the man of Stratford. He seems to have nothing to justify his claim, whereas Oxford has almost everything. It is quite inconceivable to me that Shakespeare should have got everything secondhand—Hamlet's neurosis, Lear's madness, Macbeth's defiance and the character of Lady Macbeth, Othello's jealousy, etc."

*Contested Will* misquotes Freud's remark to Zweig as: "I do not know what attracts you to the man of Stratford. He seems to have nothing to justify his claim, whereas Oxford has almost everything secondhand—Hamlet's neurosis, Lear's madness, Macbeth's defiance and the character of Lady Macbeth, Othello's jealousy, etc." This must be a mistake, but it is a striking one (a Freudian slip?) and it certainly dilutes Freud's conviction of the congruities between the man and the work. In fact, Shapiro has much less to say about de Vere in his "Oxford" chapter than he does about Freud and Looney, and much of what he does say about him is hostile, in contrast to a more sympathetic attitude toward de Vere's two advocates.

Shapiro makes the conventional claims that skepticism didn't start until scholars uncovered William's business dossier, and that skeptics err in trying to match Renaissance authors' lives and work. But, as I've said, covert skepticism started much earlier, and the work of other outstanding writers like Marlowe and Jonson reveals a lot about their lives without being overtly autobiographical. Even if autobiographical fiction is a largely post-Enlightenment phenomenon as Shapiro says, that doesn't mean that unusually talented "early modern" writers didn't inject much of their experience and personality into their work.

When Shapiro affirms William's authorship in his first and last chapters, he glosses over the dossier's lack of congruities with the canon. Like other recent biographers, he conjectures a supremely imaginative theatre professional picking plots from bookstalls and patrons' libraries and dashing off collaborative plays between rehearsals, administrative meetings, and business deals. Otherwise, he presents the same faint paper trail for William as a writer that skeptics do. He just presents it as probable or definite, which would be fair if he answered their detailed arguments against it. But except for citing them in a "Bibliographical Essay," he doesn't.

In a 2015 book, *The Year of Lear: 1606*, Shapiro returns to the strategy of his *1599*, weaving a largely conjectural William into documented history. He snubs the skeptics' "latest candidate" except in repeating some gossip about de Vere's son-in-law, Philip Herbert, who, he writes, "flirted brazenly" with bisexual King James I soon after his marriage to Susan Vere. He adds that James "visited the newlyweds while they were still in bed," hinting at a kinky threesome. He doesn't mention Philip's involvement in the First Folio's publication two decades later.

Some Stratfordian attitudes to de Vere are snappish. A.L. Rowse, one of William's biographers, says in a 1989 PBS-Frontline authorship documentary that Edward couldn't have created Shakespeare's heroines because he was "a roaring homo." In a 2005 biography, *Shakespeare: The World as Stage*, humorist Bill Bryson is whimsically genial until a chapter on skepticism. Then, after acknowledging congruities between de Vere and the canon, he snaps: "But Oxford also had shortcomings that seem not to sit well with the compassionate, steady, calm, wise voice that speaks so reliably and seductively from Shakespeare's plays. He was arrogant, petulant, and spoiled, irresponsible with money, sexually dissolute, widely disliked, and given to outbursts of deeply unsettling violence... Nothing in his behavior, at any point of his life, indicated the least gift for compassion, empathy, or generosity of spirit..."

In fact, de Vere's fiscal irresponsibility entailed some generosity to poor people, including a musician, William Byrd, on whom he bestowed an estate. According to Aubrey's *Brief Lives*, he gave a beggar ten pounds during his continental tour, then a sum large enough to "make a man." And some of his youthful poems imply a "gift for compassion," like one published in 1573:

> The labouring man that tills the fertile soil.
> And reaps the harvest fruit, hath not indeed
> The gain but pain; and if for all his toil
> He gets the straw, the lord will have the seed.
> ("Labour and Its Reward")

Bryson might as justly have written that nothing in William's behavior suggests a "gift for compassion, empathy, or generosity of spirit." Along with suing debtors for minor sums and hoarding grain during a bad harvest, he refrained from supporting Stratford opposition to enclosure of common lands—which disadvantaged the poor—because he was friends with the magnates who were enclosing them. He billed the town for some wine he'd used to entertain a visiting clergyman. But Bryson just reads the canon's "steady, calm, wise voice" into William.

Bryson is a rare Stratfordian in acknowledging congruities between Edward and the canon. *Monstrous Adversary*, a 2003 de Vere biography by an American academic, Alan Nelson, just presents uniformly snappish value judgments of his character and behavior. While taking the "monstrous" counter-accusations of his fellow plotters in 1580 at face value, it interprets Edward's original accusation against them as a reflection of his depravity. Most of its 442 pages concern lengthy documents about household and fiscal arrangements, irrelevant to the authorship question. It dismisses Oxfordian books as irrelevant because they don't concern such documents.

## A Hall of Mirrors

It is hard to see through wire mesh. Henry James complains of occluded vision in a 1907 essay on *The Tempest*: "The man everywhere, in Shakespeare's work, is so effectually locked up and imprisoned in the artist that we but hover at the base of thick walls for a sense of him; while, in addition, the artist is so steeped in the abysmal objectivity of his characters and situations that the great billows of the medium itself play with him, to our vision, very much as, over a ship's side, in certain waters, we catch, through transparent tides, the flash of strange sea-creatures."

Looney's *"Shakespeare" Identified* might have enlightened James, but who knows? Looney maintains that de Vere could not have written *The Tempest* because it is not aristocratic enough: "Prospero, the Duke of Milan, represents in no way a ducal dignity, or the function of a dukedom." Looney certainly doesn't see de Vere as a shamanic personality, writing that he couldn't have created Prospero because the character is "first and last, a magician." Like mainstream scholars, he sees Shakespeare's "special domain" as a "universal understanding of human nature." He downplays the "late romances" and ignores *The Winter's Tale*.

Some conspiracy-minded Oxfordians inflate Looney's aristocratic bias and make Edward into William's fun-house mirror image: a super-nobleman who wrote wholly from experience instead of a super-commoner who wrote wholly from imagination. A 2011 film about de Vere as Shakespeare, *Anonymous*, magnifies this. So much dynastic intrigue swirls around a snobbish, humorless Earl of Oxford that the canon sinks from sight. The film has him publishing *Venus and Adonis* not in 1593 to "perform a call" but in 1601 to mitigate the Queen's rage at Southampton's treason by reminding her of a 1570s dalliance by which they supposedly begat the youth. It ends with Robert Cecil telling him that, as Elizabeth's putative son, he might have been king if he hadn't wasted his life writing poetry.

Yet "passionately held fantasies" about Edward shouldn't condemn Oxfordians to gulags any more than ones about William should promote Stratfordians to politburos. The way the establishment "disappears" de Vere seems totalitarian, as with the old Bolsheviks purged and airbrushed out of Soviet history.

Joseph Sobran, whose tentatively Oxfordian *Alias Shakespeare* deals mainly with evidence, writes: "The impulse to scold the dissenter; the inability to acknowledge even the possibility of reasonable doubt... intense frustration with anything less than unanimity; the conviction that dissent reveals a moral or psychological defect--- these are the marks of the brittle belief systems we call cults or ideologies." Sobran might have been referring to William's main support group, the Shakespeare Birthplace Trust, which has attributed the "psychological aberration" of dissent not only to snobbery but to "ignorance; poor sense of logic; refusal, willful or otherwise, to accept evidence; folly; the desire for publicity; and even... certifiable madness."

## Literary Patrimony

Why does the dearth of evidence about William as a poet interest me more than the wealth of conjectures about him? Jonathan Bate proposes a reason: "Writers, especially American ones who want to throw off the burden of their English literary patrimony, are drawn to the anti-Stratfordian heresy out of what Harold Bloom calls 'the anxiety of influence,' the knowledge of Shakespeare's insurmountable superiority. They cannot actually kill Shakespeare, so the next best thing is to kill his name, for it is as a name that a literary father exercises authority. The works are thus displaced onto a different name which carries the weight of aristocratic instead of literary tradition."

If I want to throw off a burden of literary patrimony, however, it is not just an English one but an equally American one of a Whiggish Bard who efficiently maneuvered universal genius into status and wealth while holding day jobs as an actor, director, theater manager, and financier. That paragon didn't need life experience to write his masterpieces and they aren't expected to affect life except to fund the academic and entertainment industries and affirm progressive mythology. An everyman-superman, a demigod of success for its own sake, he perches atop his monolith, ritually invoked to discourage would-be writers:

"You think you're Shakespeare or something?"

Some establishment figures have found the model oppressive. James Shapiro complains of "the romantic myth of literary genius, which has long promoted an effortless and unfathomable Shakespeare." Edmund Wilson, twentieth century America's leading critic, writes: "So great was the need of humanity to believe in a human intellect all-self-controlled and all-wise that there had been superimposed on the plays of the great master of hatred and horror a legend which now disguised them—and the solemn, impassive don, laboring day after day at his desk, explaining, interpreting... had supplied us with what men of letters, what all mankind, had desired: a writer superhuman and humanly impossible, a writer who could never have existed—a Master, of impeccable technique and imperturbable quality, a writer who could never be supplanted and never be left behind, a writer unassailable, a classic!"

Wilson ostensibly refers to "Sophocles" here: he elsewhere dismisses "anti-Stratfordians." But he also expresses some open puzzlement about Shakespeare. Like Joseph Campbell, he prefers lofty savants: "I dare say that no other national poet presents quite the same problems as Shakespeare to the academic critics who study him. Goethe and Dante were great writers by vocation: they were responsible and always serious... But he displayed all along toward his craft a rather superior and cavalier attitude that at times even verged on the cynical... He had certainly, by the end of his life, come to see himself as Prospero, a powerful and splendid enchanter. It is difficult for the scholar to understand... a pure enchanter for whom life is not real or earnest but a dream which finally must fade like the dramas in which he reflects it."

## Chapter Fourteen

## Shakespeare's Brain

---

A medieval painting on the back cover of *Shakespeare and the Goddess*'s English paperback edition shows the naughty ninth earl of Oxford lying beside his cross-barred spear as a boar gores his groin. (Despite his predicament he sports a fancy hat like young Edward in his 1575 portrait.) But although Ted Hughes mentions the case for Francis Bacon as Shakespeare in *The Goddess*, he ignores that for de Vere despite its notoriety in the early 1990s, soon after the PBS-Frontline documentary wherein A.L. Rowse calls Edward a "roaring homo." Widely seen and sympathetic to Oxfordians, the program shows a U.S. Supreme Court Justice, John Paul Stevens, speaking at a 1987 "mock trial" on authorship. To Stratfordian testimony about de Vere misbehavior, he replies: "Sounds like the actions of a playwright."

Hughes may not have noticed the case: his penchant for abstraction involved some tunnel vision. His Coleridge essay attributes "the bellowing of rutting alligators" that influenced "Kubla Khan"'s imagery to "Purchas's account of his travels in the Carolinas." But Samuel Purchas, a seventeenth century historian, never traveled to America. Hughes overlooks the real source of the alligator account although a Coleridge study that he read, *The Road to Xanadu*, cites it from the poet's notebook: "Now Coleridge got his alligators from one of the most delightful books that he or anyone else ever read, William Bartram's *Travels*: 'The alligators' terrible roar, like heavy distant thunder...'"

Perhaps the colonial naturalist Bartram, like Thoreau, came too close to Hughes's failed American escape. He also had personal motives for overlooking de Vere. A posh wastrel like Edward was the antithesis of his thrifty, demotic values, whereas William's rise from rustic obscurity to urbane prosperity must have appealed. And, as Poet Laureate, he was vulnerable to the Tory reactionary label pinned on Looney. When in *The Goddess* he describes Shakespeare's literary debut as "announced, in typical English fashion, by a howl of indignation from an older writer," he obliquely refers to Phillip Larkin's indignation when the Queen made Hughes laureate after Larkin, disdaining the job's stuffy duties, had declined.

The way Hughes begins *The Goddess* by portraying William as the conventional media hack genius suggests an understandable desire to be inside the prickly circle of establishment discourse. But the literati received *The Goddess* coldly, derided its techno-mathematical metaphors as pseudo-science, then mostly ignored or dismissed it. In the "Bibliographical Notes" to his *The Shakespeare Wars*, Ron Rosenbaum scoffs: "Ted Hughes (yes, that Ted Hughes) … offers a mega-meta theory of All Shakespeare as a pagan allegory of the devouring female nature goddess… Everyone wants to recruit Shakespeare into their System."

A few praised *The Goddess* reservedly. Stephen Greenblatt writes in *Will in the World*'s "Bibliographical Notes" that it has "brilliant pages on *Venus and Adonis*, which he views as the key to unlocking Shakespeare's whole poetic achievement." Although Jonathan Bate ignores it in his books about Shakespeare, he reconsiders in a 2015 biography of Hughes: "*Shakespeare and the Goddess of Complete Being* remains *sui generis*, and certainly cannot be recommended to students as an introductory critical study of the plays. But it does not now seem quite so eccentric in its entirety." Bate sees "something ahead of its time, something prophetic, about some aspects of the book." He thinks Hughes anticipated new critical tendencies: a more acceptant attitude to the canon's religious side; a more biographical approach to its creation; and a "neurological literary criticism" that draws on medical technology "to ask questions about what exactly might have gone on in Shakespeare's brain as he wrote."

Bate concludes, however, that "the spectacle of Hughes reading Shakespeare is less interesting than that of Shakespeare reading Hughes." He sees *The Goddess*'s vague Tragic Equation story of William running away from Anne Hathaway, taking up with a dark lady, and finally returning to country wife Anne more as Hughes's own story of running away from Sylvia Plath to dark lady Assia Weevil and ending up with a country wife, Carol Orchard. Bate might have considered that, aside from its rustic-urbane trajectory, Hughes's story is more like Edward de Vere's than William's. But since Hughes doesn't notice de Vere, Bate doesn't have to.

## More Circumstances

Another reason for Hughes to overlook the de Vere case was that it would have confused his Tragic Equation chronology, which follows the overall Stratfordian one that William dedicated the narratives to Wriothsley in his late twenties, then went on to write two mature plays a year through his forties. Yet Stratfordian chronologies are gossamer webs of historical connections and stylistic traits. My doorstop Oxford University Press *Complete Works* places Hughes's "first" Tragic Equation play, *All's Well That End's Well,* after his "later" ones, *Hamlet and Othello*. Other chronologies place *All's Well* after *King Lear* and *Macbeth*. Anyway, Hughes doesn't let chronology disturb his assumptions of authorship:

"It can't be claimed this was the order in which the plays were actually composed: in the oeuvre of most artists there are proleptic inspirations, inexplicable yet apparently necessary regressions. I shall make no attempt to guess at that real outer order, about which nobody seems to be sure, but will look at the plays only within this ideal sequence, their order according to the evolutionary development of the tragic equations."

Beyond class solidarity, Hughes's indifference to Shakespeare skepticism doesn't entail any great enthusiasm for William. Plenty of juicy conjectures about the "lost years" and other things have accrued to the dossier, but *The Goddess* largely ignores them except for its first chapter on his conjectured relationship with Henry Wriothsley. And de Vere lurks there. Hughes cites the attempt to marry Wriothsley to "Elizabeth de Vere, daughter of the Earl of Oxford" as William's motive for the narratives' and sonnets' exhortations to procreation. Oxfordians like to ask how an actor-impresario might presume to publicly lecture even a juvenile earl on marital duties.

If he had noticed Lord Boar, Hughes could have found food for thought. John Looney first suspected that Edward wrote the canon because the Shakespeare narratives resemble de Vere poems. "All that was necessary," Looney writes of his original search, "was to observe the number and length of the lines—six lines, each of ten syllables—and the order of the rhymes: alternate rhymes for the first four lines, the whole finishing with a rhymed couplet.

"With this in mind, I turned to an anthology of sixteenth century poetry and went through it, marking off each written in the form of stanza identical with that employed by Shakespeare in his *Venus and Adonis*. There turned out to be much fewer than I had anticipated...I was left ultimately with only one: the following poem on "Women" by Edward de Vere, Earl of Oxford ..."

> But when I see how frail these creatures are
> I muse that men forget themselves so far.
>
> To mark the choice they make and how they change,
> How oft from Phoebus do they flee to Pan,
> Unsettled still like haggards wild they range,

These gentle birds that fly from man to man,
Who would not scorn and shake them from the fist
And let them fly, fair fools, which way they list?

The de Vere poem's rhyme scheme is not its only resemblance to Shakespeare: so is its easy metaphorical use of elite sporting technicalities. Its "gentle birds that fly from man to man" are peregrine falcons--"gentle" refers not to behavior but to their status as earls' heraldically appointed raptors. "Haggards" were mature falcons trapped in the wild as opposed to "eyases," birds taken from a nest and hand-raised. Haggards were better raptors but they were harder to control. Sportsmen sometimes tired of their unreliability and got rid of them. In *Othello* when the Moor begins to doubt Desdemona's chastity:

If I do prove her haggard
Though that her jesses were my dear-heart strings
I'd whistle her off and let her down the wind
To prey at fortune.
(*Othello*, 3,3)

Stratfordians try to explain the Shakespeare narratives' apparently unprecedented appearance by invoking imitation as well as a genius that needed no personal experience of things like falcony to evoke them vividly. They conjecture that William wrote them following a fashion begun in 1589 by university wit Thomas Lodge. Lodge's lengthy classical-erotic poem, *Scilla's Metamorphosis*, does have the same rhyme scheme:

But why alas should I that marble hide
That doth the one and other flank,
From when mount of quickening snow doth glide;
Or else the vale that bounds the milkwhite bank.
Where Venus and her sisters hide the fount,
Whose lovely nectar does all sweet surmount.

The awkward verse and murky imagery in *Scilla's Metamorphosis* hardly seem a model for the Shakespeare narratives, however. Lodge wasn't much of a poet: he mainly wrote novels, pamphlets, and plays. If anything, his "fount" of "lovely nectar" stanza seems like a mangled version of the famous *Venus and Adonis* one wherein the Goddess likens her body to a landscape:

> Feed where thou wilt, on mountain or in dale;
> Graze on my lips, and if those hills be dry,
> Stray lower, where the pleasant fountains lie...

Lodge called himself a "euphuist" and a habitué of "Silexedra," which Oxfordians consider an alias for de Vere's literary establishment at Fisher's Folly. If the sonnets circulated among Shakespeare's "witty friends" in manuscript, the narratives probably did too. De Vere could have written them in response to his Italian sojourn, shown them to the university wits at Silexedra, including Lodge, and later published revised versions to influence Wriothsley.

## Vision

But does De Vere's dossier reflect a "great shaman" who conceived a Tragic Equation? With his extravagances and intrigues, Edward doesn't seem much like the dignified holy man, Black Elk. Still, great shamans are human. After performing his vision, Black Elk toured in Buffalo Bill's Wild West Show, became a Christian, and uneasily participated in the Ghost Dance of the Paiute shaman, Wovoka, who hoped performance of *his* vision would restore the bison and rid the West of whites. This ended in the Army's 1890 massacre of the Lakota leader Big Foot's band at Wounded Knee, South Dakota, with its photos of machine-gunned noncombatants so prophetic of the next century. About that debacle, Black Elk said: "I had had a very great vision and I should have depended on that to guide me to the good… It is hard to follow one great vision in this world of darkness and of many changing shadows."

A poet named John Soouthern who dedicated a 1584 book to de Vere describes him as a kind of "knower":

> For who marketh better than he
> The seven turning flames of the sky?
> Or hath read more of the antique;
> Hath greater knowledge of the tongues?
> Or understandeth sooner the sounds
> Of the learner to love music?
> Or else who hath a fairer grace,
> In the Centaurian art of Thrace,
> Half horse, half man …

Shamans are repositories of natural and traditional lore, are as much musicians as poets, and have close links with animals. Dreams and visions like those that "call" them figure in both the Shakespeare canon and de Vere's known poetry. "These poems," writes Joseph Sobran of the latter, "bear hundreds of resemblances to Shakespeare's phrasing, far too many to be dismissed as insignificant. The kinship is evident in the poems' themes, turns of phrase, word associations, images, rhetorical figures, various other mannerisms, and, above all, general diction."

Edward's youthful turmoil implies powerful anxieties: an undiagnosed illness incapacitated him for months in 1569, the year his mother died. His poems manifest the "sacred horror" that Borges associates with Shakespeare. Sobran finds resemblances to *Titus Andronicus* and over twenty other plays and poems in the following verses:

> I went to gather strawberries tho' when woods and groves were fair,

And parch'd my face with Phoebus lo, by walking in the
air.
I lay me down all by a stream and banks all over head,
And there I found the strangest dream, that ever young
man had.

Methought I saw each Christmas game, both revels all
and some,
And each thing else that man could name or might by
fancy come
The substance of the thing I saw, in Silence pass it shall,
Because I lack the skill to draw, the order of them all;
Yet Venus shall not 'scape my pen, whose maidens in
disdain,
Sit feeding on the hearts of men, whom Cupid's bow hath
slain.

And that blind Boy sat all in blood, bebathed to the Ears,
And like a conquerer he stood, and scorned lovers' tears.
'I have more hearts,' quod he, 'at call, than Caesar could
command,
and like the deer I make them fall, that overcross the
land.'

As in the Shakespeare narratives, decorative conventions
turn strange. Poets often portrayed Venus and Cupid as cruel,
but not as blood-bathed cannibals. *Venus and Adonis*'s man-
eating Titian nude comes to mind. So do Grendel and his
Mother. Young Edward's tutor at Cecil house in 1563,
Lawrence Nowell, was an Anglo-Saxon scholar and owned the
*Beowulf* manuscript. Some of de Vere's early poetry has
alliteration suggestive of Anglo-Saxon verse:

My life, though ling'ring long, is lodg'd in lair of
loathsome ways;

My death delay'd to keep from life the harm of hapless days.
                    "Loss of Good Name"


If Nowell taught *Beowulf* to his pupil, Mark Anderson suggests: "the ancient poem's influence on Shake-speare becomes not inexplicable but rather expected... *Beowulf* and the original Hamlet myth ("Amleth") are cousins from the same family of Scandinavian folklore. Shake-speare uses both as sources for *Hamlet*. Once HAMLET kills his uncle CLAUDIUS, Shake-speare stops following the "Amleth" and starts following *Beowulf*. It is Beowulf who turns to his loyal comrade (Wiglaf in *Beowulf*; Horatio in *Hamlet*) to recite a dying appeal to carry his name and cause forward; and it is *Beowulf* that carries on after its hero's death to dramatize a succession struggle for the throne brought on by an invading foreign nation."

Anderson doesn't mention *Beowulf*'s more mythic side, but an adolescent's response to a tale of giants and dragons might elucidate much in the canon, from Tamora and the Moor Aaron to anomalous Caliban. Like Grendel, Caliban is the son of a fiendish mother, Sycorax, and although she doesn't appear in the play, she certainly embodies a Queen of Hell. Of course, Caliban is not a man-eating giant, yet his name is an anagram of cannibal and *The Tempest* likens him to Polyphemus and other classical monsters. Hughes writes: "Polyphemus claims descent from an international species, the cannibal cave ogre, like *Beowulf*'s Grendel, whose terrible mother lives under deep water."


## Quest


De Vere's continental tour seems a kind of vision quest: his travels through northern France and Germany in the winter of 1575 would have had mythic associations given his forebear's adventures. Little is known about that part of the journey, but it was customary for nobles to stay at castles as in *Gawain*, and hospitality often included hunts:

> I was with Hercules and Cadmus once
> When in the woods of Crete they bayed the bear
> With hounds of Sparta. Never did I hear
> Such gallant chiding; for besides the groves.
> The skies, the fountains, every region near
> Seemed all one mutual cry. I never heard
> So musical a discord, such sweet thunder.
> (*A Midsummer Night's Dream*, 4,1)

De Vere certainly crossed the Alps. He has been suggested as co-author, with Anthony Munday, of an anonymous 1580 poem that associates "Honour" with climbing:

> Lo, first the case in seeking how to climb
> With study strange how it doth beat our brain
> In climbing then our observance of time,
> Then heed to hold, lest we go down again...
> Which joy to tell is Honour high
> Which noblest minds account the greatest joy
> Which first obtained by deadly jeopardy...
> "The Paine of Pleasure"

Michel de Montaigne, who crossed the Alps to Italy in 1580, expresses a more normal outlook for pre-mountaineering times. "Honour" doesn't come into it: "I have often experienced this in our mountains hereabout (and yet I am one who is very little dismayed by such things) that I could not bear the sight of that bottomless depth without dread and a trembling in my hams and thighs, although I was not near the edge ..." But there were other outlooks. In 1543, a Swiss naturalist, Conrad Gesner, wrote: "whoever does not consider towering mountains preeminently worthy of more than ordinary attention is, to my mind, an enemy of Nature."

After Mark Anderson conjectures that Edward was "at a loss for words" in the Alps, he continues: "But his fortnight spent winding through what is now Switzerland and eastern France surely came back to him years later in Shake-spearean snapshots such as 'far off mountains turned into clouds' and 'were I tied to run afoot even to the frozen ridges of the Alps' and 'night's candles are burnt out and jocund day stands tiptoe on the misty mountaintops'."

Anderson might have cited something else: Shakespeare's rapt wildflower descriptions. After I grew up with New England's lowland deciduous forest —like southern England's—nothing impressed me more in western mountain wilderness than the abundance and diversity of wildflowers. In the Yellowstone backcountry, they didn't just grow in the herbage-- they were the herbage—big showy ones like columbine, harebell, paintbrush, and lupine. Frost that would have withered garden flowers coated them every morning but they kept blooming. They included many plant families Shakespeare mentions: primrose, buttercup, pea, violet, campanula, iris, and lily.

There was more to the sixteenth century Alps than scenery and flowers. One traveler described the country between Geneva and Lyons as "mainly inhabited by wolves and bears," and that wasn't even the high Alps. In his compendium, *History of Four-Footed Beasts*, Conrad Gesner writes that "Helvetian Alp" bears are "so strong and full of courage" that they can "tear in pieces both oxen and horses." Dead pack animals would have attracted them to travel routes-- and not just pack animals. A hospice at Mont Cenis Pass kept a "wayfarers' mortuary" that held seventeen bodies in March 1578, two years after de Vere's likely crossing. In snowstorms, the monks sent out parties to rescue lost travelers and retrieve corpses that wore rosaries or other Catholic tokens. They left dead heretics for the beasts.

*"Exits, pursued by a bear"* is definitely no joke in such places, as I found in 1972 when, hitchhiking past the St. Elias Mountains in the Yukon, I was warned that a local grizzly had

just chased a jeep. I saw many big tracks when I backpacked briefly in the area, and I later heard a rumor that a bear had pursued another hitchhiker on the same stretch of road. The Yukon bear allegedly mauled its victim's back as the Illyrian one does on *The Winter's Tale*'s "Seacoast of Bohemia," where sixteenth century bears probably scavenged beaches. Gesner's *History of Four Footed Beasts* refers to "Illyria" as a particularly wild place. Grizzlies frequented California beaches well into the nineteenth century.

*The Winter's Tale* is not the only Shakespeare play that mentions a bear attack on a beach. After King Lear invokes divine retribution against his enemies on the blasted heath, he goes on:

> Tremble, thou wretch,
> Who hast within thee undivulged crimes...
>     ...Thou'dst shun a bear,
> But if thy flight lay toward the roaring sea
> Thou'dst meet the bear in the mouth..."
>                (*King Lear*, 3,2)

For Shakespeare to repeat such an incident, and to do so in the abnormal context of punishing evil, suggests an impressive source. It may be amateur literal-mindedness to suggest that Edward de Vere saw or heard about a bear attack on a Balkan beach or Alpine pass, but then where did this strange incident which figures in two of Shakespeare's greatest plays come from? It's hard to see how the vaguely normal man of William's dossier would have invented it and interpreted it as redemptive. The normal tourists who told me the rumor about the Yukon bear's attack said it just made them hate bears. When I asked them how they liked cars, which, to put it mildly, harm more people than bears (baseball-size rocks flung up by passing vehicles were the main hazards of hitchhiking the "gravel" Yukon roads) they said that cars are useful.

If de Vere made an Adriatic voyage, it could have been an ordeal worthy of shamanic initiation. "The Venetian galley recognized no class boundaries; all were equally put upon. Vermin and lice were no strangers … The galley's design had scarcely changed since the days of Mark Antony—two masts and dozens of oars rowed by both prisoners and sailors-for hire… In the words of one contemporary Spanish traveler, galley crews 'are diligent in profiting by good fortune, lazy in a gale; in a storm they command freely and obey little; their god is their sea chest… and their pastime is watching the passengers being seasick.'"

Mark Anderson conjectures that the voyage got as far as Delphi, ruined site of the Pythian Oracle, a fit goal for a poet's vision quest: "As eagles and white-tailed Egyptian vultures soared overhead, de Vere's party would have approached the Temple of Apollo, which stood amid a collection of holy rubble that had once been the centerpiece of the ancient Greek world." The oracle, a local girl, had prophesied by sitting on a tripod above an earth fissure from which trance-inducing vapors issued. Delphi's oracle figures large in *The Winter's Tale*: after accusing his queen of adultery, the Sicilian king, Leontes, sends messengers there to seek the truth. They return soon after Leontes dispatches Antigonus to expose the infant Perdita, and deliver a terrible judgment:

> Officer: (*reads*) Hermione is chaste, Polixenes blameless… Leontes a jealous tyrant, his innocent babe truly begotten, and the King shall live without an heir if that which is lost is not found.
> (3,2)

## Performance

Of course, the possibility that de Vere visited Illyria doesn't prove he wrote *The Winter's Tale* any more than the likelihood that he visited Sicily does. Again invoking imitation to buttress genius, Stratfordians say William derived the play from *Pandosto*, a 1588 novel by Robert Greene of the "upstart Crow" pamphlet. *Pandosto* has a similar plot but with different names and reversed locations, including a jealous *Bohemian* king and a princess who is "lost" on the *Sicilian* coast. The Delphic oracle plays a part, but the bear and flowers of a wild Balkan coast don't, and the novel lacks the play's sense of redemption through wild nature. The "Hermione" queen just dies from grief at her husband's accusations and her son's death. When the "Perdita" princess returns from Sicily to a nondescript Bohemia, the "Leontes" king tries to seduce her, then plots to murder her, then gets depressed and kills himself after he learns she is his daughter.

I don't see this Renaissance bodice-ripper, which pads "sexual situations" with windy rhetoric about honor and chastity, as the original of *The Winter's Tale*. Nothing in Greene's life suggests how he might have invented the story. Along with plays and pamphlets, he turned out one or more potboiler novels a year through the 1580s, allowing little time to develop new plots, and he probably never left England. His biographer doubts "sweeping" claims of travel and adds: "critics find all his references to continental customs and landscapes brief and conventional." *Pandosto*'s geography is certainly "brief": the "lost" infant, cast away alone on a Bohemian "barque," floats off to Sicily in two days.

Northrop Frye speculates that William had been rereading "old plays that had gone out of fashion and been superseded by the highly sophisticated productions that came along in the early 1600s," implying that *The Winter's Tale* didn't derive only from the novel. But he cites only one "old play," an anonymous 1590s comedy called *Mucedorus* wherein the hero impresses the heroine by killing a bear after the villain ignominiously has fled from it. William's biographers, usually quick to trace literary borrowings, don't even speculate about such ideas. All Greene's biographer has to say on *Pandosto*'s origin is that its "emblematic situations" have "parallels" in his other works.

Another tricky aspect of this is that Shakespeare's comedy, *Twelfth Night,* is also set in Illyria, although in a city, not a wilderness. Stratfordians think William wrote it in 1601, some ten years before their conjectured date for *The Winter's Tale*, deriving it from a romance, *Appolonius and Silla*, published by a novelist named Barnaby Rich in the 1581. That story is not set in Illyria, however, but, vaguely, in Constantinople. Why would William relocate *Twelfth Night* to a coastal city in remote Illyria, evoking that obscure place more vividly than Rich does Constantinople?

Mark Anderson conjectures that *Twelfth Night*'s location was Ragusa, a prosperous city-state in what is now Croatia: "Unlike any other city on the Illyrian shores, in Ragusa de Vere would certainly have been safe to 'beguile the time and feed his knowledge with viewing of the town'… seeing sights that 'satisfied the eyes with the memorials and things of fame that do renown this city' and enjoying music that is the very 'food of love'." Oxfordians think that Edward wrote an early *Twelfth Night* version in the 1580s, citing the lost manuscript of a play listed in a 1732 catalogue as "a pleasant conceit of de Vere, Earl of Oxford, discontented at the rising of a mean gentleman at the English court, circa 1580." They think the "mean gentleman" was Elizabeth's favorite, Christopher Hatton, satirized in *Twelfth Night* as vain, posturing Malvolio.

According to Leonard Digges's eulogy in the 1640 edition of the poems, Shakespeare *didn't* borrow from writers like Greene:

> …Nor Plagiari-like from others gleane,
> Nor begs he from each witty friend a Scene
> To peece his Acts with, all that he doth write,
> Is pure his owne, plot, language, exquisite…

De Vere's "witty friends" knew him as a long-winded storyteller. "This lie is very rife with him and in it he glories greatly," wrote his co-conspirator Charles Arundell of one Italian tale. "Diversely hath he told it and when he enters into it, he can hardly out, which hath made such sport as often I have been driven to rise from his table laughing." And, according to Mark Anderson, his literary establishment at Fisher's Folly teemed with books and manuscripts. A hack like Robert Greene could have worked up a property from hearing a tale or reading a script, as his friend Lodge could have borrowed from *Venus and Adonis*. Like Lodge, Greene called himself a "euphuist" habitué of "Silexedra," and he certainly borrowed. In the year he published *Pandosto*, he imitated Christopher Marlowe's 1587 hit about an Asian tyrant, *Tamburlaine*, with a "thinly disguised rewrite" called *Alphonsus King of Aragon*, "a plodding pastiche of Marlowe's blank verse line and Grand Guingol effects."

"Wheresover Maecenas lodgeth," Greene wrote in dedicating a 1584 book to de Vere, "thither no doubt scholars will flock... your Honour being a worthy fosterer and favorer of learning." But bankrupt Edward may have tired of fostering a plot-stealing Robert, who had real underworld connections that he exploited in a series of pamphlets on "coney-catching," Elizabethan con artistry. And Edward might have done something about it. *The Winter's Tale* features a rogue named Autolycus, a self-styled "snapper up of unconsidered trifles" also absent from *Pandosto*. Like Greene, Autolycus is a once-respectable drunk: he robs clotheslines for liquor money. Perhaps de Vere repaid Greene for *Pandosto*'s lecherous, murderous, suicidal Bohemian king by revising the *Tale* to fashion a great comic rogue from a larcenous hack.

Originals are usually better than imitations, although *The Winter's Tale* was a commercial flop compared to *Pandosto*. The play's mix of tragedy and burlesque as Autolycus snaps up Act IV with his antics might have baffled early modern audiences as much as its ursine manslaughter. Although a play called *A Winter's Night's Pastime* was registered in 1594, there's no record of a performance until the one, called *A Winter's Night's Tale*, that Simon Forman described at the Globe in May 1611. (And that may be a John Payne Collier forgery.) There was a performance at court in November, 1611, but the play went unpublished until the First Folio, evidently an "unconsidered trifle." While *Pandosto* went through many editions into the 1600s, however, it is *The Winter's Tale* that lives-- the voice of experience?

> Of moving accidents by flood and field,
> Of hair breadth scapes in th'iminent breach...
> And portance of my traveller's history
> Wherein of antres vast and deserts idle,
> Rough quarries, rocks, and hills whose heads touch
> Heaven,
> It was my hint to speak...
> (*Othello*, 1,3)

## Women

Hughes's interpretation of Coleridge's poetry as inspired by a kind of Great Goddess shamanism also might apply to one of de Vere's youthful poems. Like "Kubla Khan" and "Christabel," it revolves around an archetypal apparition of womanhood:

> Sitting alone upon my thought in melancholy mood
> In sight of sea, and at my back an ancient hoary wood.
> I saw a fair young lady come, her secret fears to wail,
> Clad all in colour of a nun, and covered with a veil;
> Yet (for the day was calm and clear) I might discern her
> face
> As one might see a damask rose hid under crystal glass.

The Tragic Equation theme of men chosen by goddess-like women and then driven to destructive behavior pervaded de

Vere's life. He was Adonis-like in youth judging from court gossip, and he attracted the era's Great Goddess embodiment, Queen Elizabeth. His attitude to her vacillated between adoration and impudence-- some contemporaries saw *Venus and Adonis* as a satire on their relations-- and he spent the rest of his life bouncing between a Heavenly Queen and a Hellish one:

> She did lie
> In her pavilion-- cloth of gold, of tissue—
> O'er picturing that Venus where we see
> The fancy outwork nature.
> > (*Antony and Cleopatra*, 2, 2)

> O this false soul of Egypt! This grave charm.
> Whose eye becked forth my wars...
> Like a right gipsy hath at fast and loose
> Beguiled me to the very heart of loss.
> > (*Antony and Cleopatra*, 4, 13)

De Vere's Tarquin side emerged as he rejected his wife, plotted against the Queen's allies, and impregnated her maid, Anne Vavasour. That seduction seems to have launched Anne on a lifetime of promiscuity: when the Queen put her in the Tower she took up with her jailer, and she later had multiple husbands and lovers, possibly including de Vere. His attitude to his teenaged conquest seems to have been smugly egotistical judging from the rest of the poem about the "fair young lady... clad all in the colour of a nun."

> O heavens! who was the first that bred in me this fe*ver*?
> Vere.
> Who was the first that gave the wound whose fear I wear
> fore*ver*? Vere.
> What tyrant, Cupid, to my harm usurps thy golden
> qui*ver*? Vere.
> > "Ann Vavasour's Echo"

Reading the canon back into Edward's life as it is read into William's would suggest that he eventually felt remorse about his treatment of women, especially after Anne Cecil's early death. Callow sexual abuse can resurface painfully in the middle-aged male mind after the hormones have subsided. This could elucidate "the terrible howls from the Female" that Hughes perceives. His references to William's life and personality often seem more appropriate to Edward's, as with the canon's ubiquitous theme of marital strife.

As I've said, there's no evidence for Hughes's conjectures that a "powerful guardian" forced William to marry Anne Hathaway; that he left Stratford to escape her; or that some "bed trick" briefly reunited them. Such things do apply to de Vere's marriage to Anne Cecil: her powerful father influenced and possibly enforced it; Edward ran away to Italy; and rumor had it that Anne's first pregnancy involved a "bed trick." As Oxfordians say, this is the plot of *All's Well That Ends Well*.

Then the marriage moved into the realm of tragedy and finally, vicariously, of tragicomedy. Edward rejected Anne, as Leontes rejects Hermione, and only reunited with her near the end of her short life. Soon after her widely-mourned death, her father installed a statue of her on her tomb in Westminster Abbey, a circumstance echoed in *The Winter's Tale* with its "statue" of Hermione: "a piece many years in doing, and now newly performed by that rare Italian master Giulio Romano... they say one would speak to her and stand in hope of answer." (5,2).

The William-Edward disparity touches other woman characters. Of *King Lear*, Hughes writes: "The tragic hero, Lear, now confronts (rather like Shakespeare drafting his own will in 1606) three women, i.e. the Goddess who incorporates in some form still hidden from him, the Queen of Hell, but who mainly embodies the love on which his sanity depends." But William's relations with his family seem less like Lear's than Edward's. De Vere's youngest daughter, Susan, who scarcely knew her mother, shared his love of poetry and drama. The two eldest, Elizabeth and Bridget, grew up in Cecil's household and must have resented their father's neglect and misbehavior. De Vere performed a kind of abdication when he transferred ownership of Castle Hedingham to them and withdrew from public life, but, like Goneril and Regan, they may not have been duly grateful.

Hughes has even more trouble finding William behind *Macbeth*'s female characters. He follows the Stratfordian convention that he wrote the play soon after King James's accession to flatter the new monarch by affirming his right to the crown via his ancestor Banquo and catering to his fascination with witchcraft. But there is no evidence that James saw *Macbeth* performed, and Oxfordians doubt that a play featuring witches who encourage a Scottish king's murder would have pleased one who greatly feared assassination, having narrowly escaped a 1600 kidnapping attempt called the Gowrie Plot in Scotland. When the King's Men tried to flatter James by producing a play called *The Tragedy of Gowrie* in 1604, it was suppressed after two performances. Anyway, flattery seems a shallow motive for *Macbeth*'s deep delving into treachery.

Hughes interprets *Macbeth* as an unfolding of the Tragic Equation's second part, when Venus has morphed into the Queen of Hell, embodied by Lady Macbeth and the Weird Sisters, and Macbeth has become the Tarquin-Boar. The Scottish king that Macbeth-Tarquin murders thus becomes a kind of Lucrece:

> .... Witchcraft celebrates
> Pale Hecate's offerings, and withered murder,
> Alarumed by his sentinel the wolf,
> Whose howl's his watch, thus with his stealthy pace,
> With Tarquin's ravishing stride, towards his design,
> Moves like a ghost...
> (*Macbeth*, 2,1)

There certainly are overtones of rape in this "ravishing stride" soliloquy that Macbeth voices just before his bedroom stabbing of tender-minded King Duncan. But that would be a kinky twist of the Equation as an attempt to flatter a bisexual King James. On the other hand, if the play associates the Scottish monarchy with Mary Stuart instead of her son James, as some Oxfordians see it, the rape metaphor could make more sense. Lady Macbeth and her Tarquin-boar husband might be associated with Queen Elizabeth as she threatened and cajoled her nobles into condemning her royal cousin to a Catholic martyr's death.

Like doomed Macbeth, the dying Elizabeth couldn't sleep and "saw things." In a strange echo of the play's "they have tied me to a stake; I cannot fly" bear-baiting speech, she told Lord Admiral William Howard: "My lord I am tied with a chain of iron about my neck. I am tied, I am tied, and the case is altered with me." De Vere knew Howard, who was his commander in the Armada campaign. Perhaps *Macbeth* is short and fragmentary because a moribund man wrote it after Elizabeth's death. Of Mary's judicial murder, de Vere might have reflected on his own guilt:

> I am afraid to think what I have done,
> Look on't again I dare not.
> (*Macbeth*, 2,2)

Hughes has the most trouble fitting the females of Shakespeare's most famous tragedy into his Stratfordian Equation, devoting six pages to *Hamlet* as compared to sixteen to *Macbeth* and twenty-four to *King Lear*. He makes a vague attempt to link the Danish Prince's tangled feelings about his mother and his prospective bride to William: "Hamlet whirls unendingly in the tunnel of his bond with his mother—from which he can never break to marry Ophelia. This cyclotron effect is the one unique result of the variant Equations being combined in just this way, and adds greatly to the sense of something inexpressible in itself and at the same time rooted beneath the foundations of Shakespeare's own nature ... The fact that the work was composed at about the time when Shakespeare's father's death (which might have been some time pending) coincided with the first phase of his deliberately undertaken spiritual renewal (as intimated in *As You Like It* and *All's Well that Ends Well*) must be relevant."

But he has trouble seeing just how all this is relevant to the play's tortuous story: "As in no other play, he sets the mythic plane and the human plane in opposition, or rather he sets Hamlet's mythic destiny and Hamlet's individual will in opposition. In all the other tragedies, the hero's individual will, his Adonis will, is demolished, and taken over by the mythic Tarquinian will... But Hamlet does not merely resist change and attempt to deflect his destiny: he goes on resisting it for most of the play... It is as though Hamlet were putting out all his personal strength against what is a kind of mythic overdrive. Like the driver of a bus containing all the characters of the drama, he hurtles toward destruction, in slow motion, with his foot jammed down hard on the brakes."

Oxfordians like to ask why William, the consummate theater pro of Stratfordian doctrine, would write at such length about a prince's psycho-sexual problems that the resulting play was too long to be performed entire at the Globe. It is easier to imagine Edward writing "unendingly" about them: he *was* like the driver of a runaway bus "containing all the characters of the drama," hurtling toward destruction.

Sorcery

Hughes doesn't even try to find William in some shamanic aspects of the canon, like dream calls of demon lovers which, he writes, "project the inner experience, consistent and archetypal, of a spontaneous human transformation that always tends to produce the same end result: a healer who exercises his power through public, dramatic performances." No evidence exists outside the canon of William dreaming anything, but Edward's Catholic co-conspirators accused him of consorting with a nocturnal female spirit, bringing to mind Bottom's dream of lustful Titania.

Mark Anderson sees a likeness between the co-conspirators' panicky accusations of sorcery and heresy and the clownish constable Dogberry's accusations against the protagonists of *Much Ado About Nothing*. De Vere's main accuser, Charles Arundell testified: "First, I will detect him some of the most impudent and senseless lies that ever passed the mouth of man... to show that the world never brought forth such a villainous monster, and for a parting blow to give him his full payment, I will prove against him the most horrible and detestable blasphemy... To conclude, he is a beast in all respects and in him no virtue to be found and no vice wanting."

Dogberry testifies: "Marry, sir, they have committed false report, moreover they have spoken untruths... they have verified unjust things... Moreover, sir, which indeed is not under black and white, this plaintiff here, the offender, did call me ass... And also the watch heard him talk of someone Deformed. They say he wears a key in his ear and a lock hanging by it, and borrows money in God's name..." (5,1)

De Vere's rank and education didn't immunize him from sorcery's allure. "Nero and Heliogabalus," writes Robert Burton, "were never so much addicted to magic of old as some of our modern princes and popes are nowadays. Ericus, King of Sweden, had an enchanted cap by which, and some magical murmur or whispering terms, he could command spirits, trouble the air, and make the wind stand which way he would." Edward knew John Dee, the era's leading astrologer-physician, who consulted for many aristocratic patrons, including the Queen, and was later accused of sorcery. He may have known Giordano Bruno, the Italian natural philosopher burned for heresy in 1600. Visiting England during the 1580s, Bruno lectured at Oxford and published books in London although the printer "prudently gave

Paris or Venice as the place of publication, for the wizard's enthusiastic account of idolatry and conjuring disclosed the most shocking aspects of pagan theology."

Hamlet, who studies at the University of Wittenberg where Bruno taught, doubts the orthodox doctrine of a geocentric universe made of five essential elements in five concentric spheres, and ponders Bruno's heretical ideas of an ephemeral earth, a heliocentric solar system, and a universe infinite in time and space.

> Horatio: O day and night, but this is wondrous strange!
> Hamlet: And therefore as a stranger give it welcome.
> There are more things in heaven and earth, Horatio,
> Than are dreamt of in our philosophy..."
> (*Hamlet*, 1, 5)

Shakespeare's fascination with sorcery unnerves critics on both sides of the authorship debate, as with Looney's rejection of *The Tempest*. The witch's cauldron scene in Act IV of *Macbeth* has such detailed descriptions of fetishes and spells that scholars have decided, on "stylistic grounds" that it is an "interpolation" by a much younger man, Thomas Middleton, who wrote a play called *The Witch* around 1614. Middleton's play has a lot of lore taken from a 1584 book, Reginald Scot's *Discoverie of Witchcraft*. They think he added material to *Macbeth* to sensationalize it for a performance, and that the additions got into the First Folio, consisting of two songs, the cauldron scene (4,1), and one character, Hecate.

The songs are the same, but the two plays' cauldron scenes aren't, and their Hecates are quite different. *Macbeth*'s Hecate is a lunar deity, a Great Goddess embodiment with great powers, as Macbeth says in his Act II soliloquy: "Witchcraft celebrates / Pale Hecate's offerings." She appears in Act III and scolds the Weird Sisters for capriciously tempting Macbeth to murder Duncan. Then she passes judgment on him, consigning him to the "spirits" that will say he's safe until Birnam Wood comes to Dunsinane:

> He shall spurn fate, scorn death, and bear
> His hopes 'bove wisdom, grace, and fear;
> And you all know security
> Is mortals' chiefest enemy.
> (3, 5)

*The Witch*'s Hecate is the mortal head of village coven. Asked by the hero to stop a rival's marriage to the heroine, she can't prevent a Christian sacrament, only inflict impotence on the groom. Otherwise, the witches just stoke their cauldron with grisly objects and pursue handsome young men, providing comic relief in a vaguely Italianate revenge thriller. Middleton wrote mainly topical satires and bourgeois comedies, and he was puritanical for a playwright. Why would he imagine a Great Goddess Hecate? Anyway, *Macbeth*'s author sounds more like a feral outcast obsessed with apocalyptic heterodoxy than a shrewd property investor:

> I conjure you by that which you profess
> (howe'er you come to know it) answer me.
> Though you untie the winds and let them fight
> Against the churches...
> Though castles topple on their warders' heads;
> Though palaces and pyramids do slope
> Their heads to their foundations...
> Even till destruction sicken—answer me...
> (*Macbeth*, 4, 1)

## A Wicked Imagination

Northrop Frye makes the common claim that Shakespeare's "chief motive in writing, apparently, was to make money, which is the best motive..." The plight of most contemporaries known to have written for money doesn't support this. Robert Greene died destitute at age thirty despite his popularity: his friend Thomas Lodge abandoned literature for medicine and lived to be sixty-seven. Ben Jonson estimated his lifetime income from plays at less than two hundred pounds. Top professionals like him and Middleton got their main income from commissioned masques and revels, but no such cash cows bear Shakespeare's name.

In this milieu, the dreams, visions, and anxieties of a shamanic personality seem a more likely motive for sustained literary performance than money. In calling young Edward her "Turk," Queen Elizabeth implied religious heterodoxy along with pugnacity and sexiness. When she told historian William Lambarde, "Know ye not. I am Richard II," after Robert Devereux's deposition attempt, the startled Lambarde said: "Such a wicked imagination was determined and attempted by a most unkind gent. the most adorned creature that ever your Majesty made." Historians assume he meant Devereux, although "imagination" seems an mild term for armed insurrection.

Elizabeth replied: "He that will forget God will also forget his benefactors. This tragedy was played forty times in open streets and houses." Devereux did not "forget God": on the scaffold before his beheading, he denied ever being an atheist or a Catholic. He certainly wasn't to blame for *Richard II*'s "forty" performances.

Whether or not he was a "great shaman," de Vere did want to play a savior and prophet role in England's conflicts, first trying to preserve the old religion with his intrigues, then joining in the fight against Catholic Spain. The canon revolves ritualistically around opposed identities, and not just Catholic and Protestant ones, but male and female, human and non-human, socially dominant and socially outcast. As his attempts to resolve the conflicts through politics, war, and venture capitalism failed, he might have tried it in an Elizabeth-approved, magically-imbued dramatic role.

'Tis known I ever
Have studied physic, through which secret art,
By turning o'er authorities, I have,
Together with my practice, made familiar
To me and to my aid the blest infusions
That dwells in vegetatives, in metals, stones,
And can speak of the disturbances
That nature works, and of her cures, which doth give me
A more content in course of true delight
Than to be thirsty after tottering honor
Or tie my pleasure up in silken bags...
      (*Pericles,* 3, 2)

# IV

# ECOLOGY

---

The wretched animal heaved forth such groans
That their discharge did stretch his leathern coat
Almost to bursting, and the big round tears
Coursed one another down his innocent nose
In piteous chase…
(*As You Like It*, 2,1)

# Chapter Fifteen

## Horses and Hares

---

As I've said, Shakespeare's narrative poems seem an attempt to reach back past Christianity and classicism toward some more emotionally gratifying state, what Hughes calls "complete being." But Hughes doesn't really define complete being in *Shakespeare and the Goddess*, and his Stratfordian assumptions combine with his penchant for abstraction to mute his response to a significant aspect of the canon, particularly of *Venus and Adonis*.

Although Shakespeare describes it with his usual spareness, the poem is *set* in a "draughty, radiant Paradise of the animals":

> Lo, here the gentle lark, weary of rest,
> From his moist cabinet mounts up on high
> And wakes the morning, from whose silver breast
> The sun ariseth in his majesty,
>   Who doth the world so gloriously behold
>   That cedar tops and hills seem burnished gold.
>           (*Venus and Adonis*, 853)

### A Randy Stallion

Charlton Ogburn Jr., a State Department official turned author, was late twentieth century America's leading Oxfordian, prominently featured in the 1989 Frontline documentary. His 892-page *The Mysterious William Shakespeare*, published in

1984, revived the de Vere case after decades of Stratfordian dismissals had obscured it. Ogburn was also a nature writer: some of *The Winter Beach*, an exploration of the Atlantic Coast that he published in 1966, reads like Hughes's "draughty, radiant Paradise" essay:

"Western literature from Shakespeare to the publications of the Sierra Club is eloquent in the responsiveness it reveals to woods, mountains and rivers, birds and four-footed animals… It leads to the belief that a feeling for nature and a sense of being integral with the natural world are deep seated... Yet (and this I can never fully fathom) we were led to adopt and at times have fanatically prosecuted a religion—that is to say, a view of what life is ultimately about—in which there is no fellowship whatever of man and nature…. The God of Judah, Christianity, and Islam created the animals solely to be of use to mankind. This is made explicit in *Genesis*."

Ogburn writes similarly in *The Mysterious William Shakespeare*: "Shakespeare was the first in English literature to find solace and rewards in nature as we conceive them in our over-civilized times. As a poet of nature he has never been excelled." And although he doesn't interpret Shakespeare's narratives as shamanic initiation dreams, he brings up an aspect of *Venus and Adonis* that Hughes doesn't. He finds a striking, perhaps unprecedented, empathy for non-human life in it. Ogburn notes, for example, that the poet identifies more with Adonis's randy stallion, who breaks away to chase a mare, than he does with the prudish young demigod:

> Imperiously he leaps, he neighs, he bounds,
> And now his woven girth he breaks asunder.
> The bearing earth with his proud hoof he wounds,
> Whose hollow womb resounds like heaven's thunder.
>     The iron bit he crushes 'tween his teeth.
>     Controlling what he was controlled with.
>
> His ears up-pricked, his braided hanging mane

Upon his compassed crest now stands on end,
His nostrils drink the air, and forth again,
As from a furnace, vapors doth he send.
  His eye, which scornfully glisters like fire,
  Shows his hot courage and high desire...

What recketh he his rider's angry stir,
His flattering "Hola", or his "Stand, I say!"?
What cares he now for curb or pricking spur;
For rich caparisons or trappings gay?
  He sees his love and nothing else he sees,
  For nothing else with his proud sight agrees.
                    (*Venus and Adonis*, 265)

Ogburn's interpretation goes against the Stratfordian convention of borrower-genius William coolly contriving the narrative poems simply to establish his reputation. Biographer Peter Ackroyd writes: "The description of the horse of Adonis, often cited as a testimony to Shakespeare's knowledge of equine matters, is cribbed almost verbatim from a translation by Joshua Sylvester of *Divine Weekes and Workes* by Guillaume du Bartas." But while du Bartas's biblical epic has a passage with similarities to Shakespeare's, it is about Cain breaking a stallion for hunting and war: it doesn't empathize with equine sexuality. And Sylvester published his translation in 1605, so William couldn't have "cribbed" from it in 1593.

On the other hand, the 1584 French version of the Gascon poet's epic might have influenced multilingual Edward. And there is another possibility. According to its modern editor, Sylvester's translation takes "many liberties with the French text": the widely read *Venus and Adonis* might have influenced *it*. The part of Sylvester's horse passage that most resembles Shakespeare's is a heraldic description of equine anatomy, a more likely subject for a nobleman accomplished at jousting than a middle class translator like Sylvester.

Shakespeare's stallion passage doesn't seem like a cribber's, anyway. It seems like that of someone who knows horses not just mechanically as beasts of burden but emotionally, as feeling beings, someone who has identified with well-kept horses for much of his emotional life—who has grown up with them and lived with them from day to day.

Hughes doesn't remark on this equine empathy in *The Goddess*, however, and he doesn't even remark on something he might have been expected to notice. Considering his "draughty, radiant Paradise" essay, he might have seen empathy with animals as an aspect of Shakespeare's great shaman role, making him a "savior" of the old sense of totemic kinship with non-human life that lingered in sorcery's roots as well as a "prophet" of the new biological, eventually evolutionary, thinking that arose from natural philosophy. Hughes quotes the horse passage, but he doesn't make the connection. He sees the stallion's pursuit of the mare symbolically, as "the uncontrollable erotic energy of Venus…projected first (as a demonstration) into a sexually excited and therefore uncontrollable stallion before—frustrated—it materializes in the fatal form of the boar."

## Vulcan's Wife

Venus herself embodies the narrative poem's "draughty radiance" with her uninhibited nakedness, which seems an implicit definition of "complete being." In the "graze where thou wilt" stanza, she metaphorically *becomes* the paradise. Hughes's avoidance of that side of the poem seems linked to the ambivalence about wilderness that marked his failed American escape.

His moor-bred "way with animals" was one of the main things that attracted Sylvia Plath, as when in *Birthday Letters* he calls a tawny owl from a copse by imitating the "throaty thin woe" of a rabbit's distress call:

I made my world perform its utmost for you.

You took it all in with an incredulous joy…
"The Owl"


But Plath saw another side of it as well. On the moors just after their marriage, she astonished him by going "berserk" when he killed a badly injured grouse they found. "Like an electric shock," he recalled, he felt "a total kind of transference to me of her feelings," and he didn't want to kill birds or mammals again. Yet her outburst about what was, after all, a merciful act may have caused some resentment. Feelings about wildlife became a touchy spot with them.

In *The Goddess,* Hughes suggests that what Shakespeare's Adonis really wants is a mate without Venus's clingy needs, who will go hunting with him like Ovid's Venus. Plath, who was clingy and needy, wanted Hughes to be less like Ovid's Adonis, a detached, aggressive hunter, and more like Shakespeare's--an empathetic Orpheus who charms beasts with his art. Her gushy early descriptions of the moors perhaps overlay a sense of their violently subdued state and a desire for less subdued places. Before they moved to America, she wrote her mother: "I have seen next to nothing of England's natural beauty and feel I should." Before they went on their western camping trip, she wrote: "I am becoming more and more desirous of becoming an amateur naturalist."

Her Yellowstone story, "The Fifty-Ninth Bear," probes the touchy spot. Sadie, the wife, is naively excited about the park while her more knowing husband Norton is uneasily detached: "Timorous as Sadie was, she had no fear of animals. She had a way with them. Norton had come upon her once, feeding a wild stag blueberries out of her hand, a stag whose hooves could, in one blow, have dashed her to the ground…" Sadie's excitement is partly sentiment, partly something else. Venus loves Adonis but she is Vulcan's wife:

"She had insisted on the Dragon's Mouth, that hoarse, booming spate of mud-clogged water; and the Devil's Cauldron. He had waited for her habitual squeamishness to turn her away from the black, porridgy mass that popped and seethed a few yards from under her nose, but she bent over the pit, devout as a priestess in the midst of those vile exhalations. And it was Norton, after all, bare-headed in the full noon sun, squinting against the salt-white glare and breathing in the fumes of rotten eggs, who defaulted, overcome by headache. He felt the ground frail as a bird's skull under his feet, a mere shell of sanity and decorum between him and the dark entrails of the earth where sluggish muds and scalding waters had their source."

> There's hell, there's darkness,
> There is the sulphurous pit, burning, scalding, stench...

Norton compensates by drawing the place into an occult system: "Away from the boardwalks, the spiels of rangers, the popular marvels, Norton revived a little. His headache, withdrawn to the far edge of awareness, circled and stalled there like a thwarted bird. As a boy, Norton had developed, quite by himself, a method of intense prayer... to what he liked to think of as the genius of a place, the fostering spirit of an ash grove or a shoreline... Now, lulled by the putter of the car, and feigning sleep, Norton began to will toward him all the animals of the forest—the fog-colored, delicately striated antelope, the lumbering, tousled buffalo, the red foxes, the bears..."
Norton's prayer is a magical hunting technique, a form of abstracted control. It allays his unease but, when night comes to their camp, it is the official control behind bears conditioned to be tourist attractions that threatens the couple more than the "dark entrails" of the wilderness. Norton and Sadie would have been safer in the Yellowstone backcountry, where the closest thing to a bear scare my wife and I had during a two-week backpack was one night when we thought a large animal was moving around our tent. Crouching to tighten her boots in the morning, my wife fell over backward: a noisy mouse had amused itself by gnawing through the laces.

Hughes would have liked that mouse. He didn't much like Norton and Sadie's camping trip—the insouciant child of nature versus the testy would-be beast-master. His *Birthday Letters* poem on the real incident has Plath fleeing into their tent when bears appear and panicking the next morning about a rumor of a fatal bear attack at another campsite (a false rumor repeated obliviously by biographers-- the only Yellowstone death recorded in 1959 was a concession worker's suicide).

His resentment is understandable. Plath's story implies that Sadie feeds a big Yellowstone elk stag, but a deer that Hughes photographed her feeding at a Canadian park is a small white-tailed buck, and her expression seems as much an eye-rolling tourist's as an insouciant child of nature's. Plath didn't much like the story herself, calling it "a stiff artificial piece" with "none of the deep emotional currents gone into or developed." But she was reluctant to reread it, which suggests it went deeper than she liked.

The war of jealous Venus and resentful Adonis escalated as they returned to England. The gushy attitude of Plath's early moor descriptions changes in a 1960 poem:

> There is no life higher than the grasstops
> Or the hearts of sheep...
> ("Wuthering Heights")

In 1961, she published "The Fifty-Ninth Bear" in *London Magazine*, publicly challenging, appropriating-- even mocking— Hughes's way with animals. "I was surprised," recalled an American friend that "she made a story of the killing of a husband for her husband and their friends to see." That year she wrote a poem, "Zookeeper's Wife," about a woman who lies in a "dead lake" beside a boor who presides not over a Paradise of wild animals but an Inferno of caged ones. Hughes had considered getting a zoology degree and working at the London Zoo.

When they moved to rural Devon, the war climaxed as their marriage collapsed. Finding rabbit snares in a wood she described as a "place of force," Plath furiously tore them out as Hughes resentfully watched. Both wrote a poem about it. Plath's evokes furtive cruelty:

> I felt hands round a tea mug, dull, blunt,
> Ringing the white china...
> ...and a mind like a ring
> Sliding shut on some quick thing...
> ("The Rabbit Catcher")

Hughes's ascribes his resentment to social more than personal feeling:

> You saw blunt fingers, blood in the cuticles,
> Clamped round a blue mug. I saw
> Country poverty raising a penny,
> Filling a Sunday stewpot..."
> ("The Rabbit Catcher")

Hughes links the snares to peasant resistance to "hangings and transportations" and accuses Plath of "a rage that cared nothing for rabbits." But while her poem isn't just about rabbits, she did care about "quick things" and there is some special pleading in his. He had hunted for "a Sunday stewpot" but he'd also pursued the inedible for fun, trapping fox cubs that farmers and dogs killed before he checked the traps. Such things can cause residual traumas, which Hughes evokes cryptically in "The Rain Horse," a 1958 story about a man returning to his boyhood home on the moors. When a strangely hostile horse chases him, he repels it with stones, then flees into a shed:

"The mingled smell of paraffin, creosote, fertilizer, dust—was exactly as he had left it twelve years ago. The ragged swallows' nests were still there tucked in the angles of the rafters. He remembered three dead foxes hanging in a row from the beams, their teeth bloody.

"The ordeal of the horse… hung under his mind, an obscure confusion of fright and shame, as after a narrowly-escaped street accident. There was a solid pain in his chest, like a spike of bone stabbing …"

## Holiest of Beasts

Hughes still hunted occasionally after Plath's outburst about the wounded grouse. William's deer-poaching legend may have appealed to him. In 1997, he wrote his friend, Keith Sagar: "One of the reasons I came to Devon, thinking of living on Exmoor, was the possibility of knocking over the occasional deer—subsistence." That year he published an article warning that proposed bans on horseback hunting of deer and foxes might work against the species' survival. He had a point if, as he maintained, they had nearly vanished from the "West Country" when the Civil War suspended aristocratic game regulations, whereas democratized hunting made preserving them popular after the Restoration. Yet the article takes for granted the relentless utilitarianism that his 1970 "drafty radiant Paradise" essay rejects.

Hunting's democratized popularity didn't save wild boars, hounded from Britain in the eighteenth century. They reintroduced themselves in the 1980s, however, escaping "game farms" and establishing several wild populations. As poet laureate, Hughes might have celebrated the return of what in *The Goddess* he calls: "the holiest of Celtic and Anglo-Saxon beasts." Yet smart, prolific boars can conflict with agribusiness, and he had a farm then. In a 1980s poem, they are not real animals in landscape like his foxes and otters but symbols of frustration at streams too flooded for fishing and, marginally, of his wildlife war with Plath, who kept bees that stung him as their marriage failed:

Piglets, tusky boars, possessed, huge sows
Piling in the narrows.
> I stayed clear. "Swine,
Bees and women cannot be turned."
> ("Salmon-Taking Times")

Hughes's boars in *The Goddess* are also symbolic. His
one reference to real pigs is a footnote on the farm brood-sow,
described as "a mobile tub entirely made of female sexual parts,"
with "an elephantine, lolling mouth under her great ear flaps, like
a Breugelesque nightmare vagina, baggy with over production,
famous for gobbling her piglets." She has "supplanted all other
beasts as the elemental mother," but "she fulfills an ambiguous
lunar role… inseparable from the lethal factor of the Boar, who
carries the same vaginal grin yet is prodigiously virile—the same
swingeing, earth-searching, root-gripping mouth but with moon
sickle tusks—and who incarnates the most determined, sudden,
and murderous temperament." Hughes concludes that: "as a
country boy, and nephew of several farmers," William would
have "enjoyed a familiarity with pigs that is not irrelevant to his
myth."

William may have had "a familiarity with pigs" in
Stratford, but there is no evidence that he had any with wild
boars. On the other hand, Edward de Vere's outdoor youth and
continental travels imply experience, and his heraldic-totemic
identity implies empathy. Wild boars are not so hard to
empathize with. Sows are furry, leggy, and agile: they cooperate
to foster dozens of piglets. They may be aggressive in defending
young, but I haven't seen that. I was surprised at how confiding
the little family at the Mount Diablo trap was: I had to shout and
wave my arms to scare them away. Grown males are warier, as
when, during one hot day, I watched a big boar I'd disturbed
leave his cool wallow and depart with startling ease up a nearly
vertical hillside.

Of course, boars are "determined and sudden" at bay, as Shakespeare's Venus warns Adonis, not with Ovid's sex gossip, but with practical advice:

'Thou hadst been gone,' quoth she, 'sweet boy, ere
   this,
But that thou told'st me thou would hunt the boar.
O, be advised; thou know'st not what it is
With javelin's point a churlish swine to gore,
   Whose tushes, never sheathed, he whetteth still,
   Like a mortal butcher, bent to kill.'

'On his bow-back he hath a battle set
 Of brittle pikes that ever threat his foes.
His eyes like glow-worms shine; when he doth fret
His snout digs sepulchers where'er he goes.
   Being moved, he strikes, whate'er is in his way,
   And whom he strikes his crooked tushes slay.'

'His brawny sides with hairy bristles armed
 Are better proof than thy spear's point can enter.
His short thick neck cannot be easily harmed.
Being ireful, on the lion he will venture.
   The thorny brambles and embracing bushes,
   As fearful of him, part; through whom he rushes.'
                              (*Venus and Adonis*, 613)

The warning is dead serious, but with an undertone of appreciation for the boar's defensive strength: "eyes like glow-worms," "brawny sides with hairy bristles armed."
Although Stratfordians see Shakespeare's boar passages as William imitating Ovid, the passages really are quite different. The Roman poet's warning is perfunctory:

Beauty and youth and love
Make no impression on bristling boars and lions,

On animals' eyes and minds.  The force of lighting
Is in the wild boars' tusks...
(*Metamorphoses* 10, 549-553)

Ovid describes a boar at more length in "The Calydonian Hunt":

A boar as big as a bull, with blood-shot eyes,
A high stiff neck, and bristles rising from it
Like spears along a wall, and hot foam flecking
The shoulders, dripping from jaws that opened
With terrible grunting sounds; his tusks were long
As an Indian elephant's, and lightning flashed
Out of his mouth, and his breath would burn the grasses.
(*Metamorphoses* 8, 283-289)

This imagery clearly influenced Shakespeare's.  Yet the Calydonian Boar is a fantasy monster, not a real beast, and Ovid doesn't appreciate it or empathize with it.  His description is still perfunctory compared to his courtesan-goddess's complexion worries.  Indeed, his boar-hating Venus distorts classical paganism, which saw her as an ally of dangerous beasts, not an enemy:

Behind her moved gray wolves, fawning on her,
And bright-eyed lions, bears, and quick insatiable
panthers.
When she saw them she felt joy in her heart.
(*Homeric Hymns*)

Shakespeare's Venus doesn't hate the boar: she empathizes with its vitality at the same time she fears its danger to Adonis.  And his description implies technical knowledge as well as experience.  Boar hunts required many dogs (Titian's "Venus and Adonis" shows the young hunter holding a leash of huge hounds that pull him away from the goddess), but although

Ovid mentions the Calydonian monster "scattering the pack," he
leaves it at that.  Shakespeare goes into graphic detail:

> She hearkens for his hounds, and for his horn
>   Anon she hears them chant it lustily,
>   And all in haste she coasteth to the cry...
>
>           ... She knows it is no gentle chase,
> but the blunt boar, rough bear, or lion proud,
> Because the cry remaineth in one place,
> Where fearfully the dogs exclaim aloud.
>   Finding their enemy to be so curst,
>   They all strain court'sy who shall cope him first...
>
> Here kenneled in a brake she finds a hound,
> And asks the weary caitiff of his master;
> And there another licking of his wound
> 'Gainst venomed sores the only sovereign plaster.
>   And here she meets another, sadly scowling,
>   To whom she speaks, and he replies with howling.
>
> When he hath ceased his ill-resounding noise,
> Another flap-mouthed mourner, black and grim,
> Against the welkin volleys out his voice.
> Another, and another, answers him.
>   Clapping their proud tails to the ground below,
>   Shaking their scratched ears, bleeding as they go.
>                    (*Venus and Adonis*, 868)

Again, such familiarity seems more congruent with a
nobleman than a businessman, although a different one from the
knights in *Gawain*, who simply exult in bagging the quarry.  De
Vere knew what it was to be to be hounded-- by creditors,
pirates, and the guards who threw him in the tower for the
Vavasour affair-- and to be wounded at bay by Anne's vengeful
relative:

As a bear, encompassed round with dogs,
Who having pinch'd a few and made them cry,
The rest stand all aloof and bark at him.
                    (Henry VI, Part 3, 2)


Charlton Ogburn writes: "Shakespeare lost his taste for
hunting early in manhood, I believe, as his sympathy went out to
the victim of the chase—

'the poor frightened deer that stands at gaze,
Wildly determining which way to fly,'

as does Lucrece. In *Venus and Adonis*, the action is altogether
stopped while we watch the 'purblind hare' and

Mark the poor wretch, to overshoot his troubles
How he outruns the winds, and with what care
He cranks and crosses with a thousand doubles
    The many musits through which he goes
    Are like a labyrinth to amaze his foes.

For five stanzas, I think the most moving in the poem, in a
digression on the flimsiest excuse, we follow the tiring quarry's
desperate evasions as feelingly and circumstantially set forth as
if the poet had been in its place."
        Coming from Venus right after she urges Adonis to chase
harmless instead of dangerous animals, Shakespeare's hare
description *is* an odd endorsement for the pleasure of "coursing"
hares. Ovid's Venus feels no empathy for hares. But then, as
her 400-line lament for him shows, Shakespeare's Venus doesn't
love Adonis just as a handsome young hunter:

To recreate himself when he hath sung
The tiger would be tame and gently hear him.
    If he had spoke, the wolf would leave his prey,
    And never fright the silly lamb that day.

(*Venus and Adonis*, 1095)

As Gary Wills observes, there is "nothing normal" in Shakespeare's poem. And the least normal thing about it is the way the boar kills Adonis:

> But this foul, grim, and urchin-snouted boar,
> Whose downward eye still looketh for a grave,
> N'er saw the beauteous livery that he wore:
> Witness the entertainment that he gave
>   If he did see his face, why then, I know
>   He thought to kiss him, and did kill him so.

> Tis true. 'tis true; thus was Adonis slain;
> he ran upon the boar with his sharp spear,
> Who did not whet his teeth at him again,
> But by a kiss thought to persuade him there,
>   And, nuzzling in his flank, the loving swine
>   Sheathed unaware the tusk in his soft groin.
>                    (*Venus and Adonis*, 1105)

Adonis's death is clearly symbolic. Although Hughes doesn't mention the boar's "kiss," he might have interpreted it as a final manifestation of Venus's baffled anger at Adonis's priggish resistance or, perhaps, as a sexual innuendo playfully directed at young Henry Wriothsley. Yet, as the descriptions show, it is a real boar as well as a symbol. Boars do carry their heads close to the ground, and their distance and depth perceptions are probably limited. In light of his evident sympathy for non-human life, Shakespeare's strange end to *Venus and Adonis* might be a gesture toward some reconciliation with "the real Eden, 'excellent as the first day'."

## Venus's Own Portrait

Regarding Edward de Vere as an animal rights advocate would be anachronistic, and Charlton Ogburn doesn't: "A tender-hearted sympathy for four-footed victims of man's cruelty, surely a rarity in Tudor times, combined with a total mistrust of popular rule and an abhorrence of the vulgar crowd is the mark of a man of privileged birth and upbringing. A feeling for our fellow creatures as such is a refinement not to be looked for among those whose experience is of the brutal necessities at the margin of existence in a primitive society."

Still, few of Edward's peers had such "refinement" either. Queen Elizabeth hunted compulsively and she liked to watch killing: Robert Dudley had thirteen bears baited for her at one fete. James I was even more addicted to slaughter. Shown the "lion pit" at the Tower of London, the newly installed king had three mastiffs thrown in so he could watch the big cats maul them. (After killing two of the dogs, the lions apparently got tired of it. They retreated into their den, and James's son, Prince Henry, had the survivor rescued.) Privileged callousness was by no means confined to the aristocracy. Conrad Gesner, the Alps-loving naturalist who praises bears' strength and courage in his *History of Four-Footed Beasts,* otherwise writes mainly of ways to kill them and use their carcasses. One critic describes Shakespeare's attitude as "unique among the dramatists of his time, for he shows a sympathy with and understanding of the animal's point of view and sufferings which no one else in his age approaches."

Montaigne was another exception to the general bloody-mindedness, however, one of the period's more sensitive if less consistent nobles. His long essay, "Apology for Raymond Sebond," starts as a defense of Catholicism but veers into many pages on non-human animals, maintaining that they think, feel, and dream like us and are in many ways our superiors, mentally as well as physically. He prefers paganism's zoomorphic gods to its anthropomorphic ones: "The things about which we are most ignorant are the most suitable to be deified: therefore, to make gods of ourselves as the ancients did goes beyond extreme weakness of judgment."

Most scholars think that Shakespeare read Montaigne. If "Raymond Seybond" encouraged *Venus and Adonis*'s empathy, however, that doesn't fit with the Stratfordian assumption that William read him in John Florio's 1603 translation. But De Vere could have encountered Montaigne in the 1580 French edition. "Apology for Raymond Seybond" would have attracted him given his Catholic leanings, and the essay's sudden turn into unconventional ideas about non-human animals could have affected an imaginative soul who, given his father's outdoor pursuits, had grown up in close contact with them.

Shakespeare goes beyond Montaigne, who, despite his intellectual sympathy for the non-human, still takes pervasive human callousness for granted, indeed, rationalizes it. In another essay, "Of Cruelty," Montaigne writes: "Nature, so I fear, has herself implanted in man some instinct of inhumanity." His own sympathy didn't stop him from hunting, and wild land *per se* didn't interest him. His Alps journal largely ignores native fauna and flora. Carried across Mont Cenis Pass in a litter, he merely remarks that it isn't as rugged as he'd heard. The towns on the other side are what interest him. Shakespeare's idea that wild animals deserve wild land doesn't occur to Montaigne: he considers land only for human use.

William's documented attitude to land was similarly utilitarian. Edward's was conflicted. He sold most of his estates to pay his debts. In a letter to Burghley soon after his release from the Tower, he wrote that Queen Elizabeth had heard he "meant to cut down all my woods especially about my house, which she did not so well like as if I should sell some land elsewhere…" But another letter to Burghley about his estates shows an early conservationist attitude: "The woods were preserved, the game cherished, the forests maintained in their full state." He persistently tried to reclaim forests that had belonged to his family. His last extant letter, to King James in 1604, thanks the king for restoring two forests to him and condemns past logging and poaching in them.

Such things show a feeling for wild flora and fauna as more than things to use. The other *Venus and Adonis* hare stanzas deepen an impression of almost supernormal empathy:

> Sometimes he runs among a flock of sheep
> To make the cunning hounds mistake their smell,
> And sometimes where earth-delving conies keep,
> To stop the loud pursuers in their yell;
>     And sometimes sorteth with a herd of deer.
>     Danger deviseth shifts; wit waits on fear.
>
> For there his smell with others being mingled,
> The hot scent-snuffing hounds are driven to doubt,
> Ceasing their clamorous cry till they have singled,
> With much ado, the cold fault cleanly out.
>     Then do they spend their mouths. Echo replies,
>     As if another chase were in the skies.
>
> By this, poor Wat, far upon a hill,
> Stands on his hind legs with list'ning ear,
> To hearken if his foes pursue him still.
> Anon their loud alarums does he hear
>     And now his grief may be compared well,
>     To one sore sick who hears the passing-bell.
>
> Then shalt thou see the dew-bedabbled wretch
> Turn and return, indenting with the way.
> Each envious briar his weary legs do scratch;
> Each shadow makes him stop, each murmur stay;
>     For misery is trodden on by many,
>     And, being low, never relieved by any."
>                 (*Venus and Adonis, 685*)

Hughes interprets *Venus and Adonis*'s hare even more abstractly than its stallion, however: "Shakespeare's sensitivity to the dream-lexicon of sexual myth contrasts this stallion (Venus's irresistible sexual appetite) with Venus's own portrait of the hare which she begs Adonis to hunt instead of the lethal boar. The hare, in all mythologies and in spontaneous dream life, is the mythic animal of the menstrual cycle, the self-sacrificial victim and divinity of the womb's cycle of reproduction, the moon's own magical love creature, in oestrus, passive, appealing. Here she is Venus's prophetic image of herself as she will be, a 'dew-bedabbled wretch' searching distractedly for the hunter whom her other self—her own rejected 'lust' who was a horse and is now a boar—has already killed."

Empathy with wildlife can seem pointless in the everyday world of guns, hounds, traps and road kills. Hughes's rejection, in his *Birthday Letters* poem "Epiphany," of an "orphaned-looking, woebegone as if with weeping" fox cub for sale on a London street is common sense. Describing hunted beasts, he tends to detachment. In "The Harvesting," another story written during his wildlife war with Plath, a man shooting game flushed by a mechanical reaper becomes a hare that he has shot-- but only at the moment of death. Hughes doesn't imagine the hare's suffering as Shakespeare does.

"Tarquin is by definition partly numbed," writes Hughes in *The Goddess*, "he must numb himself, to the inner life, the vast distress, of his victim; that, after all, is his crime." Shakespeare conveys Tarquin's numbness vividly, yet, as Ogburn says, he also has an extraordinary capacity for conveying the feelings of other beings. In the narrative poems, he is Adonis and Tarquin-- and Venus and Lucrece—and the horse and hare—and "a milch doe whose swelling dugs do ache, hasting to feed her fawn." He is even a snail:

.... whose tender horns being hit

Shrinks backward in his shelly cave with pain.
And there, all smothered up, in shade doth sit,
Long after fearing to creep forth again...
        (*Venus and Adonis*, 1033-36)

Hughes sees this empathy as part of a Great Shaman identity: "In fact, the tendency of the shamanic male to evince a strongly (often predominantly) female psychology, whether based on physical actuality (with strong female characteristics) or simply regular possession by a female 'spirit'—is so usual that all over the world societies have institutionalized it." But the androgyny repels him, especially in the *Sonnets*: "His love is of an altogether peculiar kind. He submits it quite nakedly to the caprice of this powerful, unpredictable, spoiled young aristocrat. He never makes the slightest attempt to shield it from hurt. Rather the opposite: he exposes it almost willfully to abuse, and embraces every pain... not masochistically, but as opportunities to reaffirm, in new sonnets, renewed love ...

"The only voices in our literature that truly resemble Shakespeare's in his sonnets are those of his own love-smitten heroines declaring their 'total, unconditional' love, ignoring any apparent change in their beloved, ready to immolate themselves on the subjective truth and loyalty of their love. That sort of thing on a stage, in the voice of heroic girl is one thing. But seriously meant, in real life, off the stage, by a grown man..."

*Venus and Adonis*'s empathy for the horse and the hare may seem girlish, sentimental. But the Tragic Equation starts from a goddess of *complete* being, of all life. Early religions were "fertility cults" in the dismissive conventional term, but that involves more than crops, livestock, and women. Hughes's abstracted interpretation fails to reanimate Shakespeare when he evades this empathy, which seems a necessary part of whatever is "complete being." Without it, a landscape isn't radiant. And Shakespeare's landscapes-- however briefly they are evoked, whatever weight of human drama they bear— have that empathic radiance, as with the poem I spent weeks on in freshman English:

That time of year, thou may'st in me behold
When yellow leaves, or none, or few, do hang
Upon those boughs which shake against the cold,
Bare ruined choirs where late the sweet birds sang…
(*Sonnets,* 73)

# Chapter Sixteen

# Woods and Heaths

---

Mythic incongruities between Hughes's Stratfordian assumptions and his Shakespeare interpretation carry over from the poems to the plays. *As You Like It*, his Tragic Equation "overture," is an example. Its wilderness setting and empathy for hunted animals are even more explicit, if less imaginatively realized, than *Venus and Adonis*'s.

Hughes acknowledges the setting's centrality to the play: "In the symbolic language of all literatures and traditions, the Mother Forest is the wilderness that guards the mouth of the other world (for better or worse)." Yet he becomes so involved in abstractions that he pays little attention to the play's allusions to actual wilderness as a setting for retreat and contemplation:

> And this our life exempt from public haunt
> Finds tongues in trees, books in the running brooks
> Sermons in stones, and good in everything."
> (2, 1)

## Two Forests

William is supposed to have derived the play from a novel, *Rosalind*, published by the ubiquitous Thomas Lodge in 1590. Like Greene's *Pandosto,* this is a typical early modern fiction, if a less lurid one. *Rosalind*'s "forest of Arden" is vaguely located near Bordeaux in central France, a generic setting for a courtly romance with more description of costumes than of land. *As You Like It* is clearly set in "the Forest of

Ardenne" in northern France, and that setting's role as a wilderness retreat from civilized evil is central to the plot. It is where Duke Senior, banished by a usurping brother, regrets killing deer, "native burghers of this desert city." *Rosalind*'s banished king doesn't care about wild animals, and Lodge's novel lacks the play's unique character, the melancholy Jacques, whose sympathy for them echoes Montaigne's. Both his essay, "Of Cruelty," and the play describe the "grievous spectacle" of a weeping stag at bay. As a courtier tells Duke Senior:

> Today my Lord of Amiens and myself
> Did steal behind him as he lay along
> Under an oak, whose antic roots peeps out
> Upon the brook that brawls beside the wood,
> To which place a sequestered stag
> That from the hunter's aim had ta'en a hurt
> Did come to languish...
> Thus most invectively he pierceth through
> The body of the country, city, court,
> Yea, and of this our life, swearing that we
> Are mere usurpers, tyrants, and what's worse,
> To fright the animals and to kill them up
> In their assigned and native dwelling place."
>                               (*As You Like It*, 2, 1)

Unlike the *Pandosto-Winter's Tale* story, the *Rosalind-As You Like It* one has a known historical source: a fourteenth century poem, *Gamelyn*, related to the Robin Hood ballads. But *Gamelyn* is set in England, *Rosalind* in France. Why would Lodge change the setting? An impecunious hack like Greene, he didn't get to know France until he went to medical school there in 1597, and there's nothing very Gallic about *Rosalind*: one main character is named "Saladyne." Lodge said he wrote the novel while serving on a 1586 naval expedition to the Canary Islands.

Another Shakespeare comedy, *Love's Labour's Lost*, is set in France (actually in Navarre, then a kingdom between France and Spain), and also concerns a group of scholarly nobles who retreat from the everyday world, although theirs is more a conventional semi-monastic retreat than the other play's forest one. Stratfordians think William wrote *Love's Labour's Lost* in 1593, almost a decade before *As You Like It*. But if Shakespeare already knew France, as an earlier play implies, why would he derive a later play from a writer like Lodge, who probably didn't know it?

Again, as with *The Winter's Tale*, I suspect the derivation went the other way, with Lodge working up a de Vere story partly derived from the old *Gamelyn*. *Rosalind* is subtitled *Euphue's Golden Legacy Found After His Death in His Cell Silexedra*, and it ends: "If you gather any fruits by this legacy, speak well of Euphues for writing it and me for fetching it." This sounds like a tacit admission of cashing in on something from Fisher's Folly, and the novel does seem a popularized version of the play. It has the fashionable entertainments without the abnormal theme of redemption through wild nature. Like Greene's *Pandosto*, *Rosalind* was more popular than its dramatic counterpart, going through many editions in the 1590s and early 1600s while the play stayed unpublished until the First Folio. *As You Like It*'s first definitely known performance was in the 1700s. But again, it is the play that lives. The voice of experience?

Hughes associates William with a "Forest of Arden" because it was "the name of his mother's family, whose eponymous link with the real English forest of the same name, Arden, was ancient and historic." But he doesn't say how it was ancient and historic, or acknowledge that the play is actually set in a French forest. He writes that "Shakespeare's source" had "Anglicized" Ardenne to Arden, but it is Lodge's "cunningly planted groves" that seem derivative of Shakespeare's "desert city" more than the other way around. As Michael Drayton writes in *Poly-Olbion*, a lengthy poem about British history and landscape, growing population had emptied the Warwickshire "forest" of wildlife and converted most of it to farmland by Elizabethan times:

> They oft dislodged the hart, and set their houses where
> He in his broom and brakes had long time made his lair…

Despite his anti-Puritanism, Hughes was highly conscious of the Old Testament's' influence on the British imagination and particularly on Shakespeare: "This relationship included a proprietary feeling for the land itself," he writes in *The Goddess*, "for its resonant complex of sacred locations. In England, this preoccupation was acute, and continued to grow more so, right into this century…" But he doesn't factor wilderness's prophetic Biblical role into this. Instead he invokes the Puritan tradition of building a City of God: "superimposing the dream-time of Biblical Israel on Britain's topography (and on the imagination of rural and industrial workers) with a dense plantation of chapels."

Hughes's own "proprietary feeling for the land" centered on fishing for Britain's charismatic salmon—finding "books in the running brooks." He acted on this by working to save Devon's rivers from pollution. Yet he tended to a kind of tunnel vision there too. Salmon conservation emphasizes protecting old growth forests along with streams because siltation from croplands, logging and roads destroys spawning habitat. I've seen no sign that Hughes supported organizations like "Trees for Life" that try to restore native British forest. He seems not to hear the play's exhortation to find "tongues in trees." Its Ardenne forest fades into "a dense plantation" of symbols.

## Queen of Beasts

Instead of interpreting the real forest's role in the play, Hughes tries to identify William with the melancholy Jacques through pages of complicated puns, and to connect the play with the Tragic Equation via an exposition of its "ritual drama." The heroine, Rosalind, is a Venus-Lucrece as she dresses as a boy and flees to the forest to escape the wrath of Duke's Senior's usurping brother. The hero, Orlando, is an Adonis-Tarquin as he flees there to escape his own usurping brother and encounters cross-dressing Rosalind, but fails to recognize her, even scorns her, although he has already fallen in love with her undisguised self. Yet, alluding to abstractions from alchemy to psychoanalysis, Hughes makes it hard to follow. And his attempt to link the melancholy Jacques to William is particularly confusing:

"Jacques presents himself as one oppressed by the spectacle of the grisly antics of humanity. He seems to have withdrawn into the forest for a purpose. He asks leave to

Speak my mind, and I will through and through
Cleanse the foul body of the infected world.
(2, 7)

and makes it clear that his reclusive contemplation of the forest—without any hint of self-deception or bitterness—is a serious business, and a preliminary, a preparation, for something else…And Jacques is Shakespeare himself, thirty-five years old, *nel mezzo del camin*, awake in the depths of the Mother Forest, about to enter (there is even a lion!) his *Divina Comedia*."

Hughes equates the play's "preparation" for the Tragic Equation with Dante's prelude to his *Divine Comedy*. But while a forest figures in both, the poets' feelings are opposite. Dante's forest is a dark, nasty symbol of his mid-life crisis: he just wants to get out. The lion he meets tries to keep him from climbing to the light, where his guiding spirit awaits. Shakespeare's forest is real and he *likes* it: it's radiant to him. It's not a symbol of a spiritual state: it is "the thing itself." Its exotic lion is not a symbol of earthly bondage but of earthly reconciliation between the hero, Orlando, and his repentant usurper brother, Oliver, who wanders into the forest, falls asleep, and attracts the predator. Orlando passes by, is tempted to leave Oliver to his fate, but decides to save him.

The hero of Lodge's *Rosalind* also rescues his usurping brother from a lion, but it's a formulaic "king of beasts" that he conventionally conquers: "Rosader suddenly charged him with a boar spear and wounded the lion very sore at first stroke. The beast, feeling himself to have a mortal hurt, leapt at Rosader and with his paws gave him a sore pinch on the breast that he had almost fallen yet... he recovered himself and slew the lion, who at his death roared..."

*As You Like It* stands the "king of beasts" convention on its head:

> A lioness, with udders all drawn dry,
> Lay couching, head on ground, with catlike watch
> When the sleeping man should stir...
>    (4,3)

Shakespeare brings empathy to a man-eating predator: she's a nursing mother. He doesn't describe the fight in Lodge's he-man terms, just writes that she "quickly fell before him." If there is an echo of Dante here, it is not the one Hughes hears. In *The Inferno*'s "wilderness, savage, brute, harsh, and wild," Dante feels most threatened not by the lion but by a she-wolf that is "gaunt yet gorged on every kind of craving." She sounds as though, like the lioness, she is nursing cubs but Dante doesn't consider that. He says she has "blighted many a life" with her insatiable hunger and must be hounded from every town until she is extinct. She seems to symbolize female lust. If Shakespeare is echoing *The Inferno*, he conflates its lion and she-wolf into a symbol not of lust but of fertility, something also dangerously hungry, but creative.

Hughes implies that the melancholy Jacques's "reclusive self-contemplation in the forest" is a preparation for a Dante-like ascent into a higher realm. But Jacques is not contemplating

himself so much as the ills of society. His vocation is not the
Christian one of rising above earthly life, but the shamanic one
of healing earthly life through performance of a quest vision:

> O worthy fool! —one who hath been a courtier...
>                     And in his brain
> Which is as dry as the remainder biscuit
> After a voyage, he hath strange places crammed
> With observation, the which he vents
> In mangled forms.  O that I were a fool
> I am ambitious for a motley coat...
>
> Invest me in my motley.  Give me leave
> To speak my mind, and I will through and through
> Cleanse the foul body of th'infected world
> If they will patiently receive my medicine.
>                     (2,7)

Perhaps Edward de Vere, a former courtier and aspiring
performer, saw the Ardenne as wild animals' "assigned and
native dwelling place" while traveling from France to Germany
in 1575, newly if temporarily free of England's Cecils and
Dudleys: "usurpers, tyrants, and what's worse." He may have
said so in an early poem:

> Nature thought good,
> Fortune should ever dwell
> In court, where wits excel,
> Love keep the wood.
>
> So to the wood went I
> With love to live and lie,
> Fortune's forlorn.
>                     ("Fortune and Love")

## The Guest of Summer

"Shakespeare, we often feel, had a skin too few," writes Hugh Trevor Roper, "whatever he saw he felt, and he felt it far more intensely than most of his contemporaries. This too we can see in his love of nature... His sympathies are always with 'the poor hunted deer,' the trapped bird, the over driven horse, the baited bear... How did this sensitive creature, this delicate, aristocratic character so acutely aware of the pleasures and pains, the comedy and tragedy of life, himself survive the rough-and-tumble of the Elizabethan age? The answer is, I think, that he did not survive it intact... The exquisite poet of Arcadia became the greatest tragic poet of the modern world."

Yet the tragedies wouldn't be what they are without an Arcadian resonance: their evocations of flora, fauna, landscape, and weather help keep them alive. Shakespeare's feeling for wild nature offsets horrors that could otherwise be deadly monotonous, as when Banquo's observation of nesting birds on arriving at Macbeth's castle evokes a primal innocence beyond the play's sophisticated brutalities:

> The guest of summer
> The temple haunting martlet, does approve
> By his loved masonry that the heavens' breath
> Smells wooingly here. No jutty, frieze.
> Buttress, or coign of vantage but this bird
> Hath made his pendant bed and procreant cradle;
> Where they most breed and haunt I have observed
> The air is delicate."
> (1,6)

Banquo's speech vividly distinguishes these "guests" that come from some "draughty, radiant Paradise" unknown to philosophy in Shakespeare's time and the everyday world's grimly subdued "blasted heaths." That grimness is part of Macbeth and Lear's oppressive characters, and it helps to destroy them: there is finally no shelter for them in the deforested lands they rule. Lear's flight into the moors after deceitful Goneril and Regan drive him from their castles is an attempt at escape into nature that becomes a punishment because he has rejected nature in the form of his truthful daughter, Cordelia. As Duke Senior says of the Ardenne's "desert city": "this is no flattery." Nature doesn't lie. Even Birnam Wood's deceptive advance on Macbeth's castle is an ironic vindication of natural honesty.

Another natural deception injects a glimpse of innocence into the putrid miasmas of *King Lear*'s last acts. To heal the cruelly blinded Earl of Gloucester's despair, his legitimate son Edgar, who, disguised as a madman, has spent the previous scenes raving to Lear about demons and decay, paints a radiant word-picture of the white cliffs of Dover:

> The crows and choughs that wing the midway air
> Show scarce so gross as beetles. Halfway down
> Hangs one that gathers samphire, dreadful trade!
> Methinks he seems no bigger than his head.
> The fishermen that walk upon the beach
> Appear like mice, and yon tall anchoring barque
> Diminished to her cock, her cock a buoy
> Almost too small for sight. The murmuring surge
> That on th'unnumbered idle pebble chafes,
> Cannot be heard so high…

Scary as the cliffs' natural dangers are, they seem downright reassuring after the man-made horrors that preceded them. When Edgar tricks his father into ending his despair by jumping off, sightless Gloucester's imaginary fall becomes a source of regeneration. "Thy life's a miracle," cries Edgar, "speak yet again." Gloucester replies: "Henceforth I'll bear out affliction 'til it do cry out itself 'Enough, enough,' and die." As Northrop Frye says: "Nature is associated not with the credible, but with the incredible." Art—a made-up forest, an envisioned sea cliff—becomes a way not of replacing nature with a "higher" reality, but of bringing wild vitality back to a deadly everyday world.

There's certainly an element of shamanic practice in all this, of vision and performance directed to healing. Hughes sees it. "[A] crowned child with a tree in its hand... tells Macbeth that he is safe until 'Great Birnam Wood to high Dunsinane hill/Shall come against him'... Appearing here, like a blazing sign out of the storm that Macbeth invoked as the scene opened... it is the equivalent of the lightnings on the heath in *King Lear* compelling the hero to atone." Yet, again, his interpretation leads abstractedly into a "dense plantation" of symbols: "In this image, the Tragic Equation, on the mythic plane, has delivered its third and final fiat. The Divine Child Adonis is born from a tree, Osiris is resurrected from a tree, Attis and Christ are sacrificed on trees: the tree is the Goddess..."

Perhaps *Macbeth* and *King Lear*'s everyday world landscapes were too like the West Yorkshire moors at the heart of Hughes's own conflicted feelings. Despite the blasted heaths' active parts in the dramas, he doesn't try to link William to them as he does with "the Forest of Arden." And it would have been hard to link them. Stratfordians conjecture William's memories of Warwickshire house martins as the "guest of summer's source," but that doesn't account for the telling contrast between the nesting birds and the grim northern landscape. They can't associate the *King Lear* choughs with Stratford, since that corvid species inhabits sea cliffs and mountains.

There's no record that William saw Scotland or Dover, but there is that Edward did as he hurtled toward destruction on his "runaway bus." Banquo's "temple haunting martlet" could be a memory of Scottish border castles during the burnings and hangings of Elizabeth's notoriously ruthless 1570 campaign against Catholic rebels. Dover's "murmuring surge" could be a memory of stepping ashore after Dutch pirates had taken his belongings, threatened his life, and stripped him to his shirt.

## Reverted Inversions

As I've said, Shakespeare inverts the medieval convention—still found in his "early tragedy" *Titus Andronicus*—of wilderness as a realm of death and evil that civilization must redeem. In *Titus*, Tamora and her sons emerge from the northern forests like Grendel and his Mother to gruesomely menace Rome (although Rome is pretty gruesome too). But in *Macbeth*, Birnam Wood emerges from the moors to redeem gruesome Dunsinane Castle: artifice used to bring wild vitality back into a deathly everyday world.

Hughes sometimes re-inverts this inversion, as though it doesn't fit his Dante-like William. In the "late romance," *Cymbeline*, the villain, Cloten, comes to the Welsh Mountains from his evil Queen mother's palace to menace the heroine, Imogen, and it is the "wild men" of the mountains who save her by beheading him. In fact, they are her "lost" brothers. But Hughes emphasizes Cloten's bestiality as a Tarquin Boar: "the most regressive, merely brutish Boar figure that Shakespeare has created so far in the sequence." He doesn't notice that it is the wilderness that destroys Cloten.

Hughes's interpretation of the "late tragedy," *Timon of Athens*, with its proto-Darwinian catalogue of animal competition, is an extreme re-inversion. Based on a semi-legendary figure in classical literature, Timon is a rich Greek nobleman who lavishes his wealth on so-called friends but finds them stingy when it is all spent and he asks for help. Enraged, he treats them to a last "feast" of stones and hot water, then tears off his clothes and flees to a forest cave:

> Nothing I'll bear from thee
> But nakedness, thou detestable town;
> Take thou that too, with multiplying bans.
> Timon will to the woods, where he shall find
> Th'unkindest beast more kinder than mankind.

(*Timon of Athens,* 4, 1)

Digging for roots to eat, he finds gold, which draws back his erstwhile friends, including a poet and painter as well as businessmen and politicians. But Timon is through with them. He tells some senators:

> I have a tree that grows here in my close
> That mine own use invites me to cut down,
> And shortly must I fell it. Tell my friends,
> Tell Athens, in the sequence of degree
> From high to low throughout, that whoso please
> To stop affliction, let him take his haste,
> Come hither ere my tree hath felt the axe,
> And hang himself.
>                                (5, 2)

Retreat to the wilderness doesn't save Timon as it does the romances' protagonists. Although, like the Melancholy Jacques, he sees civilization's failures, he doesn't try to bring his vision back to the human world, to "perform" it as the romances' redemptive characters do. So he is tragic and he dies, perhaps a suicide as his valedictory speech implies, and lies buried by the seashore.

It's not much of a "ritual drama" by Hughes's standards. Dancing girls and prostitutes are the only female characters. He tries to fit it into his algebra by positing Athens as a Great Goddess symbol so that Timon is Adonis when he's her wealthy citizen and Tarquin when he rejects her. But why, according to the Tragic Equation sequence, would William write it right after the tentatively redemptive *King Lear*? Hughes equivocates:

"What prompted him, at the very height of his powers, to commit himself to a subject that proved so refractory? Some have supposed a conflict of motives. His wish to write another play, according to the rule that he had not broken in fifteen years, was somehow requisitioned, they suggest, by his private need to deliver a curse against mankind in general, and against 'the city' in particular. Perhaps the theme touched the traumatic public humiliation of his adolescence—his father's bankruptcy."

Stratfordians think William wrote *Timon of Athens* around 1604-06, borrowing from Plutarch and a later Greek satirist, Lucian, but I don't see why someone who wrote for money would have bothered. It is certainly not a "stirring melodrama." It was only published in the First Folio, no record of a contemporary commercial performance exists, and it inspired no popular novels. Hughes acknowledges its lack of commercial appeal: "After three acts of preparation, his Jeremiad bursts the dam, overwhelms the dramatic controls or concerns, and simply floods the audience, for the rest of the play, with execrations so vehement that there is nothing like it in the language."

But he tries hard to fit his Dante-like hack professional William into his ten-page analysis of the play. In the process, he reverses the conflict between Puritan utilitarianism and "the draughty, radiant Paradise of the animals" that he poses in his 1970 essay. Wild animals suddenly take the blame for "the last nightmare of mental disintegration and spiritual emptiness":

"When Timon searches the hearts of his friends for anything resembling the Divine Love, for any human substitute, this ideology is what confronts him—the *apelike* pursuit of a mankind whose heart is, as the proverb says, where the purse is, a mankind that has lost, in fact, the Goddess, and is plunging toward the heartless *monkeyland* of Swift and Pope, and beyond them towards *The Waste Land* and the dustbins of Beckett's *refuse-eating hominids*. Timon's volcanic eruption, in these terms, is the fountainhead of the desert of black cinders which now covers the inheritance of secular man and his works... His madness can only hurl itself against the whole of Athens, the polis of Great Goddess as the Goddess of Wisdom, now populated, in his eyes, by a kind of *baboon*." [Italics mine]

A Boar's Breakfast

Would a man who just ran away to the woods rail against wild anthropoids? In fact, Timon says nothing about non-human primates. The play has a devolutionary slur against them: "The strain of man's bred out into baboons and monkeys." (1,1) But it is voiced by a cynic philosopher, Apemantus, with whom Timon argues as to whose hatred of civilization is more justified: Apemantus's, because it has never pampered him, or Timon's because it has. Timon does liken his erstwhile friends to "affable wolves, meek bears" just before delivering the play's catalogue of beastly competition: "If thou were the lion, the fox would beguilc thee…" But he later speaks surprisingly well of "the lower animals" for the sixteenth century:

> Common mother—thou
> Whose womb immeasurable and infinite breast
> Teems and feeds all, whose selfsame mettle
> Whereof thy proud child, arrogant man, is puffed
> Engenders the black toad and adder blue,
> The gilded newt and eyeless venomed worm,
> With all th'abborred births below crisp heaven
> Whereupon Hyperion's quick'ning fire doth shine—
> Yield him who all thy human sons do hate
> From forth they plenteous bosom, one poor root.
> Ensear thy fertile and conceptious womb;
> Let it no more bring out ingrateful man.
> Go great with tigers, dragons, wolves and bears;
> Teem with new monsters whom thy upward face
> Hath to the marbled mansion all above
> Never presented.
> (4, 3)

Timon sounds like Thoreau in "Walking": "Here is this vast, savage, howling mother of ours, Nature, lying all around, with such beauty, and such affection for her children, as the leopard; and yet we are so early weaned from her breast to society, to that culture which is exclusively an interaction of man on man—a sort of breeding in and in, which produces at most a merely English nobility, a civilization destined to have a speedy limit."

When thieves come to Timon's cave and ask for gold, describing themselves as "men that much do want," he offers them a boar's breakfast instead:

> Your greatest want is, you want much of meat.
> What should you want?  Behold, the earth hath roots.
> Within this mile break forth a hundred springs.
> The oaks bear mast, the briars scarlet hips.
> The bounteous housewife nature on each bush
> Lays her full mess before you. Want? Why want?
> (4,3)

The thieves insist: "We cannot live on grass, on berries, water, as beasts and birds and fishes."
"Nor on the beasts themselves, the birds and fishes;" Timon replies: "you must eat men."  Then, speaking in surprisingly ecological terms, he gives them gold for precisely that reason, because as outlaws to civilization they are akin to nature, which neither buys nor sells:

> Do villainy; do, since you protest to do't,
> Like workmen. I'll example you with thievery.
> The sun's a thief, and with his great attraction
> Robs the vast sea. The moon's an arrant thief,
> And her pale fire she snatches from the sun.
> The sea's a thief, whose liquid surge resolves
> The moon into salt tears. The earth's a thief.
> That feeds and breeds by a composture stol'n
> From gen'ral excrement.
> (4, 3)

## The Old Common Man

Timon curses and assaults everyone else who comes to his cave except a   banished knight, Alcibiades, to whom he gives gold to make war on Athens, two whores to whom he gives gold to spread venereal disease in Athens, and his servant Flavius, who stayed faithful when Timon couldn't pay him and still doesn't want a golden handshake:

> It almost turns my dangerous nature mild.
> Let me behold thy face.  Surely this man
> Was born of woman.
> Forgive my general and exceptionless rashness,
> You perpetual sober gods!  I do proclaim
> One honest man—mistake me not, but one,
> No more, I pray--And he's a steward.
>                 (4, 3)

Timon's classical sources don't have him fleeing to the woods and railing about wildlife: the longest version, Lucian's, just describes him working as a field hand after he loses his money.  The forest retreat points to de Vere.  Oxfordians cite the existence of an "interlude," *The History of a Solitary Knight*, performed at court in 1577, and an anonymous 1585 manuscript of a play called *Timon*, conjecturing that they are earlier versions of the Folio's play.  It's not hard to see how the story would have appealed to Edward.  Timon lived during the Peloponnesian Wars, when the once self-sufficient feudal state of Athens had become a greedy mercantile empire and suffered the consequences in various disasters. His disgust with his business associates and his respect for a knight and a loyal steward place him in the old nobility.

 Timon's attitude is typical of the canon, which is less about the rise of the new common man represented by the play's politicians, artisans, and businessmen than about the fall of what might be called the old common man.  The feudal aristocracy's way of life was a vestige of the way all humans once lived: foraging and defending territory, having intimate relation with wild as well as tame fauna and flora. It was a decayed, parasitic vestige, Thoreau's "merely English nobility," but it had its version of justice. John Aubrey grudgingly, and fancifully, writes that, with its "Forests, Chases, and Parkes," the old nobility treated wildlife "as if they had been naturaliz'd, enfranchised, and Citizens of our Commonwealth."

Timon's appeal to "bounteous housewife" nature sounds like young de Vere in his early alliterative poem, "Loss of Good Name," which protests an older stepsister's attempt to disinherit him by declaring him illegitimate:

> Help man, help beasts, help birds and worms, that on the earth do toil,
> Help fish, help fowl, that flock upon the salt sea soil,
> Help echo that in air doth flee, shrill voices to resound,
> To wail this loss of my good name, as of these griefs the ground.

De Vere also comes to mind when Rosalind says to the melancholy Jacques: "I fear you have sold your own lands to see other men's." Many Shakespeare protagonists throw away land, wealth, and status as he did. Even their occasional success entails renunciation, as with Prospero's breaking his staff and drowning his book:

> To the dread rattling thunder
> Have I given fire, and rifted Jove's stout oak
> With his own bolt; the strong based promontory
> Have I made shake, and by the spurs plucked up
> The pine and cedar; graves at my command
> Have waked their sleepers, ope'd, and let 'em forth
> By my so potent art. But this rough magic
> I here abjure... (*The Tempest*, 5, 1)

# Chapter Seventeen

## A Powerful and Splendid Enchanter

---

In his final chapter, "The Dismantling of the Tragic Equation," Hughes acknowledges *Shakespeare and the Goddess*'s ethereal, pedantic side, although he blames it more on his Dante-like William than on his own penchant for abstraction: "As I have followed it, the Equation develops step by step from the two long poems to the mutation of *King Lear*, and from there, step by step, to the full Theophany [divine revelation] of *The Winter's Tale*, where it arrives at a kind of completeness. In that completeness, however, the redemption of the tragic crime is lifted right off the Earth."

But he proposes to do something about that, or to show Shakespeare doing something about it: "In *The Tempest*, Shakespeare makes the great, final necessary adjustment: he anchors his Theophany back to the Earth. And in doing so, in bringing his work to an end in this way, he finds himself facing the beginning."

I think it is Hughes more than Shakespeare who lifts *The Winter's Tale* "right off the earth" with his interpretation. He does consider that play's natural features—storm, bear, flowers-- at more length than with the tragedies. It would have been hard for him not to, since they are so vital to the plot. Yet, again, he considers them more as symbols than as a living context for the drama, and he doesn't try to link William to them except in a Dante-like way. His interpretation of the bear scene that W.H. Auden calls "the most beautiful" in Shakespeare is clearer than

Auden's, but a "dense plantation" of allusions still threatens to obscure the sacred horror:

"Leontes's atonement, as I mentioned, begins with the distant thunderclap of the Oracle, but the authentic storm centre puts the new-born Perdita into the hands of the shepherds, as the ship that carries her is wrecked.

"'O the most piteous cry of the poor souls! Sometimes to see 'em, and not to see 'em; now the ship boring the moon with her mainmast, and anon swallowed with yeast and froth, as you'd thrust a cork into a hogshead.' (4,3)

"It is intriguing to see how this marvelous shot has cannibalized various signs and sigils for his tempest. The mainmast boring the moon is a throwaway hyperbole—casual speech—yet it fits into the tragic myth like a three-point plug: it is the maddened hero's (the tossed ship's) assault on his Sacred Bride—on the Lucrece or Diana aspect of the Goddess, for which, throughout Shakespeare, the moon is the first title. The cork thrust into the hogshead is a comic reminiscence of Clarence/Adonis going head first into the butt of Malmsey. As if that were not specific enough, suddenly, in the very next sentence, a bear (almost a boar, and in fact associated with the earliest Great Goddess at Delphi. The appropriate alternative form of the boar for the play) plunges across the scene to tear out the shoulder bone of Perdita's guardian..."

## A Windy Island

*The Goddess* starts to get less confusing when it reaches *The Tempest*: it gets more like Hughes's first hundred pages on Shakespeare as a shamanic personality. There is plenty of symbolic allusion, but the story and characters seem more concrete, more alive, than with the "earlier" plays. A reason for this, I think, is that the play's bizarre setting is harder for Hughes to pass over than the forests, seacoasts, mountains, and moors of the other plays. Prospero's island is uniquely a place of sacred horror, what Hughes calls "the rocky, storm-beaten island of a terrible dead witch and her devil-god."

It may be more unique than anyone had thought. In *The Shakespeare Guide to Italy*, Richard Roe proposes that it is based not on the traditional Stratfordian version of a borrowed description of Bermuda, but on experience of a volcanic islet off Sicily's northwest coast. Part of a group called the "windy islands" for their frequent storms, the islet, "Vulcano," has many lava caves, including huge sea caves like the one wherein Ariel hides the King of Naples' ship, and smaller land ones like Prospero's "cell." It has Mediterranean flora and fauna like the "sharp furzes," "pricking gorse," and hedgehogs or "urchins" with which Ariel torments Caliban. In addition, Roe thinks the play's "yellow sands," "filthy mantled pool" and "foul lake" refer to the island's active volcanic features—shoreline sulfur deposits and smelly hot springs inland. He thinks the strange noises to which the characters refer also have volcanic origins.

Hughes didn't know of Roe's idea, but the play's imagery seems to have struck a similar chord with him. He doesn't even mention the traditional Bermuda version of the island. His sense of its setting is earthier than his Stratfordian "forest of Arden." It is the "rocky, storm-beaten" crux to the Tragic Equation, a chthonically transformative place, like Yellowstone. (His fellow poet, Seamus Heaney, likened *Birthday Letters* to a "volcanic island" in the "geology of imagination.")

As I quoted earlier, Hughes writes that *The Tempest* "invokes the Boar—Caliban—to meet its match in the magically invulnerable Prospero, and to be not only stopped in mid-charge, not only arrested, as I said, in mid-air, but *sublimated* into its transcendent form." But he doesn't see this "transcendence" as Prospero "rising above" his wild animal Caliban self in a Dante-like way. Although Caliban is a bestial grotesque, Hughes finds him a surprisingly sympathetic one. Indeed, Caliban seems a *re-inverted* version of the "refuse eating hominids" in his *Timon of Athens* interpretation. Instead of representing the "last nightmare of mental disintegration and spiritual emptiness" that Timon rejects, Caliban represents Timon.

Like Timon after his flight to the woods, Caliban greets strangers—first Prospero and Miranda, then, many years later, the King of Naples' low life servants, Trinculo and Stefano-- by offering them a boar's breakfast:

> I'll show thee the best springs; I'll pluck thee berries...
> I prithee, let me bring thee where crabs grow,
> And I with my long nails will dig thee pig-nuts,
> Show thee a jay's nest...
> > Wilt thou go with me?
> > (2, 2)

Like Timon, Caliban faces urbane men who are not interested in his subsistence offerings but in wealth and status. The King of Naples' servants are comically crass about it, but even lofty Prospero slights Caliban's generosity in favor of his own self-aggrandizing agenda. Driven from Milan by his usurper brother, he becomes a usurper: he treats Caliban as European colonists did Native Americans. He exploits his astonished belief that he is a spirit and regales him with liquor — "water with berries in't." Then, when Caliban manifests "savagery" by fancying his beautiful daughter Miranda, in effect, manifesting humanity, Prospero afflicts him with "agues," and enslaves him. When Caliban rebels, Prospero takes it as further evidence of savagery and carries on like Simon Legree:

> Hag-seed hence!
> Fetch us in fuel. And be quick, thou'rt best,
> To answer other business—Shrug'st thou, malice?
> If thou neglectest or dost unwillingly
> What I command, I'll rack thee with old cramps,
> Fill all thy bones with aches, make thee roar
> That beasts shall tremble at thy din.
> > (1, 2)

Yet, Hughes observes, Prospero's imprecations are not just a slave driver's curses. They are an acknowledgement of Caliban's mythic nature and of its relationship to himself: "Prospero calls him up, out of his cave, with three abusive terms: 'thou earth, thou," 'thou tortoise,' and 'thou poisonous slave, got by the Evil himself/Upon thy wicked dam.' This little impressionistic sketch conjures up a venomous kind of primeval reptile only just poking out of its egg—its shell—which is the Earth itself. The tortoise as the symbol of the Earth, or supporter of the Earth, a snake-headed, snake-skinned creature, in fact a snake with legs, recurs wherever there are tortoises. And so when Prospero sees this creature in Caliban, he sees him as the primal child of Earth's creatress and her consort—regarded as demons. In other words, he sees him purely and simply as the child of the rejected Goddess."

"In every play, each one dramatic just to the degree that the struggle is intense, Prospero-- as one form or another of Adonis—has fought to make sense of this monstrously difficult being whom he now, in this grand denouement to the tragic sequence, acknowledges to be his own, something in himself. Just as Alonso, Antonio, and Sebastian are brought to admit and face their crime, Prospero has been brought to confess *Caliban*, the protagonist of all the crimes."

Prospero's "transcendence" of the Caliban-Boar is an accretive incorporation of him instead of a progressive rising above him. The Boar stops being a demonized beast and becomes a person. "In spite of Prospero's triumphant restoration of civilized behavior, Caliban remains the real figure, the attractive and even fascinating bearer of the life of the play, and of uncontainable life itself. This creature who was ready to love Prospero as much as he lusted for Miranda, and for whom the heavens open (and who weeps when they close), and who speaks the poetry of the natural world, possesses a sensibility and a nature that makes his master's seem stale and sour":

Be not afeard.  The isle is full of noises,
Sounds, and sweet airs, that give delight and hurt
                                                    not.
Sometimes a thousand twangling instruments
Will hum upon mine ears, and sometimes voices
That if I had then waked after long sleep
Will make me sleep again; and then in dreaming
The clouds methought would open and show riches
Ready to drop upon me, that when I waked
I cried to dream again.

                                    (*The Tempest* 3, 2)

Hughes's sense of Caliban's transformation seems to express a change in his own feelings.  As the powerful and splendid enchanter "confesses" his kinship with Caliban, Hughes ultimately "confessed" to the "girlish" empathy for non-human life that he resisted in his wildlife war with Plath.  In a letter to Keith Sagar, who challenged his 1997 article in defense of hunting to hounds, he wrote: "I've known for some years what a hunted deer goes through physically.  And a hunted fox.  And a fish being caught, for that matter.  For years I've kept having an idea that I daren't quite formulate: why aren't wild animals simply given the legal status of fellow citizens?"

## A Hopeful Monster

As I've said, Caliban's appearance in Shakespeare signals a dawning awareness of the ethnological implications that would revolutionize literary attitudes to nature. Caliban implies that originally wild humans somehow developed into civilized ones, the implication that leads to the idea of evolution with its further implication that wild humans developed from other wild animals-- apes. He may arise partly from the devil's spawn wild men of medieval wilderness, but he is a mindful being, as he shows at the play's end:

I'll be wise hereafter,
And seek for grace.  What a thrice-double ass
Was I to take this drunkard for a god,
And worship this dull fool!
          (5, 1)

Prospero returns to Milan to meditate on his impending death.  Caliban's fate is not clear.  Prospero dismisses him at the play's end after releasing him and the loutish servants from enchantment.  Some critics think he takes him back to Italy as a servant, but Caliban is under no obligation now that Prospero has renounced his powers.  When Caliban says he'll "seek for grace" it seems unlikely that he'll seek it from the domineering Duke. He knows how to live on the island: he probably just stays, glad to be left in peace.

All things in common, nature would produce
Without sweat or endeavor.  Treason, felony,
Sword, pike, knife, gun, or need of any engine,
Would I not have; but nature would bring forth
Of its own kind all foisson, all abundance...
          (*The Tempest*, 2, 1)

It is not lowbrow Caliban who voices these ideals, but Gonzalo, "an honest old counseller" in King Alonso's retinue, echoing Montaigne's wishful praise of Brazilian "noble savages" in his essay "On Cannibals."  Such a golden age was an old convention, as Montaigne acknowledges: "'All things,' writes Plato, 'are produced either by nature, or by chance, or by art; the greatest and most beautiful are by one or other of the first two; the least by the last.'"  Yet, as in his narrative poems, Shakespeare's version of convention becomes strange.

Caliban is not a newly discovered member of a traditional indigenous society, and certainly not a noble savage.  He is more like one of the "new monsters" that Timon of Athens asks nature to spawn in his diatribe against "ingrateful man," what evolutionists call a "hopeful" monster, a sudden adaptive mutation. Although the *dramatis persona* calls him "a savage and deformed native," the play itself gives only the other characters' confused versions of him. To Prospero he is tortoise-like, to Miranda, "most brutish," to drunken sailors, fish-like or four-legged. He seems unfinished —as with the old belief that bears mouth their young into shape after birth.

> Like to a chaos, or an unlicked bear whelp
> That carries no impression like the dam...
> Seeking a way and straying from the way,
> Not knowing how to find the open air,
> But toiling desperately to find it out...
> (*The True Tragedy of Richard, Duke of York*, 3, 3)

There's no question of re-establishing a conventional golden age on the island. Miranda and Ferdinand's union may solve the Tragic Equation, but it's temporary: they too will return to the Renaissance Italy that, despite its splendors, de Vere doubted during his tour. Equations can have final solutions, not life. Caliban is the only character in the play whose future seems undecided or who learns much that is new-- to use human language, to beware of civilized promises, and to "seek for grace." To the extent that there is a "brave new world" on *The Tempest*'s island, Caliban seems to be it, although there's no hint as to what "it" might be. He has no mate (Miranda might have missed something) and prophecy has its limits.

## A Single Titanic Work

Again, it is easier to see Edward de Vere in all this than William. Edward probably sailed from Sicily back to Italy past the Windward Isles, and phenomena like Vulcano certainly interested him. What better setting for a drama about a wild man monster? And although Shakespeare clearly has positive feelings about Caliban on his forward-looking, natural philosophy side, he also has negative ones on his backward-looking, medieval side. Caliban has "sensibility" but he plots with the low life servants to kill Prospero.

The conflict is typical of de Vere. Growing up in the feudal world where human origins were not from "below" via beasts and wild men, but from "above" via divinely appointed kings, Edward had an innate sense of lofty entitlement. Yet that made him prey not only to a false protector like Robert Dudley and a false agent like Michael Lok, but to a false servant like a factotum, Rowland Yorke, who fed his suspicions about his wife's chastity during his continental tour. Oxfordians see Yorke as a model for *Othello*'s Iago.

De Vere was trapped in a socioeconomic Tragic Equation as well as a psychosexual one. Pampered scion of crumbling feudalism, he lacked the crafty ruthlessness that had always maintained it and that upstarts like Dudley used to exploit the remnants. He rebelled against both the system and its collapse in his flights, conspiracies and feuds but he had no real power except, imaginatively, in his role as an upscale court jester, a stage wild man, a Timon or Caliban. Hughes describes the humiliation of it aptly: "capering about in a public arena (on a stage!) to a drum (a jig!), not in a goatskin, like the forerunners of the Greek tragedians, but in the bristly pelt of that holiest of Celtic and Anglo-Saxon beasts—the wild boar."

Hughes is referring to William, but if he was originally a "strolling player" as Stratfordians think, it would not have been such a humiliation for him. They cite the melancholy Jacques' "all the world's a stage" speech, Shakespeare's most quoted, as proof that its author was a professional actor. Yet its cynical sentiments seem more like disillusioned Edward's than practical William's. And although it's not documented, an aspect of de Vere's disrepute may have been that he acted in his plays as well as presenting them at court:

> Alas, 'tis true, I have gone here and there
> And made myself a motley to the view…

(*Sonnets,* 110)

Shakespeare writes from a heraldic world that is collapsing, where England's Lord Great Chamberlain could end up "capering on a stage," and he intuits that this collapse will lead not to More's *Utopia* or Bacon's *New Atlantis*, but perhaps back-- via a Valley of Death-- to some distant new beginning. Prospero's farewell is that of a man who sees nothing ahead for his civilization:

> Our revels now are ended.  These our actors,
> As I foretold you, were all spirits, and
> Are melted into air, into thin air;
> And like the baseless fabric of this vision.
> The cloud-capped towers, the gorgeous palaces,
> The solemn temples, the great globe itself,
> Yea, all which it inherit, shall dissolve;
> And, like this insubstantial pageant faded,
> Leave not a rack behind.
> (4, 1)

*The Tempest* doesn't celebrate Caliban's release from bondage as it does Ariel's, but like Hughes I find it more interesting.  Maybe it's not really the canon's progressive new common man overlay that still excites people after four centuries, but an accretive old common man core.  What distinguishes the TV series, *Slings and Arrows,* may be that it shows how audiences respond to the biological "root meaning" of the canon more than to what Hughes calls the "funereal pyramid of theater conventions," the umbrellas and painted domes, piled on it.  At least, that is at the core of Hughes's Tragic Equation, despite his abstracted Stratfordian assumptions. Shakespeare festivals might undergo a "creative rejuvenation... enriched with more interpretive boldness" if they paid attention to it.  Hughes writes:

"The ideal reader would regard my idea as a sort of musical adaptation, a song. The only justification for it, perhaps, is that it might form a preliminary outline for a new kind of Shakespearean production. After all, I am addressing the whole thing to the stage, not to anyone's study. I keep reminding myself that the main point is to project the fourteen plays and their overture (*As You Like It*) as a single Titanic work, like an Indian epic, the same gods battling through their reincarnations, in a vast, cyclic Tragedy of Divine Love. That is the way to think of it: two great deities appear. They subdivide in pain—there's the opening movement. Like fighters choosing weapons, they take up their first masks (all the other future masks are dangling on threads from the heavens.) They pull on second-hand shirts. Blouses, dresses, pants. They squeeze into shoes that don't quite fit, and take a few hobbling steps. Suddenly, they begin to hear the noises of earth…"

The "root meaning" of *The Goddess* is that attempts to deny and control biotic reality inevitably start up the Tragic Equation, for which another name might be the Chain Reaction. "The story of the mind exiled from Nature is the story of Western Man. It is the story of his progressively more desperate search for mechanical and rational and symbolic securities, which will substitute for the spirit-confidence of the Nature he has lost… It is a story of decline. When something abandons Nature, or is abandoned by Nature, it has lost touch with its creator, and is called an evolutionary dead-end. According to this, our civilization is an evolutionary error."

Hughes suggests that by exploring a personal Tragic Equation, his Dante-like William may have seen beyond it, as with the "sea change" from Clarence's drowning dream in *Richard III* to Ariel's regeneration song in *The Tempest*. But it is a change that associates wealth with death and the loss of it with life. William's life didn't follow that course: Edward de Vere's did. Perhaps he wrote *Richard III* as, weighted with property, he sank into debt; perhaps he wrote *The Tempest* after Elizabeth's annuity brought him up for air. The *Richard III* dream is of lifelessness: the gems in sunken skulls' eyes are just precious stones. In Ariel's song, the skull is coral and the gems are pearls, products of life and tokens of its ancient past. Maybe Edward had learned of early fossil collectors like Conrad Gesner and Leonardo da Vinci on his way through wilderness Europe's draughty radiant Paradise:

> Full many a glorious morning have I seen
> Flatter the mountain tops with sovereign eye,
> Kissing with golden face the meadows green,
> Gilding pale streams with heavenly alchemy…
> (*Sonnets*, 33)

Chapter Eighteen

Morning Glory Pool

---

In *The Mysterious William Shakespeare*, Charlton Ogburn comments on William McFee's remark that Looney's *"Shakespeare" Identified* "is destined to occupy in modern Shakespeare studies the place Darwin's great work occupies in evolutionary theory." Ogburn acknowledges that this seems far-fetched, but concludes: "It is no small thing in itself to discover the person behind the West's supreme literature; but beyond that, where Darwin had laid to rest the notion about spontaneous generation of life-forms and showed that they evolved from earlier life forms, so Looney laid to rest the notion, based on the Stratford attribution, that works of art could come about by spontaneous generation and cleared the way for us to understand that in fact they evolve, in Mr. Looney's words, from their creators' personality and experience."

Ted Hughes discovered something like that about his own work after he wrote *The Goddess*. Publishing *Birthday Letters* made him feel that his previous refusal to write about his marriage with Plath had stunted his poetic development: "I think those letters do release the story that everything I have written since the early 1960s has been evading… If only I had done the equivalent 30 years ago, l might have had a more fruitful career—certainly a freer psychological life." One reason for that refusal had been his belief that most of the Shakespeare canon didn't come from personal experience: "Once you've contracted to write only the truth about yourself—as in some respected kinds of modern verse, or as in Shakespeare's sonnets—then you can too easily limit yourself to what you imagine are the truths of the ego that claims your conscious biography.  Your equivalent of what Shakespeare got into his plays is simply foregone." But if Shakespeare wrote his plays from experience, that's not true.

In a book about nature poetry, Jonathan Bate maintains that reading it can be a more environmentally sound way to appreciate wilderness than package tours to Third World countries, in effect, a substitute for wilderness experience. "That self-enclosed area might be called Ariel's Island… To go there in imagination is to rediscover enchantment without having to pay the price of having to destroy the ecosystems of real islands…" Maybe so, but Bate thereby implies that experience isn't required to *write* great nature poetry, since he assumes that William wrote *The Tempest* from imagination. Such Stratfordian "algebra" could lead to a deathly "final solution": "When there is no more unknown, when the last tropical rainforest has been cleared, it may then be only in art—in poetry—that we will be able to hear the cry of Rima."

But I suspect that *The Tempest*—along with *As You Like It* and *The Winter's Tale*—derives from personal experience of wild places— a Sicilian volcanic islet, a northern French forest, a Balkan coastline.  I know that much of Hughes and Plath's writing does. According to one Plath biographer, "the huge land mass of North America, with its extremes of landscape and climate and its huge magical skies… became the main source for the big, dramatic effects of land and sky in the *Ariel* poems." Without the Yellowstone "scenario," dud or not, there would be no "Fishing Bridge" or "The 59th Bear" … or "The Fifty-Ninth Bear." Or a poem from Plath's *Ariel* period which invokes a Delphic Yellowstone as an antidote to her dream well of death-- a well of life purified by volcanic anger to "a perfectly lovely shade of blue":

> Yes, yes, this is my address.
> Not a patch on *your* place, I guess, with the Javanese
> Geese and monkey trees.
> It's a bit burnt out…

Here's a spot I thought you'd love—
Morning Glory Pool!
The blue's a jewel.
It boils for forty hours at a stretch.

O I shouldn't dip my hankie in, it *hurts*!
Last summer, my God, last summer,
It ate seven maids and a plumber
And returned them steamed and pressed and stiff as
shirts.
I am bitter? I am averse?
Here's your specs, dear, here's your purse.

Toddle on home to tea now in your flat hat...
Toddle on home, and don't trip on the nurse! —

She may be bald, she may have no eyes,
But, auntie, she's awfully nice.
She's pink, she's a born midwife—
She can bring the dead to life...
("The Tour")

Morning Glory Pool is a hot spring in Yellowstone's
Upper Geyser Basin-- a cauldron descending to what William
Bartram, describing a Florida spring, called "the blue ether of
another world." It's one of over ten thousand such springs in the
park, and Plath is right about their appetite for "maids and
plumbers": They do "boil for hours" and they've scalded over
twenty unwary people to death. Walking in Mud Volcano
Geyser Field-- where Sadie and Norton visit the "Dragon's
Mouth" and "Devil's Cauldron" in "The Fifty-Ninth Bear" -- I
felt a strange discomfort. When I mentioned it to a park
naturalist, she said it was because the ground's 200 F
temperature was starting to cook my feet.

"The Tour" addresses the iconic poetess, Marianne Moore, who wore a "flat hat" and wrote about zoo animals-- "Javanese geese and monkey trees." In 1957, Moore dismissed poems Plath sent her as "grisly," and in 1961 she forced the publisher to cut ten from Plath's first book, *The Colossus*. Moore also demanded cuts from Hughes's first book, *The Hawk in the Rain*, and he dissects her in a *Birthday Letters* poem, "The Literary Life," calling her "neat and hard as an ant" among other things.

Hughes understandably left out "The Tour" in his 1965 *Ariel* edition— Moore was still alive and Plath's version had left it out too-- but he also doesn't mention it in "The Literary Life," which is unusual. Most of *Birthday Letters* refers to specific Plath poems. Perhaps it brought back Plath's anger at his own zoo poet side. He does refer to it, significantly if obliquely, at the end of the last *Birthday Letters* poem:

> Blue was your kindly spirit—not a ghoul
> But electrified, a guardian, thoughtful.
>
> In the pit of red
> You hid from the bone clinic whiteness.
>
> But the jewel you lost was blue.
>     ("Red")

Hughes's poetic "recall" of Plath through her Delphic Yellowstone imagery echoes Shakespeare's dramatic "recall" of Leontes's "loved and loathed" Hermione in *The Winter's Tale*. And he further echoes that play in a short *Birthday Letters* sequel entitled *Howls and Whispers*. In its final poem, "The Offers," Plath returns to him in three dreams. In the first, she is sitting in a subway, apparently timeless and oblivious, pallid like a statue, but he sees that her face has aged. She is like Hermione's living statue in *The Winter's Tale*. In the second, she is still an exuberant co-ed, and she tells him that it is really he who has been in the land of the dead since her 1963 suicide. She is like blossoming Perdita: he is like wintry Leontes in the years after Hermione's "death."

In the last dream, while he is running a bath, naked, Plath, suddenly appears at his back, as *The Winter's Tale's* bear attacks Perdita-exposing Antigonus. This time she is the radiant Goddess, foam-born Aphrodite, as the rushing bathwater implies. The sound echoes the rivers that were Hughes's basic connection to wilderness. So, like Perdita, the lost Plath is finally "found" in wilderness, as though the transformation that Hughes attempted in the central *Birthday Letters* poem, "Fishing Bridge," has finally worked: "The threshold of that great lake/Spilling its river... what infinite endowment/ leaned over that threshold, beckoning us..." The transformed Plath is:

> As if new made, half a wild roe, half
> A flawless thing, priceless, faceted
> Like a cobalt jewel.

## Two Myths

Morning Glory Pool was less of a jewel when I saw it in 1996 than during their 1959 visit. Echoing Plath's "dream of dreams," tourists had polluted it by tossing in coins and trash. The pool had shrunk, and a mantle of yellow covered its border. But there is a further dimension to that. Microorganisms in the boiling waters had caused the yellow color, and they are among the planet's oldest organisms. They may have evolved in energy-rich volcanic waters when the rest of the Earth was lifeless. Such places may literally be wells of life— "born midwives." Civilization has turned them into spas and hydrothermal plants in much of the world, making Yellowstone of unique value for exploring life's origins.

Three centuries before Yellowstone became the world's first democratically protected wilderness park, Shakespeare's

Venus describes herself as what its enabling legislation would call it: a "pleasuring ground":

> Within this limit is relief enough,
> Sweet bottom grass and high delightful plain,
> Round rising hillocks, brakes obscure and rough,
> To shelter thee from tempest and from rain;
>     Then be my deer, since I am such a park
>     No dog shall rouse thee, though a thousand bark.
>             (*Venus and Adonis* 235)

Venus moves in mysterious ways on her pleasuring ground. The wildest part of the Yellowstone backcountry my wife and I reached during our "noisy mouse" trek was the Buffalo Plateau on the northern border, a forest so deep that moose moved among its tangles of wind-thrown pines in spectral silence. When we came on a little lake-- a blue island in the dark green sea-- it seemed the heart of vitality. A family of otters played among ducks and coots, and a coyote nosed around the shore.

The sunny enclave incited us to sex. In the midst of this, a towering bull moose burst from the trees, waded into the lake, and urinated copiously and noisily into the water, eyeing us sidelong. I guess our smell had attracted him. Then he stalked back into the forest. I thought of him when I saw Hayao Miyazaki's animated film, *Princess Mononoke*, a Japanese version of Kipling's "Letting in the Jungle" wherein a wolf-girl summons the beasts, especially wild boars, against a forest-destroying town. A many-antlered deer god presides over a lake in the heart of that forest.

Kipling met a Venus-Perdita in Yellowstone four years before he wrote *The Jungle Books*: "a maiden—a very little maiden" who "amazed and amused" him with her "critical commendation of the wonders that she saw." She was "good enough to treat him… a sun peeled, collarless wanderer…as a human being," and accompanied him to "the glories of the Upper

Geyser Basin… mighty green fields splattered with lime beds, all the flowers of summer growing up to the very edge of the lime… But how intoxicating it was!… As we climbed the long path… we nearly fell into a little sapphire lake—but never sapphire was so blue… Then we lay in the grass and laughed at the sheer bliss of being alive… Four little pools lay at my elbow, one was black water (tepid), one clear water (cold), one clear water (hot), one red water (boiling). My newly washed handkerchief covered them all, and we two marveled as children marvel."

Yellowstone is more the new American mythology that Thoreau prophesies in "Walking" than is the American backwoodsman that excited Lawrence and Hughes. *Walden* pokes fun at the popular fiction that perpetuated their fantasies: "I think that they had better metamorphose all such heroes of universal noveldom into man weathercocks… and let them swing round till they are rusty, and not come down at all to bother honest men with their pranks." Lawrence misjudged Thoreau as just putting New England "under a lens, to examine it." He perhaps never read his account of climbing Maine's Mount Ktaadn, now a wilderness park. Thoreau knew sacred horror:

"I began to work my way, scarcely less arduous than Satan's anciently through chaos, up the nearest though not the highest peak. At first scrambling on all fours over the tops of ancient black spruce trees, old as the flood, from two to ten or twelve feet in height, their tops flat and spreading, and their foliage blue, and nipped with cold, as if for centuries they had ceased growing upward against the bleak sky, the solid cold. I walked some good rods erect on the tops of these trees… Once, slumping through, I looked down ten feet into a dark and cavernous region… These holes were bears' dens, and the bears were even then at home… This was the Earth of which we have heard, made out of Chaos and Old Night."

Although he probably never heard more than rumors of the marvelous volcanic plateau at the Yellowstone River's source, Thoreau would have understood the park's mythic role:

"To preserve wild animals generally implies the creation of a forest for them to dwell in or resort to. So it is with men... and out of such a wilderness comes the Reformer eating locusts and wild honey." A Reformer, John Muir, might have been speaking for him in 1902: "No wonder that so many fine myths have originated in springs; that so many fountains were held sacred in the youth of the world and had miraculous virtues ascribed to them. Even in these cold, doubting, questioning scientific times many of the Yellowstone fountains seem able to work miracles."

The American backwoodsman came to a mythic end in Yellowstone in 1894 when the Army stopped one from killing the park's wild bison--- the last in the U.S.—for their heads and hides, and a public outcry forced Congress to pass the first federal law against unregulated hunting. It is right that Hughes failed to escape into that myth. Civilization has done enough escaping in space, which is what the backwoodsman was about. Hughes is perceptive not to hear encouraging words in "Badlands," his grim *Birthday Letters* poem on the Great Plains, which the backwoodsman's cowboy offspring have subdued as violently as the Yorkshire moors. He did become part of Yellowstone's myth, however painfully, and if he didn't envision restoring a "draughty, radiant paradise" in Britain, he pointed that way:

> ...If I go
> To the end on the way past these trees and past these trees
> Till I get tired that's touching one wall of me
> For the moment if I sit still how everything
> Stops to watch me I suppose I am the exact center
> but there's all this what is it roots
> roots roots roots and here's the water
> again very queer but I'll go on looking.
> ("Wodwo")

Crowded Japan has boars and bears in ancient forested national parks. Boars share Mount Diablo State Park with bobcats, coyotes, mountain lions, and golden eagles a few miles from three million people. Nature writers go on about this or that "last wilderness": Britain could have the refreshing advantage of a "first wilderness." It would be a better "use" of some places than shooting coverts, stalking moors, sheep pastures, and softwood plantations: it would enhance civilization. As Thoreau told his graduating class at Harvard: "This curious world we inhabit is more wonderful than it is convenient; more beautiful than it is useful; it is more to be admired than used."

## The Real Job

Hughes's assumption that Shakespeare was an everyman-superman hack conflicts tellingly with his ideas about Plath. In his introduction to *Johnny Panic and the Bible of Dreams*, he writes that she considered poetry "an evasion from the real job" of academic and commercial success. It was only when Plath shed the everyman-superman model, Hughes thinks, that she expressed her "molten core," and that didn't arise only from her genius and imagination but from her personality, knowledge, and experience. Her realization of artistic identity involved loss of security and status, not gain. The narrator of "Johnny Panic and the Bible of Dreams" is not the everyday world's upward mobile Sylvia but a "tough" nobody who follows her instincts.

The everyman-superman Whiggish Bard is about the rise of the new common man who succeeds through gain, but art comes from before that, when humans lived "in common" with other life. The old common man's fall is virtually complete: few savages survive. But the well of life rises to us from them. Whether or not the Shakespeare canon grew out of an Elizabethan version of the shamanic initiation dream, it did grow out of ancient versions of it. For all its abstractedness, Hughes's Shakespeare interpretation shows that, and it comes closer than others to explaining my adolescent reaction to Ariel's "Full

Fathom Five." It was as though the poetic music metabolized the numbing violence around me-- as bulldozers carved out the Whiggish Bard suburb -- into a compensatory rapture.

Plath describes a similar childhood epiphany she had as her mother read her another song of underwater life: "I saw the gooseflesh on my skin. I did not know what made it. I was not cold. Had a ghost passed over? No, it was poetry... I felt very odd. I had fallen into a new way of being happy.":

> Sand-strewn caverns cool and deep,
> Where the winds are all asleep,
> Where the spent lights quiver and gleam;
> Where the salt weed sways in the stream;
> Where the sea beasts ranged all round
> Feed in the ooze of their pasture ground...

Hughes writes that true poetry "is a healing substance— the vital energy of it is a healing energy, as if it were produced, in a natural and spontaneous way, by the psychological component of the auto-immune system, the body's self-repair system." In that sense, Ariel's song is an immersion in the well of life. It echoes diagnostically as well as frighteningly in Plath's "dream of dreams."

Critics intent on social and psychological implications have neglected the ecological strain in *Ariel* poems like "Daddy," "Lady Lazarus," "Getting There," and "Totem." They condemn the totalitarian world that her dream of dreams called her to witness: the earth "scraped flat by the roller of wars, wars, wars," where everything is transported to industrial facilities — "an engine, an engine, chuffing me off"—and made into products and waste products, ending in "the sewage farm of the ages." It's no wonder that *Time* magazine, the voice of everyday normality, called Plath: "a literary dragon who in the last months of her life breathed a burning river of bale across the literary landscape." For all her suicidal abnormality, we can't deny her condemnation since it is the everyday world we live in. We turn the well of life into more bathrooms and factories, and it flows out more polluted. The draughty, radiant Paradise of the animals becomes the supermarket:

> O adding machine—
> Is it possible for you to let something go and have it go whole?
> Must you stamp each piece in purple,
> Must you kill what you can?
>            ("A Birthday Present")

To quote Thoreau's "Walking" a last time: "Some of expressions of truth are reminiscent, others merely *sensible*, as the phrase is, others prophetic. Some forms of disease, even, may prophesy forms of health... The wildness of the savage is but a faint symbol of the awful ferity with which good men and lovers meet."

Harold Bloom, who calls Plath's poetic reputation "grossly exaggerated," prizes the Whiggish Bard precisely for his acquisitive banality. "At once no one and everyone, nothing and everything, Shakespeare is the Western Canon." But where is the Western Canon going with all it drags along? Bloom's saying a Whiggish Bard created modern humanity is like Orwellian propagandists saying Big Brother did. It fosters a belief that we can succeed through acquisition forever, "sustainable growth," a formula for global disaster.

As Plath's dream of dreams foretells, success through acquisition trickles down from the affluent suburb's sparkling-blue reservoir to its stinking sewage farm. To stop polluting the well of life, we need to discard that model. Toppling the Whiggish Bard won't save the planet, but a challenge to one monolithic belief based on little evidence might encourage others. To quote a poet who, far from Shakespeare in history and culture, seems near him in mind:

One Moment in Annihilation's Waste,
One moment, of the Well of Life to taste...

Look to the Rose that blows about us— "Lo,"
Laughing she says-- "Into the World I blow:
At once the silken Tassel of my Purse
Tear, and its Treasure on the Garden throw."
*(Rubaiyat)*

# Notes

———————

## Introduction

6 "The undisputed fame": Halliday, *Shakespeare and His Critics*. pp. 105, 106.
   "He calls it "the myth of the Great Goddess": Hughes, *Shakespeare the Goddess of Complete Being,* p. 3.

## Chapter One: Monument and Monolith

10 "In 1957, around the time," Wright and LaMar, "The Author." *The Folger Library General Reader's Shakespeare.*
13 "Not only did Shakespeare": Greenblatt, *Will in the World*, p. 12.
14 "He was embalmed": Ackroyd, *Shakespeare: The Biography*, p. 514.
15 "Shakespeare has left": diary entry of October 27, 1857. Flower, *Henry David Thoreau*, p. 632.
   "English literature, from the days": "Walking" Flower, p. 540.
   "As a type of story": Northrop Frye": "Myth, Fiction, and Displacement," in *Fables of Identity.* p. 31.
16 "Nobody can reconstruct": Frye, *A Natural Perspective*, p. 54.
   "Our ancestors were savages": Flower, p. 534.
17 "In literature it is only": ibid, p. 539

## Chapter Two: Ground Water

19 "the strange squalor": Lawrence, "The Princess."

"The wild thing's": Lawrence, *Saint Mawr, The Later D.H. Lawrence*, p. 75.

"And if we go": Lawrence, *Lady Chatterley's Lover.*

23 "one anthropologist calls": Shepard, *The Others*, p. 167.

"Bear skulls artfully arranged": Baring, *The Myth of the Goddess*, p. 70.

"When James Boswell toured": Pottle, p. 212.

"A 9,000-year-old sculpture": Baring, p. 70.

25 "The monastic orders": Blair, *Anglo-Saxon England*, p. 250.

26 "According to Northrop Frye": Frye, *Fables of Identity.* p. 40.

## Chapter Three: Spring Water

31 "One critic accordingly": Bate, *The Song of the Earth*, p. 182.

32 "The landscapes described in *Don Quixote*": Borges, *The Professor*, pp. 14-15.

"In the tragedies":  Frye, *Fools of Time*, p. 25.

34 "his propitiatory name": *Northrop Fry on Shakespeare*, p. 44.

41 "With church authority crumbling": McGinn, *Shakespeare's Philosophy*, p. 15.

44 "Antigonus first tries to coax": By "gelding," Antigonus apparently means female circumcision.  How did Shakespeare know about this exotic practice?

47 "Nature provides the means": Frye, "Recognition in *The Winter's Tale*," in *Fables of Identity,* pp. 116, 118.

## Chapter Four: Downstream

51 "*The Tempest*'s wild humanoid": Halliday, *Shakespeare and His Critics*, p. 287.

52 "If any Author": Lynch, *Becoming Shakespeare*, p. 89.

"The work of a correct": Halliday, *Shakespeare and His Critics*, p. 69.

53 "When during his": Pottle, pp. 220, 299.

54 "O mighty poet!":  Halliday, p. 95.

59 "The wild animal": Lawrence, "St. Mawr," *The Later D.H.*

*Lawrence*, p. 75.

"Like Thoreau, Lawrence places": Lawrence, *Selected Literary Criticism*, pp. 90-91.

60 "A rightist utilitarian": Lewis, *The Lion and the Fox*, p. 14.

"and his famous": ibid. p. 19.

"One must accept": Auden, *Lectures on Shakespeare*, p. 56.

"Man falls": ibid. p. 284.

"In the middle of the desert": ibid. p. 293.

"Critics called them": Motion, *Philip Larkin*, pp. 242-3.

61 "England is going down": ibid, p. 410.

"But we must not regard": Auden, *Lectures on Shakespeare.* p. 57.

63 "But now, alas": Lawrence, *Selected Literary Criticism,* p. 91.

64 "His love and understanding": Ogburn, *The Mysterious William Shakespeare*, p. 312.

## Chapter Five: Two Dragons

66 "The first function": Campbell, *The Masks of God: Creative Mythology*, p. 4.

67 "The fundamental guiding ideas": Hughes, "The Environmental Revolution," *Winter Pollen*, p. 129.

68 "They said: 'We are the oak trees": "My Own True Family" appeared in a 1973 American edition of *Meet My Folks!* but not in the original 1961 edition. Maybe it seemed too scary.

"The air of wild": Hughes, "Notes on Shakespeare," *Winter Pollen*, p.104.

"In spite of its Elizabethan ruff": ibid.

69 "Long after I am gone": Van Dyne, *Revising Life*, p. 40.

"It would be": Hughes, *Shakespeare and the Goddess*, p. 86.

"Throughout history": ibid. p. 89.

70 "Queen Elizabeth held off": Hughes, "Notes on Shakespeare," *Winter Pollen*, p. 110.

"Somehow he had identified": Hughes, *Shakespeare and the*

*Goddess*, p. 83.

71 "The dreamer, Adonis": ibid. p. 87.
   "There is another": ibid. p. 90.
72 "As the shaman of the Old": ibid.
   "Shakespeare demonstrates": ibid. p. 174.
   "He was on both sides": ibid. p. 92.
73 "Hughes interprets fourteen": ibid. p. 3. In the order Hughes
   interprets them, the plays are: *All's Well That Ends Well,
   Measure for Measure, Troilus and Cressida, Othello,
   Hamlet, Macbeth, King Lear, Timon of Athens,
   Coriolanus, Antony and Cleopatra, Cymbeline, Pericles,
   The Winter's Tale,* and *The Tempest.*
   "As the Tragic Equation": ibid. p. 88.
74 "One inexorable law": ibid. p. 260.
75 "What Shakespeare did": ibid. p. 174.
76 "But in *The Tempest*": ibid. p. 457.
   "Shakespeare," Hughes writes." "Battling over the Bard."
   *London Times*, April 19, 1992.

## Chapter Six: Bear People

78 "He writes: "man, in contrast": *Creative Mythology*, p. 673.
79 "She writes": Middlebrook, *Her Husband*, p. 245.
82 "Audubon, feverish": Wallace, *The Klamath Knot.* p. 7.
83 "Eight years after my book": Craig Carpenter, letter of
   January 13, 1991: "...Let me first express my gratitude to
   you for your insights and revelations.... You, however,
   are the first "materialist" I am aware of to have been to
   have been both 'called by Nature'... AND subsequently
   'touched' by Nature..." Letter of February 8, 1991: "...I
   think you probably met 'A Giant' or 'The Giants' in one
   of their 'Strange Bear Disguises'... Since I am 'a bear
   man,' or 'belong to the bear people' myself, I was and am
   particularly interested in your 'strange bear' experiences,
   and especially in those experiences you may have had in
   this 'Klamath Knot' area which you describe so correctly

in your letter as having <u>very</u> powerful voices…" Peter Matthiessen dedicated *Indian Country*, his book about the Native American traditionalist movement, to "Craig Carpenter, my teacher and guide on my first journeys into Indian Country, whose fierce encouragement of the last traditionals among his people is one good reason why they still exist." He further writes of Carpenter: "On the grounds that the Indian Nation should not be subject to federal or state laws, Craig refuses to earn enough to pay taxes (he barters his labor) or obtain a driver's license, or otherwise appear in the white man's records, and once went to jail rather than participate in the white man's wars." (p. 67) *Indian Country* has a chapter, "The High Country," about the controversy over the Siskiyou Wilderness sacred areas.

"In the moonlight I watched": Cooper, "Siskiyou High Country," p. 28.

84 "I could think of nothing": *Black Elk Speaks*, p.134.

86 "Sorcerers are too common": quoted in Falk, *The Science of Shakespeare*, p. 240.

"Alexander Pope sensed": Lynch, *Becoming Shakespeare*, p. 89.


Chapter Seven: Nothing Normal


88 "The two long poems,": Halliday, p. 321.

"The beasts in *Venus and Adonis*": Wills, *Making Make Believe Real*, p. 52-4.

"Ovid's 'mythic' characters": Hughes abridges Venus's complexion worries in his own translation of *The Metamorphoses*:

She who had loved equally the shade
And her indolence in it, who had laboured
Only as a lily of the valley,

Now goes bounding over the stark ridges
Skirts tucked high like the huntress…
*Tales from Ovid* p. 120

94 "By modern secular definition": Hughes, *Shakespeare and the Goddess,* p. 56.

Chapter Eight: Doctor and Mrs. Fox

96 "A verse published": Sobran, *Alias Shakespeare,* 214.
98 "The tumbled Pennine stone building blocks": Middlebrook, *Her Husband,* p. 256.
99 "Some critics take": Uroff, p. 14.
   "everything in West Yorkshire." Feinstein, *Ted Hughes: The Life of a Poet,* p. 6
   "My childhood landscape": Plath, "Ocean 1212-W," *Johnny Panic and the Bible of Dreams,* p. 21.
100 "Thoreau's "Walking" might express: Flower, p. 541.
   "Maybe he felt": Lawrence, *Studies in Classic American Literature,* in Wilson, *The Shock of Recognition,* p. 1012.
101 "My emotional life": Feinstein. p. 89.
102 "Hughes dreamt": Hughes, 'The Burnt Fox," *Winter Pollen,* p. 9.
   "Plath dreamt": Plath, *Johnny Panic and the Bible of Dreams,* p. 158.
   "Critics haven't seen": Anne Stevenson quotes the "dream of dreams" as fiction in her biography, *Bitter Fame* p. 142. Tracy Brain mentions it briefly as an example of environmental concern in *The Other Sylvia Plath,* writing that it "seems to represent a collective dream life or unconscious." Jacqueline Rose says something similar more ambiguously in *The Haunting of Sylvia Plath*: "The [collective] dreams come out of a great lake— 'the sewage farm of the ages, transparence aside'—which forms the only content of her own dream." p.56.
   "The lake bears no resemblance": *Johnny Panic,* p. 158.

103 "I'm a wormy hermit": ibid. p. 165.

"In her journal": Plath, *The Unabridged Journals*, p. 436.

"She identifies": ibid. p. 337.

"She considered calling": ibid. p. 381.

104 "Her poetry": Hughes in Newman, ed., *The Art of Sylvia Plath*, p. 187.

"Her sensuousness": Plath, "The Fifty-Ninth Bear," *Johnny Panic*, p. 110.

"Her slender": ibid, p. 107.

105 "He did not see": ibid. p. 112.

"His guidance succeeds": Lowell, foreword to *Ariel*, p. vii.

106 "A liar and a vain smiler," Plath, *Unabridged Journals*, p. 390.

107 "'At any moment": "The Fifty-Ninth Bear," *Johnny Panic*, p. 117.

"Plath calls the trip": Plath's July 29 letter says that a rumor she heard at the bathhouse was about a bear killing a woman, not a man as in *Birthday Letters* (see p. 207), and that they spent another night at the same campsite, covered their car with a kerosene-soaked poncho, took tranquillizers, and "slept the sleep of the blessed." Plath, *Letters Home*, pp. 349-50.

108 "These two long poems": *Shakespeare and the Goddess*, p. 362.

## Chapter Nine: Squire Crow

111 "Hughes conjectures": Hughes, "Notes on Shakespeare," *Winter Pollen*, p. 106.

"In her Journal": Plath, *Unabridged Journals,* p. 456.

"That division of the loved": *Shakespeare and the Goddess*, p. 516.

112 "In his *Goddess* introduction": ibid. p. 42.

115 "And time dissolves": It is unclear why Digges's poem refers to a "*Stratford moniment*" instead of a "monument." "Moniment" may just be an archaic

spelling but it may mean something other than a bust with inscriptions. One archaic meaning of monument is "a written legal document or record" (Webster's).

116 "Many were the wit-combates": Sobran, *Alias Shakespeare*, p. 46. The quote is from Fuller's *The History of the Worthies of England.*

117 "Mr. Shakespeare was a natural": Sobran, *Alias Shakespeare*, p. 47.

"A modern editor": Michael Hunter, Foreword, *Brief Lives,* ix.

"Aubrey writes": *Brief Lives,* Lawson Dick editor, p. 275.

"In 1709, an actor-impresario": Sobran, *Alias Shakespeare,* p. 48.

Chapter Ten: The Nest in the Redwood

124 "In 1628, a critic": Vicar's book is *Manuductio ad Artem Rhetoricam.*

125 "When in 1747, another Stratford": Anderson, p. xxvi
"In 1769, a physician": Lawrence. *The Life and Adventures of Common Sense.* p. 146.

126 "Yet Collier's twentieth century biographer": Ganzel, *Fortune and Men's Eyes.*

"Walt Whitman remarked": Anderson, *Shakespeare by Another Name.* p. xxvi.

"Samuel Clemens": ibid. p. 369.

"Henry James": ibid. p. xxv.

"published a story": Waugh, *Shakespeare in Court*, Kindle Edition, Loc 91.

"Sigmund Freud mused": Ogburn, *Shake-speare: The Man Behind the Name.* p. 12.

"Northrop Frye, a Canadian": *Northrop Frye on Shakespeare*, p. 3.

"The theory that Shakespeare": Taylor, *Reinventing Shakespeare*, p. 211.

127 "There is a mystery": Bate, *The Genius of Shakespeare*, p.

65.

"Another American": Bloom, *Shakespeare: The Invention of the Human.* pp. 371, 487.

128 "The 'experience' argument": *Northrop Frye on Shakespeare*, p. 3.

"Language most shows": Ogburn, *The Mysterious William Shakespeare.* p. 372.

"Judging from Shakespeare's language": In *Contested Will* (p. 276) James Shapiro quotes "the leading expert on Shakespeare's language" to the effect that most modern English speakers "use at least 50,000 words," but he doesn't say how that is.

129 "Conceived out of": in Shapiro, *Shakespeare in America*, p. 221.

"Most anti-Shakespeareans": Wright and Lamar, "The Author."

"When a 2005 *New York Times* essay": Neiderkorn, William S. "The Shakespeare Code." *New York Times*, August 30, 2005.

"The idea that William Shakespeare's authorship": *New York Times*, September 4, 2005.

130 "Ralph Waldo Emerson": Wallace, *Beasts of Eden*, p. 36.

"After examining even the best": Greenblatt, *Will in the World*, p. 13.

"The elusiveness of both": Bate, *Soul of the Age*, p. 423.


Chapter Eleven: Desire and Will

132 "It is not too difficult": *Shakespeare and the Goddess* p. 86.
133 "The immediate practical function": ibid. p. 1.
134 "According to his received biography": ibid. p. 116.
135 "By the time he emerged": ibid. p. 49.
136 "My reverent dutiful thoughts": Lawlis, *Elizabethan Prose Fiction*, p. 441.
137 "Thoreau says something else": Flower, p. 632.

"He praised": "Emerson on Thoreau," in Wilson, *The Shock*

*of Recognition,* p. 224.

138 "George Greenwood": Greenwood, *The Shakespeare Problem Restated,* p. 124.

"Even more ominously": *Shakespeare and the Goddess* p. 504.

"nothing really": Hughes, "Crow on the Beach," *Winter Pollen,* p. 240.

139 "But not when the boar": *Shakespeare and the Goddess* p. 504.

"As another poet": William Scammell, "Introduction," *Winter Pollen,* p. xiii.

140 "Of the Irish Lyr's ancestry": *Shakespeare and the Goddess,* p. 268. Unfortunately, pedantry in *The Goddess* doesn't extend to end notes, a bibliography, or an index.

"From the epic of Gilgamesh": "The Snake in the Oak," *Winter Pollen,* p. 412.

141 "That poem's "Fury Form," according": ibid, p. 414.

"The Christian Self": ibid, p. 377.

142 "The subtly apotheosized": "The Environmental Revolution," ibid. p. 129.

## Chapter Twelve: Lord Boar

143 "'We must,' he concluded": Ogburn, *The Mysterious William Shakespeare.* p. 145.

"In my opinion after several readings": McFee, Introduction to *The Mysterious William Shakespeare,* 1949 edition.

146 "There is much more": Jenkins, *Elizabeth The Great,* p. 166.

"Cecil later wrote": Ogburn and Ogburn, *This Star of England,* p. 657.

147 "After passing the falls": Anderson, p. 79.

148 "Upon leaving Venetian waters": ibid, p. 86.

"For my liking of Italy": Ward, p. 119.

149 "I'll have my chamber": Anderson, p.158.

150 "A 1586 portrait": The painting's provenance seems murky: some Oxfordians refer to it; others ignore it.

"De Vere, whose fame and loyalty": From a poem published in
1589, probably by John Lyly.
151 "I cannot but find a great grief": Anderson, p. 350.
"At the end of the year": Ogburn, *Shakespeare: The Man
Behind the Name*, p. 48.
152 "His second wife asks": Ward, p. 370.
"When the book's author touches on": Bates, *Touring in
1600*, p. 87.
153 "Oxford headed": Ward, p. 174.
"Euphues replies: "Do you not know": Lawliss, *Elizabethan
Prose Fiction*, p. 134.
154 "refrained from comment": Ward, p. 328.
156 "Among the nobility": Ogburn, *The Mysterious William
Shakespeare*, p. 686.

Chapter Thirteen: The Trap at the Spring

160 "The academic establishment": In Ogburn, *The Mysterious
William Shakespeare*, p.469.
161 "A 1958 biography of Queen Elizabeth": Jenkins, *Elizabeth
the Great*, p. 166.
"Like Scott's novel": ibid, p. 193. Jenkins's book doesn't
even mention Shakespeare.
"A 2004 Marlowe biography": Riggs, *The World of
Christopher Marlowe*, p. 123.
"Oxford's remark that the Bible": ibid, p. 113. The
"remarks" come from Henry Howard and Charles
Arundell's 1581 accusations against de Vere.
162 "There were many instances": Dunn, *Elizabeth and Mary*,
p. 348.
"The story, somewhat embroidered": Aubrey, *Brief Lives*.
Oliver Lawson Dick, ed. p. 305. Aubrey gives his source
for the fart story as "Vide Stowe de hoc in Elizabeth:
about the end." John Stowe was a contemporary
chronicler who described de Vere's role in the Armada
campaign and other military affairs.

"At the 1578 royal": *The Mysterious William Shakespeare*, p. 579.

163 "What has enraged him": Ogburn, ibid., p. 692.

164 "Half a century later, Stratford vicar": ibid. p.690.

"Walt Whitman found it": Shapiro, *Shakespeare in America*, p. 221.

165 "I am Richard": Ogburn, *Shakespeare: The Man Behind the Name,* p. 93.

166 "the exact knowledge": Bate, *Soul of the Age*, p. 74.

"It seems to me": Frye, *Fables of Identity*, p. 128.

"In his earlier": Shapiro, *A Year in the Life of Shakespeare: 1599:* p. xiii. p. 347.

167 "I do not know": Freud, *The Letters of Sigmund Freud and Arnold Zweig.* p. 140. (Shapiro's misquote is on p. 185 of *Contested Will*).

168 "He snubs 'the skeptics'"": Shapiro, *The Year of Lear*, p. 144.

"But Oxford also had shortcomings": Bryson, *Shakespeare: The World as Stage*, p. 189.

"According to Aubrey's": *Brief Lives*, Oliver Lawson Dick ed. p. 305.

169 "While taking the": Nelson, *Monstrous Adversary*, pp. 254-8, 489-91.

"The man everywhere": James, "William Shakespeare," *Literary Criticism*, p. 1209.

170 "Prospero, the Duke of Milan": Looney, *Shakespeare Identified,* p. 426.

171 "The impulse to scold": Sobran, *Alias Shakespeare*, p.14.

"Writers, especially American ones": Bate, *The Genius of Shakespeare*, p. 97.

172 "James Shapiro complains": *A Year in the Life of Shakespeare: 1599*, p. 319.

"So great": Wilson, *I Thought of Daisy.* p. 154.

"I dare say": Wilson: *Literary Essays and Reviews of the 1930s and 40s,* p. 601.

Chapter Fourteen: Shakespeare's Brain

173 "His Coleridge essay": "The Snake in the Oak," *Winter Pollen*, p. 379.

"Hughes overlooks": ibid, p. 394.

"Now Coleridge": Lowes, p. 7.

174 "When in *The Goddess* he describes": Booth, *Philip Larkin,* p. 440.

"Ted Hughes (yes that": Rosenbaum, *The Shakespeare Wars*, p. 558.

"Stephen Greenblatt writes": Greenblatt, *Will in the World*, p. 404.

"*Shakespeare and the Goddess of Complete Being* remains": Bate, *Ted Hughes*, p. 471.

175 "Bate concludes": ibid. p. 472.

"It can't be claimed": Hughes, *Shakespeare and the Goddess,* p. 97.

176 "All that was necessary": Looney, p. 107.

178 "Lodge called himself": *Shakespeare by Another Name*, p. 231.

"I had had a very great vision": *Black Elk Speaks*, p. 212.

179 "A poet named John Soouthern": Ward, p. 50.

"These poems," writes Joseph Sobran": *Alias Shakespeare*, p. 232.

181 "If Nowell taught": *Shakespeare by Another Name*. p. 23.

"Polyphemus claims descent": *Shakespeare and the Goddess,* p. 433.

182 "He has been suggested": Smith, "A Reattribution of Munday's 'The Paine of Pleasure'. *The Oxfordian* 5 (2002), p. 70.

"I have often experienced": Montaigne, "Apology for Raymond Sebond," *Essays*, p. 803.

"In 1543, the Swiss naturalist": Bates, *Touring in 1600*, p. 304.

183 "But his fortnight": Anderson, p. 79.

"One traveler described": Bates, *Touring in 1600*, p. 355.

"In his compendium": Topsell, p. 29.

"A hospice on the Mt. Cenis Pass": Bates, pp. 295-6.

185 "The Venetian galley": Anderson, p. 86.

"As eagles and white-tailed Egyptian vultures": ibid. p. 88.

186 "His biographer doubts": Crupi, *Robert Greene*, p.6.

"Northrop Frye speculates": *Northrop Frye on Shakespeare*, p. 155.

"All Greene's biographer": Crupi, p. 81.

187 "Unlike any other city": Anderson, p.87. (quotes from *Twelfth Night*, 3,3; 1,1.) Some of renaissance Ragusa remains as the extant city of Dubrovnik, a location for the TV series, "Game of Thrones."

"Oxfordians think": Anderson, p. 154.

188 "This lie is very rife": ibid. p. 167.

"In the year he published *Pandosto*": Riggs, p. 122.

"Wheresover Maecenas lodgeth": Ogburn, *The Mysterious William Shakespeare*. p. 675.

190 "That seduction": Oxfordians associate Anne Vavasour with witty characters like Rosalind and Beatrice as well as the sonnets' "dark lady." Anderson, p. 174.

191 "Of *King Lear*, Hughes writes": *Shakespeare and the Goddess*, p. 257.

193 "My lord I am tied": Jenkins, *Elizabeth The Great*, p. 323.

"Hamlet whirls unendingly": *Shakespeare and TG*. p. 238.

194 "The fact that": ibid. p. 235.

"As in no other play": ibid. p. 236.

"Hughes doesn't even": ibid. p. 88.

195 "Mark Anderson sees": Anderson, p.169.

"Nero and Heliogabalus," writes Burton": *Anatomy of Melancholy,* p. 100.

"Visiting England during the 1580s": Riggs, p. 177.

196 "The witch's cauldron scene in Act IV": In 2007, Stratfordian Gary Taylor included *Macbeth*, *Timon of Athens*, and *Measure for Measure* in Middleton's *Collected Works*, implying a final solution to the authorship question: reattribute Shakespeare to more and more theatrical "collaborators" until he quietly

evaporates. "A number of theater historians over the past decade have argued that collaboration was the dominant model of textual production within the early modern theater, and that 'authorship' itself was a communal, collaborative process... The play is therefore to be understood not as the expression of the individual author's original idea, or his personality or views. Rather it is part of the transactions of the early modern stage." (O'Callaghan, *Thomas Middleton*, p. 45)

197 "Northrop Frye makes the common claim": Frye, *A Natural Perspective*, p. 38.

198 "Such a wicked imagination": Ogburn, *Shakespeare: The Man Behind the Name*, p. 93.
   "Devereux did not": Strachey, *Elizabeth and Essex,* p. 267.

Chapter Fifteen: Horses and Hares

202 "Western literature": Ogburn, *The Winter Beach*, 49.
   "Shakespeare was the first": Ogburn, *The Mysterious William Shakespeare,* p. 247.

203 "The description of the horse of Adonis": Ackroyd, *Shakespeare: The Biography,* p. 206.
   "Bartas's biblical epic": Sylvester, Joshua (translator). *Bartas: His Devine Weekes and Workes.* p. 370.
   "And Sylvester published": ibid. p. xi.

204 "He sees the stallion's pursuit": *Shakespeare and Goddess,* p. 71.

205 "Like an electric shock," Middlebrook, *Her Husband*, p. 78.
   "Feelings about wildlife": Edward Butscher cites a January, 1961, BBC "joint interview" in which Hughes "spoke of his love for hunting" yet of "how he hated the sight of the broken bodies in his hands," while Plath "insisted upon her husband's sensitivity and gentleness-- as seen in the 'fact' that he could no longer shoot rabbits." *Sylvia Plath: Method and Madness*, p. 269.
   "In *The Goddess*, Hughes suggests": *Shakespeare and*

*Goddess,* pp. 68, 380.

"I have seen next to nothing": Plath, *Letters Home*, p. 304.

"I am becoming more and more": ibid, p. 345.

"Timorous as Sadie was": "The Fifty-Ninth Bear," *Johnny Panic*, p. 109.

"She had insisted": ibid, p. 107.

206 "Away from the boardwalks": ibid, p. 109.

207 "His *Birthday Letters* poem": Yellowstone has two bear species, the American black bear (*Ursus americanus*) and the grizzly (*Ursus arctos*, like the Eurasian brown bear). The "big brown" one that ransacked H and P's car was probably a color phase of the smaller *U. americanus*. Grizzlies are uncommon and seldom visit public facilities. Lee Whittlesey, the Yellowstone N.P. historian who cites the 1959 concession worker's suicide, writes that bear-caused injuries, mostly minor, mostly involving black bears, were not unusual in the garbage feeding era. (The Park Service had stopped garbage feeding and reduced the black bear population when we backpacked there in 1978.) As of 2017, bears, all grizzlies, have killed five people in the Park. Bison, less feared so more often approached, have killed three.

"Plath's story implies": Yellowstone elk belong to the same genus, *Cervus*, as British stags, and they weigh up to a half ton. They can be quite aggressive to Park visitors.

"a deer that Hughes": Plath, *Unabridged Journals,* illustration no. 29. White-tailed deer, *Odocoileus*, are half as big as elk.

"Plath didn't much like": ibid. p. 501.

"I was surprised": Stevenson, *Bitter Fame*, p. 317.

208 "He had hunted": Faas, *Ted Hughes: The Unaccommodated Universe*, p. 60.

"The mingled smell": Hughes, *Wodwo*, p. 59.

209 "One of the reasons": Sagar, *Poet and Critic*, p. 257.

"That year he published": "The Hart of the Mystery." *Guardian*, July 5, 1997.

210 "His one reference": Hughes, *Shakespeare and the Goddess*, p. 11.

212 "Ovid describes a boar": Shakespeare's boar description resembles that of Arthur Golding's English translation of *Metamorphoses* more than it does the original Latin:

> His eyes did glister blood and fire, right dreadful was to see
> His brawned neck, right dreadful was his hair which grew as thick
> With pricking points as one of them could well by other stick
> And like a front of armed pikes set close in battle ray
> The sturdy bristles on his back stood staring up always...

> Much other Shakespeare imagery is so like that of Golding's *Metamorphoses* that some Oxfordians think the teenaged de Vere worked on the translation with his uncle. Golding was puritanical and otherwise uninterested in such racy stuff.

"Behind her moved gray wolves": Boer, *The Homeric Hymns*, p. 75.

214 "Shakespeare lost his taste": Ogburn, *The Mysterious William Shakespeare,* p. 269.

216 "A tender-hearted sympathy": ibid. p. 270.

"Queen Elizabeth hunted": Whitelock, *The Queen's Bed*, p.158.

"Shown the 'lion pit'": Bowen, *The Lion and the Throne*, p. 235.

"One critic finds": Spurgeon: *Shakespeare's Imagery and What It Tells Us*, p. 27.

"The things about which": Montaigne, "Apology for Raymond Seybond." *Essays*. p. 690.

217 ""Nature, so I fear": "Of Cruelty," ibid. p. 575.

"His Alps journal": *Montaigne's Travel Journal*, p. 40. A

secretary wrote most of the *Travel Journal*, supposedly from Montaigne's dictation, but the Mont Cenis pass description is in his own words.

"In a letter to Burghley ": Ward, p. 223.

"The woods were preserved": Sobran, p. 274.

"His last extant letter": Nelson, p. 424.

219 "Shakespeare's sensitivity": Hughes, *Shakespeare and the Goddess. P.* 73.

"In "The Harvesting," Hughes, *Wodwo*, p. 95.

"Tarquin is by definition": *Shakespeare and the Goddess.* p. 485.

220 "In fact, the tendency": ibid. p. 92.

"His love is of an altogether": ibid. p. 59.


Chapter Sixteen: Woods and Heaths


222 "In the symbolic language": *Shakespeare and the Goddess,* p. 101.

224 "If you gather": Lawlis, *Elizabethan Prose Fiction*, p. 394.

"like Greene's *Pandosto, Rosalind*": Tenney, *Thomas Lodge*, p. 104.

"Hughes associates William": *Shakespeare and TG.* p. 101.

"He writes that "Shakespeare's source": ibid. In a footnote, Hughes attributes the Ardennes' name to "the goddess Aduina, a Gallicized Diana/Cybele" but he doesn't pursue it further.

225 "This relationship included": ibid. 519.

226 "Jacques presents himself": ibid. p. 102.

227 "Rosader suddenly": Lawlis, p. 350.

229 "Shakespeare, we often feel," Ogburn, *The Mysterious William Shakespeare*, p. 271.

231 "A crowned child": *Shakespeare and the Goddess*, p. 397.

232 "the most regressive": ibid. p. 337.

233 "What prompted him": ibid. p. 283.

234 "After three acts of": ibid. p. 284.

"When Timon searches": ibid. p. 287.

235 "Timon sounds like Thoreau": Flower, p. 545.
238 "John Aubrey grudgingly": Dick, Oliver Lawson.
     "Introduction" to *Aubrey's Brief Lives*, p. xliii.

Chapter Seventeen: A Powerful and Splendid Enchanter

239 "As I have followed it,". *Shakespeare and the Goddess*, p.
     379.
240 "Leontes's atonement": ibid. p, 405.
241 "the rocky, storm beaten": ibid. p. 381.
     "His fellow poet": Wagner, *Ariel's Gift*, p. 246.
243 "Prospero calls him up": *Shakespeare and the Goddess*. p.
     466.
   "In every play": ibid. p. 497.
   "In spite of Prospero's": ibid.
244 "I've known for some years": Sagar, *The Letters of Ted
     Hughes and Keith Sagar*, p.257.
245 "'All things,'' writes Plato'": Montaigne, "Of Cannibals,"
     *Essays*, 276.
247 "Hughes describes": *Shakespeare and the Goddess*, p. 92.
248 "the 'funereal pyramid'": "Notes on Shakespeare," *Winter
     Pollen,* p. 105.
249 "The ideal reader": *Shakespeare and the Goddess,* p. 44.
     "The story of the mind": Hughes, "The Environmental
     Revolution," *Winter Pollen*, p.129.

Chapter Eighteen: Morning Glory Pool

251 "It is no small thing": Ogburn, *The Mysterious William
     Shakespeare*, p. 374.
     "I think those letters": Wagner, *Ariel's Gift.* p. 17.
     "Once you've contracted to write": Sagar, *The Laughter of
     Foxes*, p. 57.
252 "That self-enclosed area": Bate, *The Song of the Earth*, p.
     79.
     "When there is no more": ibid., p. 67. In W.H. Hudson's

classic novel, *Green Mansions*, "Rima, the bird girl," is
the last survivor of a humanoid species that lived
harmoniously in tropical forest.

"According to one Plath biographer": Stevenson, *Bitter Fame*, p.
159.

"Yes, yes, this is my address." None of the critics I've read
mention the Yellowstone reference in "The Tour," or that
the poem addresses Moore. One (Van Dyne, *Revising
Life*) calls it "another Gothic tale...a botched job." Critics
and biographers pay relatively little attention to the
Yellowstone visit. A book on Hughes's *Birthday Letters*
locates "Fishing Bridge" -- the central poem set on
Yellowstone Lake— "on the edge of Lake Superior."
(*Ariel's Gift,* p. 164.) A perfunctory critique of Plath's
"The Fifty-Ninth Bear" sets the story in "the North
Woods." (Newman, *The Art of Sylvia Plath*, p. 51.)

253 "the blue ether of another world." Bartram, *Travels*, p. 150.

254 "In 1957, Moore dismissed": Stevenson, *Bitter Fame*, p.
134.

"forced the publisher": ibid. p. 213.

256 "Kipling met a Venus-Perdita": "Rudyard Kipling Astride
the Clouds," *American Notes.*

257 "I think that they: *Walden,* Flower, p. 260.

"I began to work": Thoreau, *Ktaadn and the Maine Woods.*
Flower, p. 60.

258 "To preserve wild animals": "Walking." Flower, p. 538.

"No wonder": Muir, p. 480.

259 "This curious world": Thoreau, Harvard Commencement
Address, 1837.

260 "I saw the gooseflesh": Plath, "Ocean 1212-W," *Johnny
Panic*, p. 22.

"Sand-strewn caverns": from "Forsaken Merman" by
Matthew Arnold.

"Hughes writes that true poetry": "Keats on the Difference
between the Dreamer and the Poet," *Winter Pollen*, p.
249.

"It's no wonder": *Time*, *Ariel* review, Friday, June 10, 1966,
    p. 118.
261 "To quote Thoreau's "Walking": Flower, p. 541.
    "Harold Bloom, who calls": Bloom, *Sylvia Plath*, p. 1.
    "At once no one": Bloom, *The Western Canon*, p. 75.

# BIBLIOGRAPHY

———————

Abrams, M. H., (editor). *The Norton Anthology of English Literature*. New York: W.W. Norton, 1968.

Ackroyd, Peter. *Shakespeare: The Biography*. New York: Nan A. Talese, 2005.

Alexander, Michael J. *The Earliest English Poems: A Bilingual Edition*. Berkeley: University California Press, 1970.

Alexander, Paul, (editor). *Ariel Ascending: Writings About Sylvia Plath*: New York, Harper and Row, 1985.

Aldhouse-Green, Miranda and Stephen. *The Quest for the Shaman: Shape-Shifters, Sorcerers, and Healers of Ancient Europe*. London: Thames and Hudson, 2005.

Anderson, Mark. *Shakespeare by Another Name: The Life of Edward de Vere, Earl of Oxford, the Man who was Shakespeare*. New York: Gotham Books, 2005.

Aubrey, John. *Aubrey's Brief Lives*. Oliver Lawson Dick, editor. Boston, David Godine, 1999.

_____. *Brief Lives*. Michael Hunter, editor. London: Penguin Books, 2000.

Auden, W.H. *Lectures on Shakespeare.* Princeton, New Jersey: Princeton University Press, 2000.

Baring, Anne and Jules Cashford. *The Myth of the Goddess*. New York: Viking Penguin, 1991.

Bartram, William. *Travels*. New York: Dover Publications, 1955.

Bate, Jonathan. *Shakespeare and the English Romantic Imagination*. Oxford: Clarendon Press, 1989.

_____. *The Genius of Shakespeare.* New York: Oxford University Press, 1998.

_____. *The Song of the Earth.* Cambridge: Harvard University Press, 2000.

_____. *Soul of the Age: A Biography of the Mind of*

*William Shakespeare*. New York: Random House, 2009.
_____. *Ted Hughes: The Unauthorized Life*. New York:
    Harper Collins, 2015.
Bates, E.S., *Touring in 1600: A Study of the Development of
    Travel as a Means of Education*. New York: Burt
    Franklin, 1911.
Beauclerk, Charles, *Shakespeare's Lost Kingdom: The True
    History of Shakespeare and Elizabeth*. New York: Grove
    Press, 2010.
Black Elk, Nick. *Black Elk Speaks: Being the Life History of a
    Holy Man of the Oglala Sioux as told through John G.
    Neihardt*. Lincoln and London: University of Nebraska
    Press, 1988.
Blair, Peter Hunter. *An Introduction to Anglo-Saxon England*.
    Cambridge: Cambridge University Press, 1977.
Bloom, Harold. *Sylvia Plath*. New York: Chelsea House, 1989.
_____. *The Western Canon: The Books and School of the
    Ages*. New York: Harcourt Brace and Company, 1994.
_____. *Shakespeare: The Invention of the Human*. New
    York: Penguin, 1998.
Boer, Charles. (translator). *The Homeric Hymns*. Chicago: The
    Swallow Press, 1970.
Booth, James. *Philip Larkin: Life, Art, and Love*. New York,
    2014.
Borges, Jorge Luis. *The Professor: A Course of English
    Literature*. New York: New Directions Books, 2013.
Bowen, Catherine Drinker. *The Lion and the Throne*. Boston:
    Little Brown, 1956.
Brain, Tracy. *The Other Sylvia Plath*. Essex, England: Pearson
    Education Limited, 2001.
Brown, Norman O. *Life Against Death*. New York: Vintage
    Books, 1959.
Bryson, Bill. *Shakespeare: The World as Stage*. New York:
    Harper Collins, 2007.
Burgess, Anthony. *Shakespeare*. New York: New York, Alfred
    A. Knopf, 1970.

Burton, Robert. *The Anatomy of Melancholy*, edited by Lawrence Babb. East Lansing: Michigan State University Press, 1965.

Butscher, Edward. *Sylvia Plath: Method and Madness.* New York: Seabury Press, 1976.

Campbell, Joseph. *The Masks of God.* New York: Viking Press, 1968.

Chiljan, Katherine. *Shakespeare Suppressed.* San Francisco: Faire Editions, 2011.

Cooper, Romaine. "Siskiyou High Country." *Siskiyou Country: Life on the Slopes of the Siskiyou Mountains*, August 1983, 26-31.

Corbin, Peter and Douglas Sedge. *Three Jacobean Witchcraft Plays.* Manchester: Manchester University Press, 1986.

Crupi, Charles W. *Robert Greene.* Boston: Twayne Publishers, 1986.

Donaldson, Ian. *Ben Jonson: A Life.* Oxford: Oxford University Press, 2011.

Duerr, Peter. *Dreamtime: Concerning the Boundary Between Wilderness and Civilization.* Translated by Felicitas Goodman. New York: Basil Blackwell, 1985.

Duncan-Jones, Katherine. *Sir Philip Sidney: Courtier-Poet.* New Haven: Yale University Press, 1991.

Dunn, Jane. *Elizabeth and Mary: Cousins, Rivals, Queens.* London: Harper Collins,2003.

Eliot, T.S. *The Waste Land: A Facsimile and Transcript of the Original Drafts Including the Annotations of Ezra Pound.* Edited and with an Introduction by Valerie Eliot. New York: Harcourt Brace Jovanovich, 1971.

Ellmann, Richard and Robert O'Clair, (editors). *The Norton Anthology of Modern Poetry.* New York: W.W. Norton, 1973.

Emerson, Ralph Waldo. "Nature." In *Ralph Waldo Emerson: Essays and Lectures.* Ed. Joel Porte. New York: Library of America. 1983, 5-49.

_____. "Thoreau." In *Ralph Waldo Emerson.* Ed. Richard

Poirier. New York: Oxford UP, 1990, 475-90.

Faas, Ekbert. *Ted Hughes: The Unaccommodated Universe*. Santa Barbara: Black Sparrow Press, 1980.

Falk, Dan. *The Science of Shakespeare: A New Look at the Playwright's Universe*. New York: St. Martin's Press, 2014.

Feinstein, Elaine. *Ted Hughes: The Life of a Poet*. New York: W.W. Norton, 2001.

Fields, Bertram. *Players: The Shakespeare Mystery*. New York: Harper Collins, 2005.

Freud, Sigmund. *The Letters of Sigmund Freud and Arnold Zweig, edited by Ernst Freud*. New York, NYU Press, 1971.

Frye, Northrop. *Fables of Identity: Studies in Poetic Mythology*. New York: Harcourt Brace, 1963.

_____. *A Natural Perspective: The Development of Shakespearean Comedy and Romance*. New York: Columbia University Press, 1965.

_____. *Fools of Time: Studies in Shakespearean Tragedy*. Toronto: University of Toronto Press, 1967.

_____. *Northrop Frye on Shakespeare*. New Haven: Yale University Press, 1986.

Ganzel, Dewey. *Fortune and Men's Eyes*. London: Oxford University Press, 1982.

Gesner, Konrad: *The History of Four-Footed Beasts, Volume 1*. Edward Topsell,(editor) New York: Da Capo Press, 1967.

Gopnik, Adam. "The Poet's Hand." *The New Yorker*, April 28, 2014.

Greenblatt, Stephen. *Shakespearean Negotiations*. Berkeley: University of California Press, 1988.

_____. *Will in the World: How Shakespeare Became Shakespeare*. New York: W.W. Norton, 2004.

Greenwood, Sir George. *The Shakespeare Problem Restated*. London: The Athenaeum Press, 1937.

Greer, Germaine. *Shakespeare's Wife*. New York Harper/Collins, 2007.

Halliday, Frank E. *Shakespeare and his Critics*. New York: Schocken Books, 1958.

Harris, Frank. *The Man Shakespeare*. New York: Mitchell Kennerley, 1909.

Honan, Park. *Shakespeare: A Life*, New York: Oxford University Press, 1998.

Hughes, Ted. *Wodwo*. New York: Harper and Row, 1967.

_____. *Shakespeare and the Goddess of Complete Being*. New York: Farrar, Straus & Giroux, 1992.

_____. *Winter Pollen: Occasional Prose*. New York: Picador, 1995.

_____. *Tales from Ovid*: New York: Farrar, Straus & Giroux, 1997.

_____. *Birthday Letters*. New York: Farrar, Straus & Giroux, 1998.

_____. *Collected Poems*. New York: Farrar, Straus and Giroux, 2003.

_____. *Collected Poems for Children*. New York: Farrar, Straus, and Giroux, 2005.

_____. *Letters*. New York: Farrar, Straus & Giroux, 2007.

Humphries, Rolfe. *Ovid: Metamorphoses*. Bloomington: Indiana University Press, 1955.

James, Henry. *Literary Criticism*. New York: The Library of America, Viking Press, 1989.

Jenkins, Elizabeth. *Elizabeth The Great*. London, Victor: Victor Gollancz, 1958.

Kazin, Alfred. *A Writer's America: Landscape in Literature*. New York: Alfred A. Knopf, 1988.

Kennedy, Charles William. *The Earliest English Poetry*. London: Oxford University Press, 1943.

Kermode, Frank. *Shakespeare's Language*. New York: Farrar, Straus and Giroux, 2000.

Kroll, Judith. *Chapters in a Mythology: The Poetry of Sylvia Plath*. New York: Harper and Row, 1976.

Lawlis, Merritt (Editor). *Elizabethan Prose Fiction*. New York: Odyssey Press, 1967.

Lawrence, D.H. *The Later D.H. Lawrence.* New York: Alfred A. Knopf, 1959.

_____. *Reflections on the Death of a Porcupine and other Essays.* Bloomington: University of Indiana Press, 1963.

_____. *Studies in Classic American Literature.* New York: Viking, 1966.

Lawrence, Herbert. *The Life and Adventures of Common Sense.* New York: Garland Publishing Inc., 1974.

Leopold, Aldo. *Sand County Almanac.* New York: Oxford University Press, 1987.

Lewis, C.S. *The Discarded Image.* Cambridge: Cambridge University Press, 1970.

Lewis, Wyndham. *The Lion and the Fox.* New York: Barnes and Noble, 1927.

Looney, J. Thomas. *"Shakespeare" Identified in Edward De Vere, Seventeenth Earl of Oxford.* Port Washington, New York: Kennicat Press, 1975.

Lowes, John Livingston. *The Road to Xanadu: A Study in the Ways of the Imagination.* New York: Vintage Books, 1959.

Loyn, H.R. *Anglo Saxon England and the Norman Conquest.* New York: Saint Martin's Press, 1962.

Lucian. "Timon, or the Misanthrope". *Lucian, Volume II.* London: Loeb Classical Library, 1960.

Lynch, Jack. *Becoming Shakespeare: The Unlikely Afterlife that Turned a Provincial Playwright into the Bard.* New York: Walker and Company, 2007.

Malcolm, Janet. *The Silent Woman.* New York: Knopf, 1993.

Matthiessen, Peter. *Indian Country.* New York: Viking Press, 1984.

McGinn, Colin. *Shakespeare's Philosophy: Discovering the Meaning Behind the Plays.* New York: Harper Collins, 2006.

Middlebrook, Diane. *Her Husband: Hughes and Plath—A Marriage.* New York: Viking, 2003.

Montaigne, Michel de. *Essays.* Translated by George B. Ives.

New York: Heritage Press, 1946.

_____. *Montaigne's Travel Journal*: San Francisco: North Point Press, 1983.

_____. *Shakespeare's Montaigne: The Florio Translation of the Essays, A Selection.* Edited by Stephen Greenblatt and Peter G. Platt. New York: New York Review of Books, 2014.

Motion, Andrew: *Philip Larkin: A Writer's Life*. New York: Farrar, Straus and Giroux, 1993.

Muir, John. *John Muir: The Eight Wilderness Discovery Books.* London: Diadem Books, 1992.

Myers, Lucas. *Crow Steered Bergs Appeared: A Memoir of Ted Hughes and Sylvia Plath.* Sewanee, Tennessee: Proctor's Hall Press, 2001.

Neiderkorn, William S. "The Shakespeare Code, and Other Fanciful Ideas from the Traditional Camp." *New York Times*, August 30, 2005.

Nelson, Alan H. *Monstrous Adversary: The Life of Edward de Vere, 17th Earl of Oxford*. Liverpool: Liverpool University Press, 2003.

Newman, Charles, ed. *The Art of Sylvia Plath: A Symposium.* Bloomington: Indiana University Press, 1970.

Nicholls, Charles. *The Lodger Shakespeare: His Life on Silver Street.* New York: Viking Penguin, 2008.

O'Callaghan, Michelle. *Thomas Middleton: Renaissance Dramatist.* Edinburgh: Edinburgh University Press, 2009.

Ogburn, Charlton Jr. *The Winter Beach*. New York: William Morrow, 1966.

_____. *The Mysterious William Shakespeare: The Myth & The Reality.* McLean, Virginia: EPM Publications Inc., 1992.

Ogburn, Dorothy, and Charlton Ogburn Sr. *This Star of England "William Shake-speare" Man of the Renaissance,* Westport, Connecticut: Greenwood Press, 1952.

Ogburn, Dorothy, and Charlton Ogburn Jr. *SHAKE-SPEARE:*

*The Man Behind the Name*. New York: William Morrow and Company, 1962.

Orgel, Stephen. *Imagining Shakespeare: A History of Texts and Visions*. London: Palgrave MacMillan, 2003.

Ovid, *Fasti*. Translated by James George Frazer. Cambridge: Cambridge University Press, 1996.

_____. *Metamorphoses*. Translated by Rolphe Humphries. Bloomington: Indiana University Press, 1955.

Plath, Sylvia. *Ariel*. New York: Harper and Row, 1966.

_____. *Letters Home*. New York: Harper and Row, 1975.

_____. *The Collected Poems*, New York: Harper and Row, 1981.

_____. *The Journals of Sylvia Plath*: New York, Random House, 1982.

_____. *Johnny Panic and the Bible of Dreams*. New York: Harper Collins, 2000.

_____. *The Unabridged Journals*. New York: Random House, 2000.

Plutarch. *Plutarch's Lives, Volume IX (Life of Mark Antony)*. London: Loeb Classical Library, 1959.

Pottle, Frederick A. (editor) *Boswell on the Grand Tour: Germany and Switzerland*, New York: McGraw-Hill, 1953.

Price, Diana. *Shakespeare's Unorthodox Biography: New Evidence of an Authorship Problem*. Westport CT: Greenwood Press, 2001.

Rasmussen, Eric. *The Shakespeare Thefts*. New York: Palgrave Macmillan, 2011.

Riggs, David. *The World of Christopher Marlowe*. New York: Henry Holt, 2004.

Roberts, Neil. *Ted Hughes: A Literary Life*. New York: Palgrave MacMillan, 2007.

Roe, Richard Paul. *The Shakespeare Guide to Italy*. New York: HarperCollins, 2011.

Rose, Jacqueline. *The Haunting of Sylvia Plath*. Cambridge: Harvard University Press, 1991.

Rosenbaum, Ron. *The Shakespeare Wars*. New York: Random House, 2006.

_____. "Ten Things I Hate About *Anonymous*." *Slate*. Oct. 24, 2011.

Rowland, Beryl. *Blind Beasts: Chaucer's Animal World*. Ohio: Kent State University Press, 1971.

Sagar, Keith. *The Laughter of Foxes: A Study of Ted Hughes*. Liverpool: Liverpool University Press, 2006.

_____. *Poet and Critic: The Letters of Ted Hughes and Keith Sagar*. London: The British Library, 2012.

Schaeffer, Susan. *Poison: A Novel*. New York: W.W. Norton, 2006.

Scigaj, Leonard. *Ted Hughes*. Boston: G. K. Hall & Co., 1991.

_____. *Critical Essays on Ted Hughes* (editor). New York: G.K; Hall and Co., 1992.

Shapiro, James. *A Year in the Life of William Shakespeare: 1599*. New York: Harper Collins, 2005.

_____. *Contested Will: Who Wrote Shakespeare?* New York: Simon & Schuster, 2010.

_____. *Shakespeare in America* (editor). New York: The Library of America, 2013.

_____. *The Year of Lear: Shakespeare in 1606*. New York: Simon and Schuster, 2015.

Shepard, Paul. *The Others: How Animals Made Us Human*, Washington: Island Press, 1996.

Smith, Sarah. "A Reattribution of Anthony Munday's 'The Paine of Pleasure.'" *TheOxfordian*, 5, 2002, 70-118.

Sobran, Joseph. *Alias Shakespeare: Solving the Greatest Literary Mystery of All Time*. New York: The Free Press, 1997.

Spurgeon, Caroline. *Shakespeare's Imagery and What It Tells Us*: London, Cambridge University Press, 1935.

Stevenson, Anne. *Bitter Fame: A Life of Sylvia Plath*. Boston: Houghton Mifflin, 1989.

Stewart, Doug. *The Boy Who Would Be Shakespeare: A Tale of*

*Forgery and Folly.* Cambridge, MA: Da Capo Press, 2010.

Strachey, Lytton. *Elizabeth and Essex: A Tragic History.* New York: Harcourt Brace, 1956.

Sylvester, Joshua (translator). *Bartas: His Devine Weekes and Workes.* Gainesville, Florida: Scholars' Facsimiles and Reprints, 1965.

Tacitus, Gaius Cornelius. "Germany and its Tribes," *Complete Works.* New York: Modern Library, 1942.

Taylor, Gary. *Reinventing Shakespeare: A Cultural History from the Restoration to the Present.* New York: Weidenfeld and Nicholson, 1989.

Tennant, Emma. *Sylvia and Ted: A Novel.* New York: Henry Holt, 2001.

Tenney, Edward Andrews. *Thomas Lodge.* New York: Russell & Russell, 1969.

Thoreau, Henry David. *Walden or Life in the Woods; The Maine Woods;* "Walking." In *Henry David Thoreau: Essays, Journals, and Poems.* Ed. Dean Flower. Greenwich CT: Fawcett Publications, 1975.

Tillyard, E.W. *The Elizabethan World Picture.* New York: Random House, 1962.

Tolstoy, Leo. "Shakespeare and the Drama," in *Recollections and Essays.* London: Oxford University Press, 1946, p. 307.

Uroff, Margaret Dickie. *Sylvia Plath and Ted Hughes.* Urbana: University of Illinois Press, 1979.

Van Dyne, Susan R. *Revising Life: Sylvia Plath's Ariel Poems.* Chapel Hill: University of North Carolina Press, 1993.

Wagner, Erica. *Ariel's Gift: Ted Hughes, Sylvia Plath, and the Story of Birthday Letters.* New York: W.W. Norton, 2001.

Wallace, David Rains. *The Dark Range: A Naturalist's Night Notebook.* San Francisco: Sierra Club Books, 1978.

_____. *The Klamath Knot: Explorations in Myth and Evolution,* San Francisco: Sierra Club Books, 1983.

_____. *The Untamed Garden: Personal Essays*. Columbus: Ohio State University Press, 1986.

_____. *Bulow Hammock: Mind in a Forest*. San Francisco, Sierra Club, 1989.

_____. *Yellowstone National Park: Official National Park Handbook*. Washington, D.C., U.S. Government Printing Office, 1998.

_____. *Beasts of Eden*. Berkeley: University of California Press, 2004.

_____. *Articulate Earth: Adventures in Ecocriticism*. Kneeland, California: Backcountry Press, 2014.

Ward, Bernard M. *The Seventeenth Earl of Oxford*. London: John Murray, 1928.

Waugh, Auberon. *Shakespeare in Court*, Kindle Single, 2014.

Wells, Stanley. *Shakespeare & Co.: Christopher Marlowe, Thomas Dekker, Ben Jonson, Thomas Middleton, John Fletcher and Other Players in His Story*. New York: Pantheon, 2006.

_____, and Gary Taylor. *William Shakespeare: Complete Works*. Oxford, Clarendon Press, 1986.

Whalen, Richard F. *Shakespeare: Who Was He?* Westport, CT: Praeger, 1994.

White, Gilbert. *The Natural History of Selbourne*. New York: Dutton, 1976.

Whitelock, Anna. *The Queen's Bed: An Intimate History of Elizabeth's Court*. New York: Farrar Strauss and Giroux, 2013.

Whittemore, Hank. *100 Reasons Shake-speare Was the Earl of Oxford*. Somerville MA: Forever Press, 2016.

Whittlesey, Lee H. *Death in Yellowstone: Accidents and Foolhardiness in the First National Park*. Boston: Roberts Rhinehart Publishers, 1995.

Wills, Gary, *Making Make-Believe Real: Politics and Theater in Shakespeare's Time.* New Haven: Yale University Press, 2014.

Wilson, Angus. *The Old Men at the Zoo*. London: Secker and

Warburg, 1961.

Wilson, Edmund. *The Shock of Recognition* (editor). New York: Doubleday, 1943.

_____. *I Thought of Daisy.* Iowa City: University of Iowa Press, 2001.

_____. *Literary Essays and Reviews of the 1930s and 40s.* New York: Library of America, Penguin Putnam, 2007.

Wood, Michael. *In Search of Shakespeare.* New York: Basic Books, 2003.

Wright, Louis B. and Virginia Lamar, (editors). *The Folger Library General Reader's Guide to Shakespeare.* New York: Washington Square Press, 1957.

37334529R00166

Made in the USA
San Bernardino, CA
29 May 2019